AND IT CAME TO PASS

AND IT CAME TO PASS

THE BOOK OF MORMON CHRONICLES

CHRISTINE C. MERRICK

CFI
Springville, Utah

ISBN 13: 978-1-59955-152-4

Published by CFI, an imprint of Cedar Fort, Inc., 2373 W. 700 S., Springville, UT, 84663
Distributed by Cedar Fort, Inc., www.cedarfort.com

LIBRARY OF CONGRESS CATALOGING-IN-PUBLICATION DATA

    Merrick, Christine C.
    And it came to pass / Christine C. Merrick.
      p. cm.
    ISBN 978-1-59955-152-4 (alk. paper)
    1. Book of Mormon—Chronology. I. Title.

    BX8627.M47 2008
    289.3'22—dc22

2007052903

Cover design by Nicole Williams
Cover design © 2008 by Lyle Mortimer
Edited and typeset by Kimiko M. Hammari

Printed in the United States of America

10 9 8 7 6 5 4 3 2 1

Printed on acid-free paper

To my grandmother,
Abigail Amanda Hintze Florence,
whose love and mastery of
the Book of Mormon
have inspired me throughout my life.

CONTENTS

Preface xi

Jerusalem in 600 BC xv

1. Leaving Jerusalem (1 Nephi 1–2) 1

2. The Brass Plates (1 Nephi 3–5) 4

3. The Joining of Two Families (1 Nephi 7) 9

4. The Vision of the Tree of Life (1 Nephi 8) 11

5. Two Sets of Plates (1 Nephi 9) 15

6. Nephi's Vision (1 Nephi 10–16) 18

7. The Liahona (1 Nephi 16) 22

8. Nephi and His Broken Bow (1 Nephi 16) 24

9. The Death of Ishmael (1 Nephi 16–17) 26

10. Nephi Builds a Ship (1 Nephi 17–18) 28

11. Sailing to the Promised Land (1 Nephi 18) 31

12. Two Nations Are Born (1 Nephi 18–19; 2 Nephi 1–5) 33

13. Jacob, the Brother of Nephi (Jacob 1–3) 36

14. Jacob Contends with Sherem (Jacob 7) 38

15. Enos and His Mighty Prayer (Enos) 40

16. Short Record Keeping (Jarom; Omni) 42

17. Discovering the Mulekites (Omni 1:12–22) 45

18. The Words of Mormon (Words of Mormon) 48

19. King Benjamin (Words of Mormon 1:12–18; Mosiah 1–6) 50

20. Finding the Land of Lehi-Nephi (Mosiah 7–8) 54

21. Overzealous Zeniff (Omni: Mosiah 9–10) 58

22. The Wicked King Noah (Mosiah 11) 61

23. Abinadi (Mosiah 11–17) 63

24. In Hiding with Alma (Mosiah 17–18, 23) 66

25. Prophecies Fulfilled (Mosiah 19) 68

26. The Lamanite Daughters and the Priests of Noah (Mosiah 20) 70

27. The Deliverance of King Limhi's People (Mosiah 21–22) 72

28. Alma and His People Are Led to Zarahemla (Mosiah 23–25) 75

29. A Recapping of Events 79

30. Alma the Younger and the Sons of Mosiah (Mosiah 26–27; Alma 36) ... 81

31. The Reign of the Judges Begins (Mosiah 28–29) 85

32. Nehor Introduces Priestcraft (Alma 1) 87

33. Amlici Seeks to Become King (Alma 2–3) 89

34. Alma Resigns as Chief Judge (Alma 4–8) 92

35. Rejection in Ammonihah (Alma 8–10) 94

36. Contending with Zeezrom (Alma 9–14) 96

37. Alma and Amulek Are Imprisoned (Alma 14–15) 99

38. Zeezrom Is Baptized (Alma 15) 102

39. The Destruction of Ammonihah (Alma 16) 104

40. Ammon Protects the King's Flocks (Alma 17) 106

41. The Conversion of King Lamoni (Alma 18–19) 109

42. On the Way to Middoni (Alma 20–21) 114

43. Teaching Lamoni's Father (Alma 22–23) 117

44. The Anti-Nephi-Lehies (Alma 23–26) 120

45. A New Home in Jershon (Alma 27–28) 124

46. Korihor, the Antichrist (Alma 30) 127

47. A Mission to the Zoramites (Alma 31–35) 130

48. Alma Counsels His Sons (Alma 35–42) 134

49. Moroni Leads the Nephite Army (Alma 43–44) 137

50. The Title of Liberty (Alma 45–46) 141

51. Amalickiah Becomes King of the Lamanites (Alma 47) 144

52. Amalickiah's Plans Are Thwarted (Alma 48–49) 147

53. Morianton Disrupts the Peace (Alma 50) 151

54. The Rise of the King-Men (Alma 51) 153

55. Amalickiah Is Slain (Alma 51–52) 155

56. The City of Mulek Is Retaken (Alma 52–53) 157

57. Rescuing the Nephite Prisoners (Alma 54–55) 160

58. Helaman's Two Thousand (Alma 53, 56) 164

59. The Two Thousand Are Spared Again (Alma 57) 168

60. Retaking the City of Manti (Alma 58) 171

61. Moroni's Scathing Letter (Alma 59–60) 174

62. Pahoran's Humble Reply (Alma 61) 176

63. Moroni Aids Pahoran (Alma 62) 178

64. The Valiant Teancum Is Slain (Alma 62–63) 180

65. Migrations to the Land Northward (Alma 63) 182
66. The Lamanites Take Zarahemla (Helaman 1) 184
67. Gadianton's Secret Band (Helaman 2) 187
68. Settling the Land Northward (Helaman 3–4) 189
69. Encircled by Fire (Helaman 5) 192
70. The Gadianton Robbers Take Over (Helaman 6) 195
71. Nephi Prays on His Tower (Helaman 7–10) 198
72. Nephi Calls Down a Famine (Helaman 10–11) 202
73. Samuel the Lamanite (Helaman 13–16) 205
74. The Savior Is Born (3 Nephi 1–2) 209
75. Nephites Under Siege (3 Nephi 3–5) 212
76. Dividing Into Tribes (3 Nephi 6–7) 216
77. Tempests, Earthquakes, Fires, and Whirlwinds (3 Nephi 8) 219
78. A Voice from the Darkness (3 Nephi 9–10) 221
79. The Savior Appears (3 Nephi 11–12) 224
80. The Sermon on the Mount, Part I (3 Nephi 12) 227
81. The Sermon on the Mount, Part II (3 Nephi 13–14) 231
82. "Other Sheep I Have" (3 Nephi 15–17) 235
83. The Sacrament Is Instituted (3 Nephi 18–24) 238
84. The Three Nephites (3 Nephi 26–29) 241
85. A Season of Righteousness (4 Nephi) 244
86. Mormon Commands the Nephite Armies (Mormon 1–2) 247
87. A People Without Hope (Mormon 3–5) 250
88. The Final Battle at Cumorah (Mormon 6–9) 254
89. Ordinance Prayers (Moroni 1–6) 258
90. Further Counsel from Mormoni (Moroni 7–9) 260
91. A Testimony of the Book of Mormon (Moroni 10) 263
92. Leaving the Tower of Babel (Ether 1–2) 265
93. The Jaredite Barges (Ether 2–6) 269
94. Shule—A Righteous King (Ether 6–7) 272
95. Secret Combinations (Ether 8–9) 275
96. A Famine and Poisonous Serpents (Ether 9) 278
97. A Succession of Kings (Ether 10–11) 280
98. Prophecies of Destruction (Ether 11–12) 283
99. Ether's Warning (Ether 13–14) 286
100. Coriantumr—The Last Jaredite (Ether 15) 290
Postscript 293
About the Author 294

PREFACE

The Book of Mormon was written centuries ago, yet we are told that it was written expressly for those of us living in the last days. The ancient inhabitants of the Americas never had this book. Their historians were inspired to write those things that we would need for our day. The prophet Moroni stated: *Behold, I speak unto you as if ye were present, and yet ye are not. But behold, Jesus Christ hath shown you unto me, and I know your doing* (Mormon 8:35).

President Ezra Taft Benson said, "No member of this church can stand approved in the presence of God who has not seriously and carefully read the Book of Mormon."[1] *And It Came to Pass: The Book of Mormon Chronicles* was written to help the members of the Church in their study of the Book of Mormon. It was never intended to be a replacement for it.

So, just what is *And It Came to Pass: The Book of Mormon Chronicles*?

Let me first explain what it is not. It is not a doctrinal commentary; there are many excellent books available for that purpose. Neither is it a verse-by-verse or chapter-by-chapter summary of the Book of Mormon. Rather, *And It Came to Pass* tells the story line of that ancient text. The information for each story in the *And It Came to Pass* might have been pulled from just one chapter of the Book of Mormon, or several. One of my objectives in writing this book was to allow the events to flow smoothly, while preserving the beauty and spirit of the Book of Mormon.

How can *And It Came to Pass* be a tool in studying the Book of Mormon?

Considerable effort has been taken to make the story line of the Book of Mormon as easy to follow as possible. It was also written with great detail, although the narrative is not embellished in any way. Occasionally, background information is given at the beginning of a chapter to set the scene. Sometimes information from outside sources has been added to illuminate events. Quotes from Latter-day Saint scholars have been included that give insight and enrich our understanding of the stories. There is frequent cross-referencing of scriptures so that all related information is included in each chapter.

Whenever I have quoted from the Book of Mormon—whether it is a word, a phrase, or an entire verse—that text appears in italics. I have quoted liberally for important reasons. Some verses could not be interpreted without great poetic license, so it seemed best to quote directly from scripture. But often the original text was just too beautiful, or poignant, or even chilling, to phrase any other way.

And It Came to Pass came about in a very roundabout way.

I did not start out to write a book. Many years ago our family ran into the same challenge with scripture study that countless others have when you have children with a wide range of ages. How do you keep the attention of the younger ones while reading and discussing the Book of Mormon? The answer for us was to hold a separate scripture study for our three youngest boys. I looked for Book of Mormon stories more on their level, but what I found was either too simple, or the scriptural account was embellished too much. The crazy notion came into my head to write a handful of stories myself. I started with Lehi and his family leaving Jerusalem, and then I just kept going. But an interesting thing happened along the way—my target audience was no longer children. There was also a driving force behind this undertaking that I couldn't explain. Fifteen years and countless revisions later, I decided it was time to call the book finished.

Writing _And It Came to Pass_ has been a joy from beginning to end, and that is the miracle of it. With a large household to run and Church callings to attend to, the task should have been overwhelming. It should have gotten tedious to the point of losing interest. Instead, the hours spent on this endeavor became the most enjoyable time of my day.

The sweetest rewards were the many spiritual experiences I had while writing this book: words that so often flowed into my heart and onto the page; direction that came in answer to prayer on myriad "What do I do here?" issues; and insights that were given to me about the Book of Mormon.

I have always had a testimony of the Book of Mormon, but the years of working on this project have made it absolutely unshakable. If I could step across the veil and meet those who transcribed their history onto the plates, I could have no stronger witness that the book is true than I do now. I also know that the Book of Mormon bears irrefutable testimony that Jesus is the Christ, our Savior and Redeemer.

My sincerest desire is that *And It Came to Pass* will help you know the Book of Mormon better and love it even more.

—Christine Cobb Merrick

Note
1. In Conference Report, Oct. 1961, 18.

Jerusalem in **600** BC

The story of the Book of Mormon begins in the land of Jerusalem about six hundred years before Christ was born. It was a time of great wealth, including large personal fortunes, due mostly to commercial trading with Egypt. The people were heavily influenced by Egyptian culture because in that day the superiority of that civilization was absolute and unquestioned. It was not uncommon for wealthy citizens of Jerusalem to read and write Egyptian.

The country of Judah, which for the previous three years had been controlled by the Egyptians, had just been conquered by the Babylonians. They set twenty-one-year-old Zedekiah on the throne, but he was nothing more than a weak puppet king. During this first year of his reign he made a military alliance with Egypt and was scheming to make a break from Babylon. This put the country on a suicidal course because the powerful Babylon was moving against Egypt.

The prophet Jeremiah told King Zedekiah that Jerusalem was going to be destroyed if the people did not repent and heed the Lord's admonition to align themselves with Babylon instead of Egypt. Jeremiah was later put in prison for being a traitor. The impending doom of Jerusalem was not caused only by political reasons, but by rampant immorality and corruption. The Lord sent many prophets this same year, each testifying that Jerusalem was about to be destroyed if the people did not repent. Each prophet's life was in great peril for heeding the call.

W. Cleon Skousen explained:

> It was right at this precise time in the historical setting described by the Bible that the Book of Mormon branches off. The ominous cloud of calamity about to descend on Jerusalem made it a good time for the Lord to lead away a group of choice

servants and shepherd them to the Western Hemisphere where the Lord had been planning to start a whole new civilization. The Lord had told Joseph (who was sold into Egypt) all about it centuries before.

And now the Lord was about to raise up another valiant servant whom the people would also try to kill. His name was Lehi.[1]

Lehi lived on an estate in the country, outside the walls of Jerusalem. He had become very wealthy as a merchant and trader and would of necessity have been an expert in caravan travel. He was also proficient in the Egyptian language, as were his sons.

Being a deeply religious man, Lehi was troubled by the doomsday prophecies and prayed for the welfare of his people. This resulted in a remarkable vision where he found out firsthand that Jerusalem would be destroyed. Knowing that repentance was their only hope, he immediately joined the other prophets in trying to stave off destruction.

The country was divided into two factions—pro-Egyptian and pro-Babylonian, and these two parties existed side by side in the land. The ruling party and probably most of the people favored Egypt, while the prophet Jeremiah and his followers advised submission to Babylon. By openly siding with Jeremiah, Lehi instantly went from well-respected citizen to traitor and was forced to flee with his family from Jerusalem. This helped to create the rift between him and his two oldest sons that would exist for the remainder of his life. His sons were staunch defenders of their affluent lifestyle, which meant "business as usual" with Egypt. Against their will they gave this up to become nomads of the desert.

About eleven years after Lehi and his family fled Jerusalem, the Babylonians invaded the city. For a year and a half prior to this they had held Jerusalem under siege. The siege alone caused horrendous suffering and death. As the city fell, many people were killed by the sword, others were taken captive, and still others fled to surrounding nations. King Zedekiah was forced to watch the execution of his sons (except one, which we learn about in Helaman 8:21). Then he was blinded and led away captive, and subsequently died in prison. The temple was looted and the city was burned. Even the great walls around Jerusalem were broken down.

Note
1. W. Cleon Skousen, *The Fourth Thousand Years* (Salt Lake City, Utah: Ensign Publishing, 1966), 582.

·1·

LEAVING JERUSALEM
1 NEPHI 1–2

I, Nephi, having been born of goodly parents . . . and having seen many afflictions in the course of my days, nevertheless, having been highly favored of the Lord . . . I make a record of my proceedings. (1 Nephi 1:1)

ephi was the youngest son of Lehi and Sariah and had three older brothers—Laman, Lemuel, and Sam. (In 2 Nephi 5:6 we learn that there were also sisters.) Nephi was an obedient son who trusted his father, but more important, he trusted God. Like Joseph who was sold into Egypt, he was chosen by the Lord to lead his older brothers. It was he who wrote this record.

The country of Judah was experiencing tumultuous times. Babylon had just conquered them, yet they were looking toward the weaker Egypt for deliverance. Even though King Zedekiah was making decisions that would soon prove to be their downfall, the political scene was not their major problem—moral decay was.

During this year many prophets came to Jerusalem, warning the people to repent or else the Lord would destroy their great city. Lehi was troubled by this and had been praying *with all his heart, in behalf of his people.*

> *And it came to pass as he prayed unto the Lord, there came a pillar of fire and dwelt upon a rock before him; and he saw and heard much; and because of the things which he saw and heard he did quake and tremble exceedingly.* (1 Nephi 1:6)

Lehi returned to his house and *cast himself upon his bed, being overcome with the Spirit and the things which he had seen.* He then had an extraordinary vision in which the heavens opened and he saw God sitting upon

1

his throne, surrounded by *numberless concourses of angels* singing praises to him. During the course of the vision, Lehi was handed a book from which he read prophecies concerning the destruction of Jerusalem. Many of the inhabitants would be killed by the sword and others would be carried away captive.

Lehi saw many other marvelous things and his *soul did rejoice.* He knew that God was merciful and if the people would only turn to Him they would not perish. He joined the ranks of the prophets trying to save Jerusalem and went among the people prophesying of the things he had just seen and heard in his vision. He taught about the coming of a Messiah and the redemption of the world, but he also *testified of their wickedness and their abominations.* First the Jews mocked him; then they became angry, and *even as with the prophets of old, whom they had cast out, stoned, and slain,* they tried to kill Lehi.

The Lord spoke to Lehi in a dream and told him that because he had been faithful in preaching those things that had been commanded of him, the people sought his life. He was instructed to take his family into the wilderness.

> *And it came to pass that he departed into the wilderness. And he left his house, and the land of his inheritance, and his gold, and his silver, and his precious things, and took nothing with him, save it were his family, and provisions, and tents, and departed into the wilderness.* (1 Nephi 2:4)

In 600 BC Lehi and his family left Jerusalem. They traveled to the Red Sea, a distance of about 180 miles. After three days' journey beyond this point, staying close to the Red Sea, they reached a valley. Here they pitched their tents by the side of a river. (This became their base camp until they received the Liahona. See chapter 7 of *And It Came to Pass.*)

Lehi built an altar of stones and made an offering unto the Lord to give thanks. He named the river after his oldest son, Laman, and urged him to be like it, *continually running into the fountain of all righteousness.* Lehi named the valley after Lemuel and admonished him to be *firm and steadfast and immovable in keeping the commandments of the Lord.*

> *Now this he spake because of the stiffneckedness of Laman and Lemuel; for behold they did murmur in many things against their father, because he was a visionary man, and had led them out of*

the land of Jerusalem, to leave the land of their inheritance, and their gold, and their silver, and their precious things, to perish in the wilderness. And this they said he had done because of the foolish imaginations of his heart. (1 Nephi 2:11)

Laman and Lemuel did not know the *dealings* of God and did not believe that the great city of Jerusalem could be destroyed.

And they were like unto the Jews who were at Jerusalem, who sought to take away the life of my father. (1 Nephi 2:13)

Lehi, being filled with the Spirit, spoke to Laman and Lemuel with such power that *their frames did shake before him.* For a time they dared not speak against their father and did as he commanded them to do.

And it came to pass that I, Nephi, being exceedingly young, nevertheless being large in stature, and also having great desires to know of the mysteries of God, wherefore, I did cry unto the Lord; and behold he did visit me, and did soften my heart that I did believe all the words which had been spoken by my father; wherefore, I did not rebel against him like unto my brothers. (1 Nephi 2:16)

Nephi told his brothers the things that the Lord had revealed to him. Sam believed all Nephi said, but Laman and Lemuel did not. This brought Nephi great sorrow, and he cried unto the Lord about his two eldest brothers. The Lord commended Nephi for his faithfulness and told him that if he kept the commandments, he would prosper and be led to a land of promise. He would also be made a ruler and a teacher over his brothers. Nephi was further told that if his brothers did rebel against the Lord they would be a *scourge unto [his] seed, to stir them up in the ways of remembrance.* This prophecy would later prove to be of great significance.

·2·

THE BRASS PLATES
1 NEPHI 3–5

Lehi had a dream in which the Lord commanded him to send his sons back to Jerusalem. Living in Jerusalem was a distant relative by the name of Laban, who had in his possession a set of records that Lehi needed to take with him on his journey.

This record, called the plates of brass, was a volume of sacred scripture. The brass plates were a more extensive work than our current Old Testament (see 1 Nephi 13:23). They contained a record of the Lord's dealings with his people from the Creation down to the time of the prophet Jeremiah, who was a contemporary of Lehi. Mosiah 1:3–4 tells us that they were written in Egyptian. Included on the plates were the five books of Moses, the genealogy of the Nephites' ancestors, and prophecies spoken down through the ages. The brass plates would prove essential in preserving the Nephite nation over the next thousand or so years.

Laman and Lemuel did not want to return to Jerusalem, saying this was a hard thing their father required of them. Book of Mormon scholars agree it was over a 400-mile round-trip journey through some of the most rugged territory in that part of the country and would take at least three weeks. The area was also infested with marauders. Their biggest objection might have been that they knew of Laban's evil nature before the trip back to Jerusalem was ever made. Our only clue comes from 1 Nephi 5:5, where Sariah is worried that her sons had perished when they had not yet returned with the plates. Lehi reassured her that the Lord would **deliver them out of Laban's hands**. It is understandable why Laman and Lemuel did not want to undertake such a dangerous journey for a set of plates they probably cared little about.

Lehi reminded them it was the Lord who had commanded them to go. Then Nephi said to his father:

*I will go and do the things which the Lord hath commanded, for
I know that the Lord giveth no commandments unto the children of
men, save he shall prepare a way for them that they may accomplish
the thing which he commandeth them.* (1 Nephi 3:7)

Nephi and his three older brothers, Laman, Lemuel, and Sam, loaded
up their tents and supplies and set off for Jerusalem. Upon their arrival,
the brothers cast lots to see which of them would speak to Laban. The lot
fell to Laman, and he went into the house and visited with Laban. Laman
asked if he could have the plates of brass, at which time Laban became
angry and threw Laman out of his house, calling him a robber and threat-
ening to kill him! Laman ran and, upon finding his brothers, told them
all that had transpired. At this news all the brothers were *exceedingly sorrowful,* but Laman, Lemuel, and Sam had given up hope of getting the
plates and were about to return to the wilderness.

*But behold [Nephi] said unto them that: As the Lord liveth,
and as we live, we will not go down unto our father in the wilderness until we have accomplished the thing which the Lord hath commanded us.* (1 Nephi 3:15)

Nephi reminded his brothers that Jerusalem was about to be destroyed
because the people had rejected the words of the prophets. He rehearsed
to them why the plates were so important: the language of their fathers
needed to be preserved, as well as the words of all the holy prophets.

Nephi came up with another plan. They would go back to the house
they had abandoned in Jerusalem, gather up all their gold and silver and
precious things, and trade them for the plates. After retrieving their valuables, they again went to Laban's house and presented their offer to him.

*And it came to pass that when Laban saw our property, and
that it was exceedingly great, he did lust after it, insomuch that he
thrust us out, and sent his servants to slay us, that he might obtain
our property.* (1 Nephi 3:25)

The four brothers ran for their lives, leaving their property behind in
the hands of the wicked Laban. They managed to outrun Laban's servants
and hide in a cave in the wilderness. Laman and Lemuel were very angry
at this turn of events and began yelling at Nephi and Sam, going so far
as to beat them.

> *As they smote us with a rod, behold, an angel of the Lord came and stood before them, and he spake unto them, saying: Why do ye smite your younger brother with a rod? Know ye not that the Lord hath chosen him to be a ruler over you, and this because of your iniquities? Behold ye shall go up to Jerusalem again, and the Lord will deliver Laban into your hands.* (1 Nephi 3:29)

No sooner had the angel departed than Laman and Lemuel began to murmur again, saying,

> *How is it possible that the Lord will deliver Laban into our hands? Behold, he is a mighty man, and he can command fifty, yea, even he can slay fifty; then why not us?* (1 Nephi 3:31)

Nephi reminded his brothers that because the Lord was mightier than all the earth, why wouldn't he be mightier than Laban's fifty—or even his tens of thousands? He asked them how they could doubt when an angel of the Lord had just spoken to them. Laman and Lemuel agreed to go back, even though they murmured all the way. They arrived at night, and Nephi told his brothers to hide outside the walls of the city. All alone, Nephi crept into the city toward the house of Laban.

> *And I was led by the Spirit, not knowing beforehand the things which I should do.* (1 Nephi 4:6)

As Nephi came near the house, he found a man lying on the ground in a drunken stupor. It was Laban! He drew Laban's sword from its sheath. The hilt was made of pure gold, and *the workmanship thereof was exceedingly fine.* The blade was of *the most precious steel.* Nephi was *constrained by the Spirit* to kill Laban!

> *But I said in my heart: Never at any time have I shed the blood of man. And I shrunk and would that I might not slay him.* (1 Nephi 4:10)

The Spirit told Nephi that the Lord had delivered Laban into his hands. Into Nephi's mind came three indictments against Laban: he had attempted to take Nephi's life, he would not keep the commandments, and he had stolen all of Lehi's property. *Again* the Spirit told Nephi to kill Laban, explaining,

Behold the Lord slayeth the wicked to bring forth his righteous purposes. It is better that one man should perish than that a nation should dwindle and perish in unbelief. (1 Nephi 4:13)

Nephi knew that his people would be led to a land of promise and that without the scriptures on the brass plates they could not keep the commandments of the Lord. The future of Nephi's people depended upon his obtaining the brass plates.

Nephi obeyed the voice of the Spirit and cut off Laban's head with the sword. Then he donned Laban's clothes and armor and headed for the treasury. Seeing Laban's servant who had the keys to the treasury, Nephi *commanded him in the voice of Laban* to go with him into the treasury. So good was Nephi's impersonation that the servant carried on a conversation with him. Laban had recently been out with the Jewish elders, and the servant mentioned this. Nephi spoke up, saying that he wanted to carry the brass plates to his elder brethren who were outside the city walls. Then he asked the servant to follow him. Because the servant thought Nephi was speaking of the elders of the church, he followed him without question.

When Laman, Lemuel, and Sam saw who they thought was Laban approaching, they feared for their lives and started running. Nephi called after them, and they recognized his voice and stopped. Now it was the servant's turn to fear, and he began to run.

And now I, Nephi, being a man large in stature, and also having received much strength of the Lord, therefore I did seize upon the servant of Laban, and held him, that he should not flee. (1 Nephi 4:31)

Nephi made an oath to the servant, Zoram, that if he would hearken to what Nephi had to say, he would have no need to fear. Then Nephi promised him that if he followed them back to the wilderness, he could be part of their family and be a free man. He took courage at Nephi's words and made an oath in return to live with Nephi's family from that time forth. After Nephi and his brothers heard Zoram's oath, their *fears did cease concerning him.*

Now we were desirous that he should tarry with us for this cause, that the Jews might not know concerning our flight into the wilderness, lest they should pursue us and destroy us. (1 Nephi 4:36)

(Also, without Zoram, one of the young women in the group would have had no husband!)

When the four sons, including the newest member of the family, Zoram, finally returned to Lehi and Sariah, there was much rejoicing. In their long absence, Sariah had complained against Lehi, calling him a *visionary man* who had led their family from the land of their inheritance. She had supposed that her sons were dead and that she and Lehi too were going to perish in the wilderness. With the arrival of her sons and the news of their miraculous experiences, Sariah was comforted and knew that the Lord had protected them. The family offered *sacrifice and burnt offerings unto the Lord* and gave thanks to God.

Through the genealogy that had been recorded on the plates, Lehi found that he was a descendant of Joseph who had been sold into Egypt. Laban was also a descendant of Joseph and had inherited the responsibility of caretaker of the plates.

·3·

THE JOINING OF TWO FAMILIES
1 NEPHI 7

It came to pass that the Lord spake unto him again, saying that it was not meet for him, Lehi, that he should take his family into the wilderness alone; but that his sons should take daughters to wife, that they might raise up seed unto the Lord in the land of promise. (1 Nephi 7:1)

The Lord commanded Nephi and his brothers to make a second trip back to Jerusalem, this time to bring Ishmael and his family back with them to the wilderness. After they arrived and told Ishmael's family of their plan, the Lord softened the hearts of Ishmael and all of his household so that they agreed to take the journey.

In the *Journal of Discourses*, 23:184–85, there is additional information given by Joseph Smith that shows a previous tie between the two families. He said that Ishmael's sons had already married into Lehi's family. This helps to explain why there is no record of Laman and Lemuel's complaining against a second trip back to Jerusalem so soon and why Ishmael's family so willingly joined Lehi's group.

And it came to pass that as we journeyed in the wilderness, behold Laman and Lemuel, and two of the daughters of Ishmael, and the two sons of Ishmael and their families, did rebel against us; yea, against me, Nephi, and Sam, and their father, Ishmael, and his wife, and his three other daughters. (1 Nephi 7:6)

They had changed their minds about leaving Jerusalem. Nephi spoke up and chastised Laman and Lemuel for being so hardhearted and not doing as the Lord had commanded them. He reminded them that they had just seen an angel of the Lord and had been miraculously delivered from the hands of Laban. Nephi preached many other things to them, including the impending doom of Jerusalem, which would be their fate also if they returned.

> *And it came to pass that when I, Nephi, had spoken these words unto my brethren, they were angry with me. And it came to pass that they did lay their hands upon me, for behold, they were exceedingly wroth, and they did bind me with cords, for they sought to take away my life, that they might leave me in the wilderness to be devoured by wild beasts.* (1 Nephi 7:16)

Nephi prayed to the Lord with great faith, asking for strength to break the cords that were binding him. The cords suddenly loosened, and he began to speak to his brothers again. They were about to lay their hands on him a second time when three members of Ishmael's family pleaded with the others to spare Nephi's life. Hearts were softened, and the newly penitent members of the group bowed down to Nephi and pleaded with him to forgive them for what they had done. Nephi generously forgave them and suggested that they pray to the Lord for forgiveness. This they did, and then the travelers resumed their journey until they were reunited with Lehi and Sariah.

At a later time, Nephi, his three older brothers, and Zoram each took one of Ishmael's daughters as a wife (see 1 Nephi 16:7).

·4·

THE VISION OF THE TREE OF LIFE
1 NEPHI 8

While Lehi was in the wilderness, he had another dream, a very remarkable vision called the vision of the tree of life. Elder Boyd K. Packer, one of the Twelve Apostles of the current dispensation, said that this vision is the central message of the Book of Mormon (see Conference Report, April 1986, 76). In this chapter, the Book of Mormon account of Lehi's dream is paraphrased, followed by endnotes that explain the symbolism in the dream.

In his dream Lehi saw a *dark and dreary wilderness*. Then a man dressed in a white robe appeared and asked him to follow him. As Lehi followed him, he found himself in **a dark and dreary waste**.[1]

> *And after I had traveled for the space of many hours in darkness, I began to pray unto the Lord that he would have mercy on me.* (1 Nephi 8:8)

After praying, Lehi saw **a large and spacious field**.[2] In the field was a **tree whose fruit was desirable to make one happy**.[3] Lehi went to the tree and partook of the fruit, finding it to be the sweetest fruit he had ever tasted. He also noticed that the fruit was whiter than anything he had seen before. As Lehi ate the fruit, *it filled [his] soul with exceedingly great joy.* He wanted very much for his family to partake of the fruit so they too could have this great joy.

As Lehi looked around for his family, he saw a **river**[4] running near the tree. At the head of the river, he saw Sariah and his sons Sam and Nephi looking as though they did not know which direction to go. Lehi called to them in a loud voice, telling them to come to him and eat of the fruit *which was desirable above all other fruit.* They came and partook of the fruit. Wanting Laman and Lemuel to partake of the fruit too, Lehi looked and found them at the head of the river, but they would not come.

Then Lehi noticed a **rod of iron**[5] that extended along the riverbank, leading to the tree. A ***strait and narrow path***[6] followed alongside the rod of iron all the way to the tree.

> *[The path] also led by the head of the fountain, unto a large and spacious field, as if it had been a world.* (1 Nephi 8:20)

Lehi saw throngs of people, so many that he could not number them. **Many of these people were *pressing forward*, trying to get to the path that led to the tree.**[7] As they began walking on the path, a ***mist of darkness***[8] arose. The darkness was so great that they could no longer see their way and they wandered off and became lost. Other people pressing forward on the path caught hold of the rod of iron, and because they clung to it, they were able to get through the awful mist of darkness and reach the tree and eat of its fruit.

> *And after they had partaken of the fruit of the tree they did cast their eyes about as if they were ashamed.* (1 Nephi 8:25)

Lehi saw what was making the people feel ashamed. On the other side of the river was ***a great and spacious building***[9] that seemed to stand in the air, high above the earth. It was filled with people of all ages, *both old and young. Their manner of dress was exceedingly fine; and they were in the attitude of mocking and pointing their fingers* at the people who were eating the fruit.

> *And after they had tasted of the fruit they were ashamed, because of those that were scoffing at them; and they fell away into forbidden paths and were lost.* (1 Nephi 8:28)

Other multitudes came pressing forward. They too caught hold of the rod of iron, and by holding tightly to it they reached the tree and partook of the fruit. The scoffing people in the building had not deterred them.

Throngs of people purposely headed towards the *great and spacious building.* Many were drowned in the great fountain, and others became *lost from [Lehi's] view, wandering in strange roads.*

> *And great was the multitude that did enter into that strange building. And after they did enter into that building they did point the finger of scorn at me and those that were partaking of the fruit*

also; but we heeded them not. (1 Nephi 8:33)

This was the end of the dream. Because Laman and Lemuel did not make it to the tree and partake of the fruit, Lehi was afraid that this was a prophecy of their future.

And he did exhort them then with all the feeling of a tender parent, that they would hearken to his words, that perhaps the Lord would be merciful to them, and not cast them off. (1 Nephi 8:37)

Notes

1. "This seems to be symbolic representation of fallen man in the lone and dreary world." (Joseph Fielding McConkie, Robert L. Millet, *Doctrinal Commentary on the Book of Mormon* [Salt Lake City, Utah: Bookcraft, 1999], 1:56)

2. The world (see 1 Nephi 8:20).

3. The love of God (see 1 Nephi 11:21, 22). John 3:16 says, *For God so loved the world, that he gave his only begotten Son, that whosoever believeth in Him should not perish, but have everlasting life.* So, more specifically, the tree and its fruit represent our Savior and his atoning sacrifice for us.

4. The fountain and the river in the dream are both symbolic of the same thing—the depths of hell (see 1 Nephi 12:16) and filthiness (see 1 Nephi 15:27). The source of the river is the fountain and has been depicted in paintings as a serenely beautiful waterfall. A more apt description might be a gushing torrent of putrid water springing from hell itself. The river is also described as *an awful gulf, which separated the wicked from the tree of life* (see 1 Nephi 15:28). When a person chooses a life of wickedness, or even a life in which divine heritage is not acknowledged, he is creating his own gulf between himself and God.

5. Picture the rod of iron as a handrail extending alongside the path. It represents the word of God (see 1 Nephi 11:25). Clinging to the rod of iron means living our lives according to counsel from the scriptures and living prophets.

6. Baptism is the gate that gets you onto the path (see 2 Nephi 31:17–18), and walking along the path symbolizes following the Savior. However, it is not possible to stay on the path without clinging to the iron rod.

7. The scriptural footnotes lead to D&C 123:12, which talks about many people *who are blinded by the subtle craftiness of men . . . and who are only kept from the truth because they know not where to find it.* The purpose of missionary work is to help people find the truth and bring them to baptism so they might follow the path that leads to eternal life.

8. *The temptations of the devil, which blindeth the eyes, and hardeneth the hearts of the children of men* (see 1 Nephi 12:17).

9. The pride, wisdom, and vanity of the world (see 1 Nephi 11:35–36, 12:18).

·5·

TWO SETS OF PLATES
1 NEPHI 9

In the first verse of the Book of Mormon we learn that Nephi was the record keeper (and would remain so throughout his life). He had been taught to read and write Egyptian in his youth. He spoke Hebrew, but when he engraved his history on the plates, he used a reformed Egyptian script. This allowed him to convey more information with fewer words, no doubt a great benefit considering the space constraints of the metal plates and the arduous task of engraving on them.

First Nephi, chapter 9, consists of six verses in which Nephi informs us that the Lord commanded him to keep two sets of plates, or records. This bit of information is many years out of context, so it is a little confusing unless we bear in mind that Nephi is writing in retrospect. Neither set of plates was started until after he reached the New World.

The first set of plates is called the *large plates of Nephi*. On this set Nephi first engraved a condensed version of his father's record. Then he began his own history of the people, which included their wars and the reigns of their kings. This history was more of a historical, or secular, account and was begun within a few years of arriving in the New World. The large plates became the official record of the Nephites until the end of their civilization.

About twenty years after starting the large plates, Nephi was commanded to make another set of plates, referred to as the *small plates of Nephi*. Our present day Book of Mormon begins with this set of plates and then switches over to the large set of plates with the book of Mosiah. The small plates were to be reserved for sacred writings such as the prophecies and teachings of the prophets and other religious leaders. It is important to understand that both sets of plates began with Lehi's story. So, although the account on the small plates covered the same period of history as could be found in the beginning of the large plates, the record of historical events on the small plates was more condensed.

This double set of record keeping continued until the book of Omni was written, about 130 BC, when the small plates were literally full and no more could be written on them (see Omni 1:30).

The Book of Mormon Student Manual gives us more information about the Lord's purpose behind the dual record keeping:

> Nephi did not understand why he was to make a second set of records, but he had faith that it was "for a wise purpose in him [the Lord], which purpose I know not" (1 Nephi 9:5). Nearly a thousand years later, the prophet Mormon echoed words similar to Nephi's when he testified that along with his abridgment of the large plates of Nephi he was including the small plates of Nephi "for a wise purpose" (Words of Mormon 1:7).
>
> Joseph Smith started the translation of the Book of Mormon with Mormon's abridgment of the large plates of Nephi. He had completed 116 manuscript pages when Martin Harris pleaded with Joseph to let him take the manuscript and show it to family members. Joseph pleaded with the Lord and eventually Martin's request was granted. The manuscript fell into the hands of wicked men (see D&C 10:8) and became known as the "Lost Manuscript."
>
> The loss of the manuscript makes it apparent why the Lord commanded Nephi and Mormon to do what they did. Joseph Smith was told not to retranslate the portion he had already completed, but to translate the small plates of Nephi (see D&C 10:30, 38–45).
>
> "The Lord knoweth all things from the beginning; wherefore, he prepareth a way to accomplish all his works among the children of men" (1 Nephi 9:6). The Lord inspired Nephi and Mormon to do the necessary things that would allow his work to be accomplished by Joseph Smith, even though they were all separated from each other by hundreds of years.[1]

The Book of Mormon prophet Jacob gives us some insight pertaining to the difficult task of record keeping:

Now behold, it came to pass that I, Jacob, having ministered much unto my people in word, (and I cannot write but a little of my words, because of the difficulty of engraving our words upon plates) and we know that the things which we write upon plates must remain;

But whatsoever things we write upon anything save it be upon plates must perish and vanish away; . . .

. . . and we labor diligently to engraven these words upon plates, hoping that our beloved brethren and our children will receive them with thankful hearts. (Jacob 4:1–3)

Note

1. *The Book of Mormon Student Manual for Religion 121 and 122* (Salt Lake City, Utah: The Church of Jesus Christ of Latter-day Saints, 1989), 51–52.

·6·

NEPHI'S VISION
1 NEPHI 10–16

After listening to his father speak of the things he had seen in his vision of the tree of life, Nephi also wanted to *see, and hear, and know of these things, by the power of the Holy Ghost.*

> *Believing that the Lord was able to make them known unto me, as I sat pondering in mine heart I was caught away in the Spirit of the Lord . . . into an exceedingly high mountain, which I never had before seen, and upon which I never had before set my foot.* (1 Nephi 11:1)

While on this mountain, Nephi beheld a marvelous vision. He was shown the tree from his father's dream, and it was *exceeding of all beauty* and whiter than the driven snow. He knew that the tree was *precious above all.* When Nephi asked for the interpretation, he was shown various scenes from the life of the Savior—as an infant held in the arms of his mother, ministering among the people, healing the sick, and casting out devils and unclean spirits. Then Nephi saw the Savior lifted upon the cross and slain for the sins of the world. The tree of life symbolized the love of God, but even more, it was the representation of the Atonement of his Son.

> *For God so loved the world that he gave his only begotten Son, that whosoever believeth in him should not perish, but have everlasting life.* (John 3:16)

Nephi was then shown the future history of the Nephites and Lamanites, and during these scenes more of his father's dream was interpreted. He was given a panoramic view of the promised land that his family would soon be led to. He beheld multitudes of people, seemingly as many as the sands of the sea, and cities too numerous to count. Then he saw the inhabitants of this land fighting against each other, resulting in *great slaughters with the sword among [his] people.*

Nephi witnessed the terrible destruction that came to the land just prior to Christ's appearance on this continent. A mist of darkness covered the face of the land, and there were terrible storms and earthquakes. He saw the earth tear apart and mountains tumble into pieces. He watched as cities sank into the sea and many others were burned (this prophecy was fulfilled in 3 Nephi 8).

When the destruction stopped and the vapor of darkness was gone, Nephi saw multitudes of people whom the Lord had spared. Then the heavens opened and *the Lamb of God* descended out of heaven and showed himself unto the people.

Twelve disciples were ordained to minister unto the people of the promised land. Nephi watched as three generations and many people of the fourth generation passed away in righteousness. He saw the last great and terrible battle between the Nephites and Lamanites, in which the Nephites were utterly destroyed.

The next part of Nephi's vision concerned the Gentiles (non-Jews) who would later inhabit this land. Nephi was shown how the Spirit of God guided a man (Columbus) to discover America (1 Nephi 13:12). Then other Gentiles who were seeking freedom were led across the waters. Because of the multitudes of new settlers now inhabiting this land, Nephi watched as the Lamanites were *scattered before the Gentiles and . . . smitten.*

> *And I beheld the Spirit of the Lord, that it was upon the Gentiles, and they did prosper and obtain the land for their inheritance. . . .*
> *. . . [And they] did humble themselves before the Lord; and the power of the Lord was with them.* (1 Nephi 13:15–16)

The mother countries of these Gentiles gathered together upon the land and the sea to battle against them.

> *And I beheld that the . . . wrath of God was upon all those that were gathered together against them to battle.*
> *And I, Nephi, beheld that the Gentiles . . . were delivered by the power of God out of the hands of all other nations.* (1 Nephi 13:18–19)

Nephi was shown a book that was carried forth among the Gentiles, which was the Bible.

> *The book . . . is a record of the Jews, which contains the covenants of the Lord, which he hath made unto the house of Israel; and it also containeth many of the prophecies of the holy prophets.* (1 Nephi 13:23)

It was explained that the Bible was a record similar to the brass plates, but smaller. When the record was first written, it contained the fulness of the gospel, but it did not remain that way.

> *For behold, they have taken away from the gospel of the Lamb many parts which are plain and most precious; and also many covenants of the Lord have they taken away.*
>
> *And all this have they done that they might pervert the right ways of the Lord, that they might blind the eyes and harden the hearts of the children of men.* (1 Nephi 13:26–27)

Nephi was told that in the last days the Lord would be merciful to the Gentiles. He would bring forth the writings of the Nephites (the Book of Mormon), which would restore many of the plain and precious parts that were taken from the Bible. Other latter-day scripture would combine with the Book of Mormon *unto the convincing of the Gentiles and the remnant of the seed of my brethren, and also the Jews who were scattered upon all the face of the earth, that the records of the prophets and the twelve apostles of the Lamb are true.* (1 Nephi 13:39)

After his incredible vision, Nephi returned to the tent of his father. He walked into an argument that his brethren were having concerning Lehi's teachings of the allegory of the olive tree. Nephi acknowledged that the things his father taught were hard to understand unless one inquired of the Lord. But because they were so hardhearted, *they did not look unto the Lord as they ought.*

In his vision, Nephi had just witnessed the destruction of the entire Nephite nation. To come home and find his family arguing with each other caused Nephi to be overcome with grief. He went on to teach them about the things they did not understand and urged them *with all the energies of [his] soul, and with all the faculty which [he] possessed* to keep the commandments. When he finished speaking, they continued to murmur, saying that he had declared hard things unto them, *more than we are able to bear.* Never one to mince words with his brothers, Nephi replied,

The guilty taketh the truth to be hard, for it cutteth them to the very center. (1 Nephi 16:2)

Nephi continued to admonish them to hearken to the truth and to walk uprightly before God. They finally humbled themselves, giving Nephi *joy and great hopes [for] them.*

·7·

THE LIAHONA
1 NEPHI 16

One night the Lord spoke to Lehi and told him to resume their journey on the following day. The next morning, when Lehi went to his tent door, *to his great astonishment he beheld upon the ground a round ball of curious workmanship; and it was of fine brass. And within the ball were two spindles; and the one pointed the way whither we should go into the wilderness.* (1 Nephi 16:10)

This instrument was similar to a compass, except that instead of pointing north, it pointed in the direction they were to travel. Messages even appeared on it from time to time. Also, unlike our compass that operates on a magnetic principle, it worked according to faith. Much later in the Book of Mormon narrative, in Alma 37:38, this instrument is called the *Liahona* for the first time.

The family gathered their tents and the remainder of their provisions and departed into the wilderness. They traveled for four days, in a south-southeast direction, and then set up camp again in a place they named Shazer. The men took their bows and arrows and went hunting to obtain food for their families. Then the family again set out, following the directions on the Liahona, which led them *in the more fertile parts of the wilderness* in the borders near the Red Sea.

At one point in the journey, the Lord chastised Lehi for murmuring (see the "broken bow" incident, covered in the next chapter) and then told him to see the things that were written on the Liahona. This seems to be the first time any messages appeared on the Liahona.

> *And it came to pass that when my father beheld the things which were written upon the ball, he did fear and tremble exceedingly, and also my brethren and the sons of Ishmael and our wives.* (1 Nephi 16:27)

It soon became apparent that the pointers in the Liahona worked *according to the faith and diligence and heed* that Lehi's group gave to them. The messages that were written on the Liahona were *plain to be read, which did give us understanding concerning the ways of the Lord; and it was written and changed from time to time.* (1 Nephi 16:29)

The group sadly discovered that when they murmured against the Lord, disobeyed his commandments, or fought or argued, the Liahona quit working altogether. When they repented of their wrongdoings and humbled themselves, the Liahona would again point the direction they were to follow.

·8·

NEPHI AND HIS BROKEN BOW
1 NEPHI 16

And after we had traveled for the space of many days, we did pitch our tents for the space of a time, that we might again rest ourselves and obtain food for our families. (1 Nephi 16:17)

While the men were out hunting, Nephi's bow broke, even though it was made of fine steel. Because the bows of the other hunters had lost their spring, the hunting expedition was a failure.

And it came to pass that we did return without food to our families, and being much fatigued, because of their journeying, they did suffer much for the want of food. (1 Nephi 16:19)

Laman and Lemuel and the sons of Ishmael began to complain angrily because of their sufferings and afflictions. Even the great patriarch, father Lehi, began to murmur against the Lord upon facing starvation. Everyone had lost faith—except Nephi.

Nephi reprimanded the group for murmuring against God, and they humbled themselves because of his words. Then Nephi set about to remedy the situation.

And it came to pass that I, Nephi, did make out of wood a bow, and out of a straight stick, an arrow; wherefore, I did arm myself with a bow and an arrow, with a sling and with stones. And I said unto my father: Whither shall I go to obtain food? (1 Nephi 16:23)

Lehi prayed to find out where to send Nephi to hunt. The voice of the Lord came to Lehi and *truly chastened* him because of his murmuring, so much so that *he was brought down into the depths of sorrow.* The Lord told

Lehi to look upon the Liahona to see what was written. Nephi followed the directions and went to the top of a mountain, where he found good hunting. He returned to camp bearing the animals he had slain.

> *And now when they beheld that I had obtained food, how great was their joy! And it came to pass that they did humble themselves before the Lord, and did give thanks unto him.* (1 Nephi 16:32)

·9·

THE DEATH OF ISHMAEL
1 NEPHI 16–17

T he family once again took up their journey, *traveling nearly the same course as in the beginning.* After traveling for many days, they made camp and rested for a while.

It was here, in a place they called Nahom, that Ishmael died and was buried. Ishmael's daughters took his death very hard and did *mourn exceedingly.* They complained against Lehi because he had brought them out of Jerusalem.

> *Our father is dead . . . and we have wandered much in the wilderness, and we have suffered much affliction, hunger, thirst, and fatigue; and after all these sufferings we must perish in the wilderness with hunger.* (1 Nephi 16:35)

Ishmael's daughters wanted to return to Jerusalem. Laman said to Lemuel and to the sons of Ishmael:

> *Let us slay our father, and also our brother Nephi, who has taken it upon him to be our ruler and our teacher, who are his elder brethren.*
>
> *Now, he says that the Lord has talked with him, and also that angels have ministered unto him. But behold, we know that he lies unto us; . . . and he worketh many things by his cunning arts, that he may deceive our eyes, thinking, perhaps, that he may lead us away into some strange wilderness; and after he has led us away, he has thought to make himself a king and a ruler over us.* (1 Nephi 16:37–38)

It is difficult to understand how Laman could have said these things when he himself had been reprimanded by an angel face to face! When Laman finished speaking, the voice of the Lord spoke to him and to the other unfaithful members of the group and chastised them at great length. They repented of their sins and the Lord again blessed them with food.

The family resumed their journey, traveling *nearly eastward from that time forth*. During the years that they traveled in the wilderness, the women bore children. Even Sariah had two more sons, Jacob and Joseph.

Nephi writes that during these years they suffered so many afflictions *that we cannot write them all*. Though they encountered many hardships, the Lord greatly blessed them. They were not allowed to make many fires (presumably because they were traveling through hostile territory), and so the Lord caused the raw meat to taste sweet. The nursing mothers had plenty of milk for their babies, and the women were strong, *even like unto the men*. The people began to bear their nomadic life without complaining.

> *And thus we see that the commandments of God must be fulfilled. And if it so be that the children of men keep the commandments of God he doth nourish them, and strengthen them, and provide means whereby they can accomplish the thing which he has commanded them.* (1 Nephi 17:3)

·10·

NEPHI BUILDS A SHIP
1 NEPHI 17–18

Lehi and his family *did sojourn* for eight years in the wilderness. (To sojourn means to live somewhere temporarily, which describes their lifestyle of moving from camp to camp. It obviously did not take them eight years to travel from Jerusalem to the sea.)

The last place they set up camp was in a land by the sea. They named the land Bountiful because of its plentiful fruit and wild honey. Several days after their arrival, the voice of the Lord came to Nephi, saying, *Arise, and get thee into the mountain.* Nephi obeyed and ascended the mountain, where the Lord said to him,

> *Thou shalt construct a ship, after the manner which I shall show thee, that I may carry thy people across these waters.* (1 Nephi 17:8)

Demonstrating great faith, Nephi asked the Lord where he could find ore with which to forge tools needed to build the ship and was told where the ore could be found. After the tools were made, Nephi was ready to begin building the ship. When Laman and Lemuel heard what he was about to do, they made great fun of him.

> *Our brother is a fool, for he thinketh that he can build a ship; yea, and he also thinketh that he can cross these great waters.* (1 Nephi 17:17)

Not believing that Nephi could build a ship or that God had instructed him, the brothers refused to help. Nephi became very sorrowful for the hardness of their hearts, which made his brothers all the more glad.

> *We knew that ye could not construct a ship, for we knew that ye were lacking in judgment; wherefore, thou canst not accomplish so great a work.*

And thou art like unto our father, led away by the foolish imagi-
nations of his heart. (1 Nephi 17:19–20)

The brothers complained that because of their father they had wandered many years in the wilderness, where their women had given birth to their children and suffered all things except death. They added that the sufferings of their wives had been so great that it would have been better if they *had* died instead of being subjected to such terrible afflictions. If the family had not left Jerusalem, they could have been enjoying their riches and *might have been happy.* Then one of the brothers said,

And we know that the people who were in the land of Jerusa-
lem were a righteous people; for they kept the . . . commandments,
according to the law of Moses. (1 Nephi 17:22)

(In reality, the people in Jerusalem were in such a state of apostasy that they tried to kill all the prophets sent to call them to repentance! And at this point in history, those "righteous people" were very soon to face unimaginable horrors as the Babylonians invaded Jerusalem.)

After listening to his brothers' rantings, Nephi was determined to get through to them. He first gave them the example of how Moses led the children of Israel out of Egypt. He explained that it was by the Lord's direction and power that the Israelites were led out of bondage to a land of promise. Nephi was trying to show his brothers that they, too, were being led to a land of promise by the hand of the Lord.

Nephi explained *again* why they had to leave Jerusalem and how the Jews had tried to kill their father. Boldly, Nephi told his brothers that they were just like the Jews in Jerusalem—they were murderers in their hearts because they, too, had wanted to kill their father. He reminded them that they had seen an angel and had heard the voice of the Lord from time to time. And then he told them,

He hath spoken unto you in a still small voice, but ye were past
feeling, that ye could not feel his words. (1 Nephi 17:45)

Nephi ended his lecture by telling them that his soul was torn with anguish and his heart was pained because of them and that he was afraid they would be cast off forever. With these last words, his brothers became so angry that they decided to throw Nephi into the depths of the sea. As they were about to grab him, Nephi gave them this stern warning:

> *In the name of the Almighty God, I command you that ye touch*
> *me not, for I am filled with the power of God, even unto the consum-*
> *ing of my flesh; and whoso shall lay his hands upon me shall wither*
> *even as a dried reed; and he shall be as naught before the power of*
> *God, for God shall smite him.* (1 Nephi 17:48)

Nephi also told them that God had commanded him to build a ship and
that they had better help him. Because of his great faith it was all very
simple to Nephi. He explained to his brothers that if God had told him
to turn the water into earth, it would be done. Since God had already
performed greater miracles among the children of men, *how is it that he*
cannot instruct me, that I should build a ship?

Nephi said other things to his brothers, leaving them *confounded* and
unable to argue against him. For many days they dared not touch Nephi,
being afraid that they would wither as he had warned.

> *And it came to pass that the Lord said unto me: Stretch forth*
> *thine hand again unto thy brethren, and they shall not wither before*
> *thee, but I will shock them, saith the Lord, and this will I do, that*
> *they may know that I am the Lord their God.* (1 Nephi 17:53)

As Nephi did this they received a shock intense enough to shake them!
Now knowing for sure that the Lord was with Nephi, they fell down
before him and were about to worship him. Nephi stopped them and told
them that it was the Lord they should be worshipping. At last he had the
help of all the brothers to build the ship.

> *And the Lord did show me from time to time after what manner*
> *I should work the timbers of the ship.* (1 Nephi 18:1)

Since they were using the Lord's blueprints, the construction of the ship
was unlike anything man had ever built before. Nephi described the work
as *curious workmanship.*

> *And it came to pass that after I had finished the ship, . . . my*
> *brethren beheld that it was good, and that the workmanship thereof*
> *was exceedingly fine; wherefore, they did humble themselves again*
> *before the Lord.* (1 Nephi 18:4)

·11·

SAILING TO THE PROMISED LAND
1 NEPHI 18

The Lord told Lehi that the time had come for crossing the sea. The group loaded the ship with provisions such as fruit, honey, and meat. Upon setting sail, they were driven by the winds toward the promised land. After many days at sea, Laman, Lemuel, and the sons of Ishmael and their wives *began to make themselves merry* with singing and dancing. (The footnotes to 18:9 refer the previous verse to the Topical Guide under Rioting and Reveling.) They had forgotten that the ship was being guided by the Lord's power.

> *And I, Nephi, began to fear exceedingly lest the Lord should be angry with us, and smite us because of our iniquity, that we should be swallowed up in the depths of the sea.* (1 Nephi 18:10)

Nephi tried to speak to his brothers, but that only made them angry. They were not going to be ruled by their younger brother. In a very rough manner Laman and Lemuel took Nephi and bound him so tightly that he could not move. When they did this, the Liahona quit working and they did not know which direction to steer the ship. Then there arose a great and terrible storm that drove them back for three days. Those who had caused this calamity were greatly afraid that they would be drowned in the sea, but even facing death they would not untie Nephi!

Lehi tried to reason with Laman and Lemuel and also with the sons of Ishmael. It was to no avail because they threatened anyone who spoke in Nephi's defense. Because of the grief and sorrow caused by their wicked sons, Lehi and Sariah *were brought down . . . upon their sickbeds . . . near to be cast with sorrow into a watery grave.* Even the tears of Nephi's wife and children did not soften the hearts of these cruel and stubborn men.

On the fourth day the storm became so violent that it seemed as though at any moment the ship would be swallowed up by the sea. Laman and Lemuel and the sons of Ishmael could see that the judgments of God were upon them. Knowing they would all perish unless they repented, they finally untied Nephi. His wrists and ankles were tremendously swollen and sore, but never once had Nephi complained to God during his tortuous ordeal. Instead, he *did praise him all the day long.* He knew that the Lord had allowed this to happen in order to show forth his power. Nephi took the compass, and it began to work again. As he prayed to the Lord, a great calm replaced the storm, and once again they sailed toward the promised land. Finally, their long voyage ended with their arrival in the New World.

·12·

TWO NATIONS ARE BORN
1 NEPHI 18–19; 2 NEPHI 1–5

Upon arriving in the promised land, Lehi's party pitched their tents and began to till the earth, planting the seeds they had brought with them from Jerusalem. Their crops flourished, and the people were blessed abundantly. As they explored this new land, they found animals in the forest of every kind—cows, oxen, donkeys, goats, horses, and all types of wild animals. They also discovered that precious ores such as gold, silver, and copper were plentiful.

Within a few years after their arrival, the Lord commanded Nephi to make *plates of ore* so that the history of his people could be recorded on them. Nephi began by abridging the records of his father, which included accounts of leaving Jerusalem and traveling in the wilderness. Then he began his own history of the people. It was the Lord's plan that these plates be handed down from generation to generation as a permanent record of his people.

Lehi was coming to the end of his days. He rehearsed unto his children the great blessings the Lord had given to them, particularly being led out of Jerusalem.

> *For, behold, . . . I have seen a vision, in which I know that Jerusalem is destroyed; and had we remained in Jerusalem we should also have perished.* (2 Nephi 1:4)

Then Lehi spoke about their new homeland. He taught that this land would be a land of promise to *all those who should be led out of other countries by the hand of the Lord.*

> *And behold, it is wisdom that this land should be kept as yet from the knowledge of other nations; for behold, many nations would overrun the land, that there would be no place for an inheritance.* (2 Nephi 1:8)

Lehi promised his family that as long as they kept the commandments, they and future generations would prosper in the land. But if they or their descendants did not keep the commandments, they would be cut off from the presence of the Lord and be *scattered and smitten* by other nations that would be allowed to possess the land.

After Lehi had blessed each member of his household, including Ishmael's family, he died. Not many days after his death, Laman and Lemuel and the sons of Ishmael became angry with Nephi *because of the admonitions of the Lord.* Nephi was once again commanded to counsel his brothers, but their anger only increased against him.

> *Our younger brother thinks to rule over us; and we have had much trial because of him; wherefore, now let us slay him, that we may not be afflicted more because of his words. For behold, we will not have him to be our ruler; for it belongs unto us, who are the elder brethren, to rule over this people.* (2 Nephi 5:3)

The Lord warned Nephi to take all those who would go with him and flee into the wilderness. Those who followed Nephi were *those who believed in the warnings and revelations of God.* They included Nephi's family, Zoram and his family, Sam and his family, Jacob and Joseph, and Nephi's sisters. (2 Nephi 5:6 is the only mention in the Book of Mormon that Nephi had sisters.) They took their tents and what provisions they could and also the brass plates and the Liahona. They traveled in the wilderness for many days and then pitched their tents in a place they named Nephi. They called themselves the people of Nephi. The little band of Nephites kept the commandments in all things, and so the Lord blessed them. They had bountiful harvests from the crops they planted and raised flocks and herds and animals of every kind. The people began to prosper and multiply in the land.

The people in the other group were now known as Lamanites, and their hatred of the Nephites continued to grow. Fearing that they might try to destroy his people, Nephi made swords using the sword of Laban as a pattern.

> *And [Nephi] did teach [his] people to build buildings, and to work in all manner of wood, and of iron, and of copper, and of brass, and of steel, and of gold, and of silver, and of precious ores, which were in great abundance.* (2 Nephi 5:15)

Nephi also built a temple, constructing it after the manner of Solomon's temple, *save it were not built of so many precious things; . . . and the workmanship thereof was exceedingly fine.* (2 Nephi 5:16)

In addition, Nephi taught his people to be industrious and to labor with their hands. His followers wanted him to be their king, which was contrary to Nephi's desire. *Nevertheless, [he] did for them according to that which was in [his] power.*

The Lamanites had cut themselves off from the presence of the Lord through their disobedience, fulfilling the prophecy given to Nephi. The threat of destruction by the Lamanites was the one thing that would cause future generations of Nephites to repent and turn to the Lord for help. Nephi consecrated his younger brothers, Jacob and Joseph, to be priests and teachers, and the people *lived after the manner of happiness.*

Twenty years after starting his first set of plates (the large plates), Nephi was commanded to begin another set of plates (the small plates). Not knowing of the Lord's purpose for the second set, Nephi was nevertheless obedient. He was instructed to reserve the small plates for more sacred writings, such as prophecies and accounts of the ministry. For over four hundred years a dual record of the people was kept. (See chapter 5 of *And It Came to Pass* for an explanations of Nephi's two sets of plates.)

Within forty years of leaving Jerusalem, the Nephites had already experienced wars and contentions with the Lamanites.

(Note: There are twenty-eight additional chapters in 2 Nephi that include Nephi's teachings and prophecies, some of the teachings of his brother Jacob, and a great many passages from the prophet Isaiah that Nephi copied from the brass plates. These same passages of Isaiah's teachings are also found in the Old Testament, with slight variations.)

·13·

JACOB, THE BROTHER OF NEPHI
JACOB 1–3

It had been fifty-five years since the people left Jerusalem, and Nephi had labored all this time for the welfare of his people. He had been their protector and was greatly loved. Knowing that his time on earth was coming to an end, Nephi anointed a man to be a king and a ruler over his people. He also turned the plates over to his brother Jacob so that he could continue recording the history of their people. Then Nephi died. Because the people held Nephi in such high esteem, they wanted to remember his name. All those who reigned after Nephi were called Second Nephi, Third Nephi, and so forth. Under the reign of the second king, the people *began to grow hard in their hearts and indulge themselves . . . in wicked practices.* They also began to search for gold and silver and to be lifted up in pride.

Jacob and Joseph, Nephi's younger brothers, magnified their callings as teachers and priests. They felt that the sins of the people would be on their own heads if they did not teach them the word of God with all diligence. The brothers labored with all their might among the people, persuading them to come unto Christ.

Jacob preached to his people and boldly testified to them of their wickedness. It grieved him to have to speak in this way in the presence of the women and children, *many of whose feelings [were] exceedingly tender and chaste and delicate.* He exhorted the people to seek first for the kingdom of God. Then they could seek for riches *if* their intent was to do good—to clothe the naked, feed the hungry, and administer to the sick and afflicted.

Jacob went on to speak about a more serious sin. The people were indulging in whoredoms with the excuse that these same things had been practiced by David and Solomon of old.

Behold, David and Solomon truly had many wives and concu-
bines, which thing was abominable before me, saith the Lord. (Jacob
2:24)

It would seem that Jacob is denouncing the practice of plural marriage,
but he is only speaking to the Nephites, who had no authorization to practice it. At various times, God has called upon his people to enter into plural
marriage. Examples would include Abraham, Isaac, Jacob, and the Saints
in the early days of this dispensation. We learn in D&C 132:37–39 why
Jacob condemns the actions of David and Solomon—*in nothing did they sin
save in those things which they received not of me.* David was not authorized
to take Bathsheba for a wife; and Solomon, after being commanded not to,
took wives *who turned away his heart after other gods* (see 1 Kings 11:1–6).

Bruce R. McConkie, an apostle of this last dispensation, made this
statement: "All who pretend or assume to engage in plural marriage in this
day, when the one holding the keys has withdrawn the power by which
they are performed, are guilty of gross wickedness."[1]

The brethren were told not to have more than one wife and not to have
any concubines. They were never to cause sorrow to come upon the fair
daughters of their people.

Behold, ye have done greater iniquities than the Lamanites. . . .
Ye have broken the hearts of your tender wives, and lost the confidence
of your children, because of your bad example before them; and the
sobbings of their hearts ascend up to God against you. (Jacob 2:35)

The people were warned that if they did not soon repent, the time
would quickly come when the Lord would lead away the righteous from
among them. The Lamanites would then take possession of their land.
(This prophecy was fulfilled in Omni 1:12–14.)

In a very forthright statement, Jacob told the people that the Lamanites
were more righteous than they were because they observed the command-
ment to have only one wife. Furthermore, the Lamanite husbands and
wives loved each other and their children. Their unbelief and hatred of the
Nephites was because of the traditions of their fathers.

Note
1.   Bruce R. McConkie, *Mormon Doctrine* (Salt Lake City, Utah: Bookcraft,
     1966), 579.

·14·

JACOB CONTENDS WITH SHEREM
JACOB 7

After some years had passed away, a man named Sherem came among the people of Nephi and began to preach that there would be no Christ. He taught many things *which were flattering unto the people, . . . that he might overthrow the doctrine of Christ.*

Sherem was a well-educated man with *a perfect knowledge of the language of the people.* By using *much flattery and power of speech,* he led many people away from the truth.

Knowing that Jacob believed Christ would come, Sherem sought an opportunity to speak with him. Because of his success with the people, he thought he could also convince Jacob that there would be no Christ. What Sherem did not know was that Jacob had not only faith in Christ but also a sure knowledge of him. Jacob had received many revelations and witnessed many miracles. Angels had ministered unto him, and the voice of the Lord had spoken to him *in very word* from time to time. Moreover, Nephi tells us in 2 Nephi 11:3 that Jacob had actually *seen* the Savior. Having experienced all these things, Jacob *could not be shaken* in his belief.

Sherem finally got his audience with Jacob. Addressing him as *Brother Jacob,* he accused him of leading the people away from *the right way of God.* Sherem said it was blasphemy for any man to preach of a Christ who would be coming hundreds of years in the future, for no man could know of things to come. The debate went on for some time, but the Lord poured out his Spirit upon Jacob, who was able to *confound [Sherem] in all his words.* Finally, Sherem said, *Show me a sign by this power of the Holy Ghost, in . . . which ye know so much.* Jacob replied:

> *What am I that I should tempt God to show unto thee a sign . . . ?*
> *Yet thou wilt deny it, because thou art of the devil. Nevertheless, not my*
> *will be done; but if God shall smite thee, let that be a sign unto thee that*
> *he has power, . . . and also, that Christ shall come.* (Jacob 7:14)

As soon as Jacob had spoken these words, the power of the Lord came upon Sherem and he fell to the ground. For many days he had to be cared for. Knowing that he was about to die, he asked that all the people be gathered together so that he could speak to them. The next day Sherem spoke plainly to the multitude, admitting that what he had taught them was not true and that he had been deceived by the power of the devil. He was afraid that he had *committed the unpardonable sin* by denying the Christ.

> *And because I have thus lied unto God I greatly fear lest my case shall be awful; but I confess unto God.*
> *And it came to pass that when he had said these words he could say no more, and he gave up the ghost.* (Jacob 7:19–20)

The multitude was astonished at the words Sherem had spoken. The power of God came upon them, and they fell to the earth. Jacob was pleased at what happened to the people because he had prayed for it. Peace was again restored as the people searched the scriptures and *hearkened no more to the words of this wicked man.*

Many attempts were made to restore the Lamanites to the truth, but these efforts were all in vain.

> *For they delighted in wars and bloodshed, and they had an eternal hatred against us. . . . And they sought . . . to destroy us continually.* (Jacob 7:24)

The Nephites' only choice was to arm themselves against the Lamanites and to put their trust in God. So far, they remained *conquerors of their enemies.*

> *And it came to pass that I, Jacob, began to be old; . . . and . . . our lives passed away like as it were unto us a dream, we being a lonesome and a solemn people, wanderers, cast out from Jerusalem, born in tribulation, in a wilderness, and hated of our brethren, which caused wars and contentions; wherefore, we did mourn out our days.* (Jacob 7:26)

Before Jacob died, he turned the plates over to his son, Enos, and then bid his readers farewell.

·15·

ENOS AND HIS MIGHTY PRAYER
THE BOOK OF ENOS

One day while Enos was hunting in the forest, his thoughts turned to his father, Jacob. He was pondering his father's teachings about *eternal life and the joy of the saints.* His *soul hungered,* and he knelt down and cried unto the Lord in mighty prayer. He prayed all day long in supplication for his own soul, and when the sun went down he was still raising his voice to the heavens. Then Enos heard the voice of the Lord tell him that his sins were forgiven, and that he would be blessed. He knew that God could not lie, and his guilt was *swept away.* He asked the Lord how his sins had been forgiven.

> *Because of thy faith in Christ, whom thou hast never before heard nor seen. And many years pass away before he shall manifest himself in the flesh; wherefore, go to, thy faith hath made thee whole.* (Enos 1:8)

After hearing these words, Enos felt a desire for the welfare of his people, the Nephites, and he poured out his whole soul unto God for them.

> *And while I was thus struggling in the spirit, behold, the voice of the Lord came into my mind again, saying: I will visit thy brethren according to their diligence in keeping my commandments. I have given unto them this land, and it is a holy land; and I curse it not save it be for the cause of iniquity.* (Enos 1:10)

Enos's faith now began to be unshakable, and he prayed for his brethren, the Lamanites. Up until this time, any efforts to convert the Lamanites to the truth had been in vain. Instead, *they swore in their wrath* that they would destroy the Nephites and their record. Enos knew that if the Nephites fell into transgression, this might happen. It was his desire that the Lord would preserve the Nephite record and at some future time bring forth these sacred writings to the Lamanites so that they might *be brought unto salvation.*

Enos *labored with all diligence* in behalf of the Lamanites. Then the Lord told him that his desire would be granted because of his faith and the faith of others before him. He covenanted with Enos that he would bring forth the records unto the Lamanites *in his own due time.* Knowing that the Lord kept his promises, Enos's soul was at peace.

Enos went among the people of Nephi, testifying of the things that he had seen and heard and prophesying of things to come. The Nephites continued their efforts to restore the Lamanites to the truth, but *their hatred was fixed.* Enos gives this description of them:

> *They were led by their evil nature that they became wild, and ferocious, and a blood-thirsty people, full of idolatry and filthiness; feeding upon beasts of prey; dwelling in tents, and wandering about in the wilderness with a short skin girdle about their loins and their heads shaven; and their skill was in the bow, and in the cimeter, and the ax. And many of them did eat nothing save it was raw meat; and they were continually seeking to destroy us.* (Enos 1:20)

On the other hand, the Nephites were a more settled and industrious people who tilled the ground and raised fruits and grains. They also raised animals of every kind, including cattle, goats, and horses.

Even though there were many prophets among the Nephites, the people were not diligent in keeping the commandments. They had to be continually taught that destruction would come upon them if they were wicked. They also had to be reminded of *the duration of eternity* in order to *keep them in the fear of the Lord.*

Enos witnessed many wars between the Nephites and the Lamanites and spent all his days preaching and prophesying to the people. It had now been 179 years since Lehi left Jerusalem. Before he died, Enos passed the plates to his son, Jarom.

> *And I soon go to the place of my rest, which is with my Redeemer;*
> *. . . Then shall I see his face with pleasure, and he will say unto me: Come unto me, ye blessed, there is a place prepared for you in the mansions of my Father. Amen.* (Enos 1:27)

·16·

Short Record Keeping
THE BOOKS OF JAROM AND OMNI

T he writings of the next six authors span about 290 years yet take up fewer than five pages in the Book of Mormon. Not much was recorded during this period because the Nephites were in a state of growing apostasy. The following is a brief summary of their writings.

Jarom, the Son of Enos

Jarom was in charge of the plates nearly his whole lifetime, but during those years he wrote only a brief history. He did not want to record his prophecies or revelations, *for what could I write more than my fathers have written?*

Many times the Lamanites came to battle against them, but because the Nephites were led by righteous men who taught the people the ways of the Lord, they withstood their enemies and drove them out of their lands.

During Jarom's lifetime the people multiplied and spread across the face of the land. They *became exceedingly rich in gold, and in silver, and in precious things.* They were skilled in the *fine workmanship of wood, in buildings, and in machinery.* They processed iron, copper, brass, and steel, and with these metals they made weapons of war such as the arrow, the dart, and the javelin. They also made tools of every kind to till the ground.

The prophets and priests and teachers labored diligently with the people, persuading them to keep the commandments. Jarom said *that by so doing they kept them from being destroyed upon the face of the land.*

Jarom passed the plates to his son, Omni.

Omni, the Son of Jarom

Omni wrote only three verses before passing the plates on. He recalled that in his days he *fought much with the sword to preserve [his] people,* but the Nephites also had many seasons of peace. Omni included this confession in his brief record:

> *I of myself am a wicked man, and I have not kept the statutes and the commandments of the Lord as I ought to have done.* (Omni 1:2)

He later conferred the plates to his son Amaron. It had been 282 years since Lehi left Jerusalem.

Amaron, the Son of Omni

Amaron also kept the plates for many years. The central message in the five verses he wrote was this promise from the Lord: *Inasmuch as ye will not keep my commandments ye shall not prosper in the land.* He added that 320 years had now passed since Lehi left Jerusalem, during which time *the more wicked part of the Nephites were destroyed.*

Amaron delivered the plates to his brother, Chemish.

Chemish, the Brother of Amaron

Chemish wrote only one verse!

> *Now I, Chemish, write what few things I write, in the same book with my brother; for behold, I saw the last which he wrote, that he wrote it with his own hand; and he wrote it in the day that he delivered them unto me. . . . And I make an end.* (Omni 1:9)

The plates were then given to his son Abinadom.

Abinadom, the Son of Chemish

In the two verses written by Abinadom, we are told that Abinadom witnessed many wars between the Nephites and Lamanites. With his own sword he took the lives of many of the Lamanites in the defense of his people. He then added that he knew of no revelation or prophecy that had not already been written, so he ended his record. His son Amaleki then received the plates.

Amaleki, the Son of Abinadom

Amaleki gave us nineteen verses that contain critical information. The people of the Book of Mormon are the product of three migrations led by the Lord from Asiatic lands to America: First the Jaredites, then

Lehi's family, and then the Mulekites. Only in Amaleki's writings do we find out how these three groups tie in to one another (this will be explained in the following chapter).

Amaleki was born in the days of the first King Mosiah. He lived to see the death of King Mosiah and to see Mosiah's son Benjamin appointed king. During the reign of King Benjamin there was much bloodshed between the Nephites and the Lamanites, but under his righteous leadership the Nephites were able to drive their enemies out of their land.

When Amaleki became old, and not having any sons, he delivered up the plates to King Benjamin. At the end of his record, he left us these stirring words:

> *Come unto Christ . . . and offer your whole souls as an offering unto him, and continue in fasting and praying, and endure to the end; and as the Lord liveth ye will be saved.* (Omni 1:26)

·17·

DISCOVERING THE MULEKITES
(WHO HAD ALREADY DISCOVERED THE JAREDITES)
OMNI 1:12–22

Amaleki was born during the reign of the first King Mosiah, who was the father of King Benjamin. Amaleki tells us this important story: Mosiah was warned by the Lord that he should flee out of the land of Nephi and take with him as many of the people who would go. The Lord guided them through the wilderness until they came to a land called Zarahemla.

(From this point on in the Book of Mormon, the Lamanites are headquartered in the land of Nephi, having taken it over when the Nephites left, and the Nephites are headquartered in the land of Zarahemla.)

King Mosiah and his followers discovered a people residing in Zarahemla that they never knew existed. These people had also been led to America by the hand of the Lord. They left Jerusalem just a few years after Lehi did, during the destruction of that city.

(At the time that Jerusalem was destroyed, the king of Judah was Zedekiah. Before Zedekiah was carried away captive by the Babylonians, he was forced to witness the execution of his sons [see Jeremiah 52:10]. Unintentionally, the Babylonians missed one son by the name of Mulek, and his life was spared [see Helaman 8:21]. All of Zedekiah's sons had to be quite young since the king was only twenty-one years old when his reign of eleven years began. We are given few details about Mulek except that he was with a group of people who left Jerusalem about 587 BC, journeyed through the wilderness, and were brought by the Lord across the ocean and into the land where Mosiah discovered them. We commonly refer to them as Mulekites, although they are never called that in the Book of Mormon. The Mulekites and the descendants of Lehi lived on this same continent for over three hundred years, until about 270 BC, without either group knowing of the other. This was made possible because, as we are told in Helaman 6:10, *the Lord did bring Mulek into the land north, and Lehi into the land south.*)

Surprisingly, there was great rejoicing among the inhabitants of Zarahemla upon the arrival of the Nephites. The newcomers had brought with them the brass plates, which not only proved their common ancestry but also contained long-forgotten teachings of God. Because the Mulekites brought no scriptures with them when they migrated to the New World, they gradually lost this precious knowledge. Their language had also become corrupted to the point where the Nephites could not understand them. By the time Mosiah discovered the people of Zarahemla, they had become *exceedingly numerous* and had had many wars among themselves.

The Nephites taught the people of Zarahemla their language. The two groups of people joined together, and Mosiah was appointed king over all the people.

Sometime after Mosiah became king, the Mulekites brought him a large engraved stone that had been in their possession for many years. Mosiah interpreted the engravings using the Urim and Thummim. (This is an instrument prepared by God for the purpose of translation. Joseph Smith used this same Urim and Thummim to translate the Book of Mormon.) The writing on the stone made reference to the Jaredite civilization that was on this continent from around 2200 BC until 600 BC or later. These people were led to America at the time of the Tower of Babel and because of wars had become extinct.

The engravings also told of a man named Coriantumr. He was discovered by the Mulekites and lived with them for nine months before he died. Coriantumr was the last Jaredite king; in fact, he was the last remaining Jaredite! The book of Ether is the record of the Jaredite people. In Ether 13:20–21 a prophet warned Coriantumr of what would happen in the future if he did not repent: Every soul would be destroyed except him, he would live to see the prophecy fulfilled that spoke of another people receiving this land for their inheritance, and he would receive a burial by these people. All three prophecies were fulfilled. It is not known how long Coriantumr wandered alone before he was discovered by the Mulekites. (See "Postscript" at the end of chapter 100 herein.)

During the days of the second King Mosiah, who was the grandson of the King Mosiah of this chapter, the land of the Jaredite civilization was discovered by the people of King Limhi.

[It] was covered with bones of men, and of beasts, and was also covered with ruins of buildings of every kind . . . [and] had been peopled with a people who were as numerous as the hosts of Israel. (Mosiah 8:8)

Breastplates, swords, and twenty-four gold plates were brought back from this land. The second King Mosiah translated these plates, and this history of the Jaredite people is found in the book of Ether. It is summarized in chapters 92 through 100 of *And It Came to Pass.*)

·18·

THE WORDS OF MORMON
WORDS OF MORMON

Victor L. Ludlow gives a concise explanation of Mormon's purpose in inserting the Words of Mormon where he did, even though this put the insertion about five hundred years out of chronological order.

The Words of Mormon, which he inscribed at the end of the small plates of Nephi, provide further insights into the various records maintained by the Nephites. Mormon lived five centuries after Amaleki and he received a vast library of various plates from the earlier generations of Nephites. He sought to abridge these records into one set of plates, the plates of Mormon. He started with the time of Lehi and had completed his abridgment down to the time of King Benjamin. . . . In searching for further records of this period, he discovered the small plates of Nephi, which basically overlapped the whole period of his abridgment to that point. However, the small plates of Nephi contained a more spiritual account of these earlier generations, along with a more complete record of key prophecies, revelations, and teachings. Mormon decided to insert this whole record into his own set of plates, and he wrote a few words at the end of the plates to bridge the last years of the reign of King Benjamin.[1]

When Joseph Smith started his translation of the Book of Mormon, he first began with Mormon's abridgment of the large plates of Nephi. After the loss of the first 116 pages of the manuscript (see chapter 5 of *And It Came to Pass* for more details), Joseph was told not to retranslate from the same record. Instead, he was directed to translate the small plates, which had a duplicate history. Because Joseph was now combining two different sets of plates, without the earlier inclusion of the Words of

Mormon we would have missed part of the history of King Benjamin and his people. (The next chapter will cover this information.)

It is interesting to note that the first six books of the Book of Mormon, taken from the small plates of Nephi and *not* abridged, are written in first person by the various authors. The remainder of the Book of Mormon, which Mormon abridged from the large plates of Nephi, is written in more of a narrative form, with many comments from Mormon interspersed throughout.

Note
1. Victor L. Ludlow, *Studies in Scripture Vol. 7*, ed. Kent P. Jackson (Salt Lake City: Deseret Book, 1988), 202.

·19·

KING BENJAMIN
WORDS OF MORMON 1:12–18; MOSIAH 1–6

King Benjamin was a holy man who governed his people in righteousness. He spent his days in the service of his people, but as he himself said, *I have only been in the service of God.* As king he never sought for gold or any manner of riches from his people. Instead, he labored with his own hands to support himself so that his people would not be laden with taxes. He taught his people to keep the commandments of the Lord, knowing that by so doing they would prosper in the land and be protected from their enemies. His humility is evident in this verse:

> *And I, even I, whom ye call your king, am no better than ye yourselves are; for I am also of the dust.* (Mosiah 2:26)

During the early years of King Benjamin's reign, the Lamanite army from the land of Nephi came to fight against his people. (Remember, the land of Nephi is now the headquarters for the Lamanites and will be for the rest of the Book of Mormon.) King Benjamin gathered his armies together and with the sword of Laban led them into battle. *In the strength of the Lord* they killed many thousands of the Lamanites and drove the rest out of their land.

During King Benjamin's reign there were many false Christs and false prophets trying to lead the people astray. They were all punished according to their crimes. There was also contention among the people. With the help of the holy prophets and *by laboring with all the might of his body and the faculty of his whole soul,* King Benjamin once again established peace in the land. He had continual peace all the remainder of his days.

King Benjamin had three sons: Mosiah, Helorum, and Helaman. These sons were taught how to read and write the reformed Egyptian language so that they would be able to diligently search the holy scriptures and become *men of understanding.* They were also taught to keep all of God's commandments.

King Benjamin grew old and knew that his time to die was approaching. It became necessary to confer the kingdom upon one of his sons, so he had Mosiah brought before him.

> *My son, I would that ye should make a proclamation throughout all this land among all this people . . . that thereby they may be gathered together; for on the morrow I shall proclaim unto this my people . . . that thou art a king and a ruler over this people.* (Mosiah 1:10)

Mosiah was also given charge of the brass plates, the plates of Nephi, the sword of Laban, and the Liahona.

The people gathered at the temple from throughout all the land to hear King Benjamin speak—so many that they could not number them. They brought the firstlings of their flocks to offer as a sacrifice unto the Lord, according to the law of Moses. Because the multitude was too great to teach within the walls of the temple, King Benjamin had a tower built from which he could speak to them. As they arrived, they pitched their tents around the temple in groups of families. The door to every tent was facing the temple so they could remain in their tents and hear King Benjamin speak. Still, not everyone could hear him, so he had his words written down and circulated among those who were not within the sound of his voice.

In King Benjamin's opening remarks, he told the people that he had not gathered them together for them to *trifle* with his words; what he had to say was of the utmost importance. An angel of the Lord had stood before him and had given him a glorious message that he was to share with his people (see Mosiah 3:2–4). Also, King Benjamin wanted to die with a clear conscience, knowing that he had done everything in his power to teach them correct principles. He did not want their sins upon his own head.

The message from the angel was about the coming of the Savior. (This address was given about 124 years before Christ was born.) King Benjamin taught his people about the Savior's upcoming ministry and about his death and resurrection. Most important, he explained to them how Christ's Atonement would relate to them. For those who sinned in ignorance, the blood of Christ would atone for their sins. But *wo unto him* who had been taught the commandments and then knowingly rebelled against God without repenting.

When King Benjamin finished delivering the angel's message, he looked around at the multitude and saw that they had all fallen to the earth.

And they had viewed themselves in their own carnal state, even less than the dust of the earth. And they all cried aloud with one voice, saying: O have mercy, and apply the atoning blood of Christ that we may receive forgiveness of our sins, and our hearts may be purified; for we believe in Jesus Christ. (Mosiah 4:2)

After having said these words, the Spirit of the Lord came upon them. They were filled with joy because they had been forgiven of their sins.

King Benjamin taught his people many things during the course of his sermon. He taught of the goodness of God and of his enduring patience with us. He taught that if we obeyed the Lord's commandments we would be blessed both spiritually and temporally.

Service was also an important theme of his sermon.

When ye are in the service of your fellow beings ye are only in the service of your God. (Mosiah 2:17)

King Benjamin gave us this valuable counsel concerning our responsibility to our children. Not only are we to see to their physical needs, but we should not *suffer that they transgress the laws of God, and fight and quarrel one with another* (see Mosiah 4:14).

Eleven verses in a row teach about imparting our substance to the poor. Four of these verses clearly explain our moral obligation to those who are less fortunate than we are:

Ye will administer of your substance unto him that standeth in need; and ye will not suffer that the beggar putteth up his petition to you in vain, and turn him out to perish.

Perhaps thou shalt say: The man has brought upon himself his misery; therefore I will stay my hand, and will not give unto him of my food, nor impart unto him of my substance that he may not suffer, for his punishments are just—

But I say unto you, O man, whosoever doeth this the same hath great cause to repent; and except he repenteth . . . he perisheth forever. . . .

For behold, are we not all beggars? Do we not all depend upon the same Being, even God, for all the substance which we have . . . and for all the riches which we have of every kind? (Mosiah 4:16–19)

Toward the end of his sermon, King Benjamin gave this advice that especially applies to our generation:

> *And see that all these things are done in wisdom and order; for it is not requisite that a man should run faster than he has strength.* (Mosiah 4:27)

After King Benjamin finished his address, he found that the people had experienced a mighty change in their hearts—they had *no more disposition to do evil, but to do good continually.* All of the people took upon themselves the name of Christ and entered into a covenant with God to be obedient the rest of their lives. King Benjamin had the names taken of those who entered into this covenant and found that he was not missing a single name, with the exception of the children who were too little to understand.

The last two official acts of King Benjamin's reign were to consecrate his son Mosiah to be the new king and to appoint priests to teach the people. Then he dismissed the multitude, and they returned to their homes.

> *And Mosiah began to reign in his father's stead. And he began to reign in the thirtieth year of his age. . . .*
> *And king Benjamin lived three years and he died.* (Mosiah 6:4–5)

Mosiah was also a righteous king, walking in the ways of the Lord and keeping the commandments in all things. Like his father had done before him, Mosiah labored with his own hands so that he would not become a burden to his people.

> *And there was no contention among all his people for the space of three years.* (Mosiah 6:7)

·20·

FINDING THE LAND OF LEHI-NEPHI
MOSIAH 7–8

Chapter 17 of this book explains how the first King Mosiah and his people were led by the Lord to the land of Zarahemla. There they joined with the Mulekites, and from that point on the Nephite nation was headquartered in Zarahemla. During the reign of this first King Mosiah, a group of Nephites led by a man named Zeniff decided to return to the land of Nephi. They wanted to live in the land of their inheritance, even though the Lamanites now possessed this land. Nothing was heard from these people during the remainder of King Mosiah's reign, nor was anything heard from them during all the years that King Benjamin reigned.

It had been three years since King Benjamin had conferred the kingdom upon his son Mosiah, who was the grandson of the first King Mosiah. The people had not forgotten about the colony of Nephites who set out for the land of Lehi-Nephi so many years before, and they *wearied* King Mosiah with their questions concerning them. (Lehi-Nephi was a part of the land of Nephi.) Finally, King Mosiah appointed sixteen of his strongest men to go in search of these people.

Their leader was *a strong and mighty man* named Ammon, who was a Mulekite, being a descendant of the original inhabitants of Zarahemla. Because they did not know the exact direction to take, they wandered for forty days in the wilderness. After coming to a hill north of the land of Shilom, they pitched their tents.

Ammon took three men and went down into the land of Nephi. There they happened to run into the king of that land, who was with his guards just outside the city walls. The king's guards surrounded Ammon and his men, bound them, and threw them into prison. After being in prison for two days, they were brought before the king, who began his questioning by introducing himself:

> *Behold, I am Limhi, the son of Noah, who was the son of Zeniff, who came up out of the land of Zarahemla to inherit this land, which was the land of their fathers.* (Mosiah 7:9)

The king asked Ammon how they could be so bold as to come that close to the walls of the city, particularly since he was also outside the gate with his guards. He added that their lives had been spared just for that question to be answered! Then he allowed Ammon to speak. Ammon bowed himself before the king and said,

> *O king, I am very thankful before God this day that I am yet alive, and am permitted to speak. . . .*
> *For I am assured that if ye had known me ye would not have suffered that I should have worn these bands. For I am Ammon, and am a descendant of Zarahemla, and have come up out of the land of Zarahemla to inquire concerning our brethren, whom Zeniff brought up out of that land.* (Mosiah 7:12–13)

King Limhi was *exceedingly glad* to hear this because now he knew for sure that the people in the land of Zarahemla were still alive! He explained that he and his people were in bondage to the Lamanites.

> *And now, behold, our brethren will deliver us . . . out of the hands of the Lamanites, and we will be their slaves; for it is better that we be slaves to the Nephites than to pay tribute to the king of the Lamanites.* (Mosiah 7:15)

Guards were sent to bring Ammon's twelve remaining men camped on the hill. All sixteen were fed and then allowed to rest themselves from their arduous journey, for they had suffered greatly.

A proclamation was sent among the people, asking them to gather at the temple to hear the good news. When the people had gathered, King Limhi excitedly told them that the time was near at hand when they would be delivered from their enemies. He rehearsed to his people the events that had led them into bondage. When Zeniff brought his people into the land of the Lamanites, he was *over-zealous* to inherit the land of his fathers. He allowed himself to be deceived by the *cunning and craftiness* of the Lamanite king, who willingly gave Zeniff part of the land for the sole purpose of bringing the people into captivity. It wasn't too many years before this happened, but only because Zeniff's people gradually fell into transgression.

Limhi recounted how the people had put the prophet Abinadi to death. He had been sent by God to warn the people that there would be consequences to their wickedness. Abinadi prophesied that they would be brought into bondage if they did not repent, and they were now living the fulfillment of that prophecy. At the present time they were forced to pay one-half of all their grain, one-half of the increase of their flocks and herds, and one-half of all the rest they possessed to the Lamanites.

King Limhi told the people to put their trust in God, who would deliver them out of bondage. He had complete faith that Ammon and his men had been sent as a means of deliverance.

Ammon was asked to stand before the multitude and rehearse all that had happened in Zarahemla since their ancestors had left with Zeniff. Ammon did this and also taught them the last words of King Benjamin. Then the multitude was dismissed to return to their homes.

The king had a great mystery on his hands and unfolded the story to Ammon, hoping he could help solve it. Sometime prior to Ammon's arrival, he had sent forty-three of his men to find the land of Zarahemla, in hopes that their brethren there would deliver them out of bondage. They never did find the land of Zarahemla, having wandered around lost for possibly months, but they did make a great discovery.

> *[They had] traveled in a land among many waters, having discovered a land which was covered with bones of men, and of beasts, and was also covered with ruins of buildings of every kind, having discovered a land which had been peopled with a people who were as numerous as the hosts of Israel.* (Mosiah 8:8)

(Mosiah 21:25–28 tells us that when Limhi's men found this land covered with bones and ruins, they thought it was the land of Zarahemla, probably dashing any hopes for deliverance. The men arrived home just a short time before the coming of Ammon.)

King Limhi's men brought back several items as proof of their discovery. There were large breastplates, which were *perfectly sound*, made of brass and copper. There were swords, but the hilts had perished and the blades had cankered with rust. The most important find was a set of twenty-four gold plates. The engravings on them most likely contained information about the people who had been destroyed, but because they were written in a different language, the mystery remained unsolved.

Ammon was asked if he could translate the plates. He answered that he could not, but knew of someone who could. King Mosiah had in his possession a set of interpreters that would allow him to translate the record. (This was the Urim and Thummim that Joseph Smith would later use to translate the Book of Mormon. In Mosiah 28:13 they are described as *two stones which were fastened into the two rims of a bow.* In verse 14 it says that they *were handed down from generation to generation, for the purpose of interpreting languages.*) No one could use the interpreters unless he had authority from God, which Mosiah did.

(The land that Limhi's people discovered was where the Jaredites had built their great civilization. King Mosiah later translated the twenty-four gold plates, and the record is called the book of Ether, which is found in the Book of Mormon.)

A record had also been kept of King Limhi's people, from the time Zeniff led the people out of Zarahemla until they were delivered out of bondage. It is referred to as the record of Zeniff and is found in Mosiah, chapters 9–22. This record is summarized in the next eight chapters of *And It Came to Pass.*

·21·

OVERZEALOUS ZENIFF

OMNI 1:27–30; MOSIAH 9–10

Zeniff was a well-educated man who had followed Mosiah to the land of Zarahemla (see the first paragraph of chapter 17 of *And It Came to Pass*). The land of Nephi, which the Nephites had deserted, was subsequently taken over by the Lamanites. Zeniff was part of a large army of Nephites who traveled back to the land of Nephi because they *were desirous to possess the land of their inheritance.* He was sent as a spy among the Lamanites to assess their forces but found that there was *good among them.* He went back to his army in the wilderness and suggested that they make a treaty with the Lamanites instead. The leader was *a blood-thirsty man* and commanded his men to kill Zeniff.

> But I was rescued by the shedding of much blood; for father fought against father, and brother against brother, until the greater number of our army was destroyed in the wilderness; and we returned, those of us that were spared, to the land of Zarahemla, to relate that tale to their wives and their children. (Mosiah 9:2)

All but fifty of the men were slain during that uprising (see Omni 1:28). Zeniff, *over-zealous* to get back the land that once belonged to them, gathered a *considerable number* of people who were willing to go with him and again set out for the land of Nephi. On their journey they suffered from hunger and had other *sore afflictions* because, as Zeniff explains, *we were slow to remember the Lord our God.*

After many days of traveling in the wilderness, they arrived at the place where so many had died before. Here they pitched their tents. Zeniff and four of his men went into the city to speak with the king, whose name was Laman, *that I might know of the disposition of the king, and that I might know if I might go in with my people and possess the land in peace* (Mosiah 9:5).

King Laman made a treaty with Zeniff that they could possess the land of Lehi-Nephi and also the land of Shilom, and ordered his own people out of those lands. Zeniff was unaware of the king's ulterior motive, which was to bring his people into bondage. The Nephites set to work constructing buildings and repairing the walls of the two cities.

> *And we began to till the ground . . . with seeds of corn, and of wheat, and of barley, and with neas, and with sheum, and with seeds of all manner of fruits; and we did begin to multiply and prosper in the land.* (Mosiah 9:9)

After Zeniff's people lived in the land for twelve years, King Laman began to grow uneasy. He was afraid that the Nephites were getting too numerous and too strong to be overpowered and taken into bondage.

> *Now [the Lamanites] were a lazy and an idolatrous people; therefore they were desirous to bring us into bondage, that they might glut themselves with the labors of our hands; yea, that they might feast themselves upon the flocks of our fields.* (Mosiah 9:12)

King Laman decided it was time to *stir up* his people, and *there began to be wars and contentions in the land.* In the thirteenth year, as the Nephites were working in the fields of Shilom, a large group of Lamanites came upon them. They began to slay them and steal their flocks and the corn of their fields. Some of the people were able to flee to the city of Nephi for protection. Zeniff armed his people with weapons of war—bows and arrows, swords and cimeters, clubs and slings, and any weapon they could devise. They cried *mightily* for deliverance and in *the strength of the Lord* they went forth to battle against the Lamanites.

God heard their cries and answered their prayers. In one day and a night they killed 3,043 of the Lamanites and drove the rest out of their land. To their great sorrow, they discovered that 279 of their own brethren had been slain. To protect his people, Zeniff had more weapons made and guards stationed throughout the land. Never again would they allow the Lamanites a surprise attack. For the next twenty-two years there was peace in the land and the people prospered.

King Laman died, and with his son in power, the era of peace came to an end. The new king incited his people to prepare for war. Zeniff makes mention here of the long-standing tradition that the Lamanites had of hating the Nephites, which they had been taught to do down through the ages. They believed that their ancestors, Laman and Lemuel, had been wronged by Nephi and Lehi every step of the way from the time they left Jerusalem. Because of this supposed injustice, they felt it their duty to do all in their power to destroy the Nephites.

Zeniff's guards spotted a large army of Lamanites north of the land of Shilom. They were armed with all types of weapons and had their heads shaved and were wearing only loin cloths. Zeniff had the women and children hide in the wilderness and then organized the remainder of the people into an army. He placed the men in ranks according to their age, including those young men and old men who were able to bear arms. Even though Zeniff was an old man, he too went with his people to fight the Lamanites. The Nephites were outnumbered; nevertheless, they put their trust in the Lord. The Lamanites knew nothing concerning the Lord, but they were strong and eager to shed the blood of the Nephites.

> *And it came to pass that we did drive them again out of our land; and we slew them with a great slaughter, even so many that we did not number them.* (Mosiah 10:20)

Zeniff and his people returned to their land and again began to tend their flocks and till the ground. Being an old man, Zeniff conferred the kingdom upon his son Noah.

·22·

THE WICKED KING NOAH
MOSIAH 11

N oah was not a good king like his father, Zeniff. He did not keep the commandments of God but committed all kinds of wickedness. He had many wives and concubines and caused his people to *do that which was abominable in the sight of the Lord*. In order to finance his wicked lifestyle, he taxed his people one-fifth of all they possessed. He removed all the priests who had been consecrated by his father and chose new ones. They were also lifted up in the pride of their hearts and, like King Noah, had many wives and concubines. The people began to worship idols *because they were deceived by the vain and flattering words of the king and his priests*.

> *Yea, and thus they were supported in their laziness, and in their idolatry, and in their whoredoms, by the taxes which king Noah had put upon his people; thus did the people labor exceedingly to support iniquity.* (Mosiah 11:6)

King Noah built many large and elegant buildings, including a temple and a palace, and adorned them with fine woodwork and precious metals. In the temple the seats for the high priests were ornamented with pure gold and set higher than all the rest.

> *And he caused a breastwork to be built before them, that they might rest their bodies and their arms upon while they should speak lying and vain words to his people.* (Mosiah 11:11)

King Noah built a tower near the temple that stood so high that it could overlook not only the lands of his people, but also the Lamanite lands. Many more buildings were built in the land round about, as well as a second tower on the hill north of Shilom.

And it came to pass that he placed his heart upon his riches, and he spent his time in riotous living with his wives and concubines; and so did also his priests spend their time with harlots. (Mosiah 11:14)

King Noah planted vineyards and built winepresses, and great quantities of wine were made and consumed by the people. While the people were living in this abominable state, the Lamanites began to come upon small numbers of them and slay them as they were working in their fields and tending their flocks. King Noah sent guards to keep watch, but he did not send a sufficient number, and so the slayings continued. King Noah finally sent his army against them, and for a time the Lamanites were driven back.

And now, because of this great victory they were lifted up in the pride of their hearts; they did boast in their own strength, saying that their fifty could stand against thousands of the Lamanites; and thus they did boast, and did delight in . . . the shedding of the blood of their brethren, and this because of the wickedness of their king and priests. (Mosiah 11:19)

·23·

ABINADI
MOSIAH 11–17

The Lord sent a prophet named Abinadi to give a strong warning to the people of King Noah:

> *Wo be unto this people, for I have seen their abominations, and their wickedness, and their whoredoms. . . .*
>
> *And except they repent . . . they shall be brought into bondage. . . .*
>
> *. . . When they shall cry unto me I will be slow to hear their cries. . . .*
>
> *And except they repent . . . and cry mightily to the Lord their God, I will not hear their prayers, neither will I deliver them out of their afflictions.* (Mosiah 11:20–21, 24–25)

When the people heard these words, they were angry with Abinadi and tried to take his life, but the Lord delivered him out of their hands. After hearing what Abinadi was preaching, King Noah was also angry.

> *Who is Abinadi, that I and my people should be judged of him, or who is the Lord, that shall bring upon my people such great afflictions?* (Mosiah 11:27)

King Noah commanded his guards to bring Abinadi in so he could be put to death, but it was not the Lord's plan for him to be taken at this time.

Two years later, Abinadi came to preach to the people again. This time he went among them in disguise, and at first they didn't know him. Because they had not repented, harsher words were added to his earlier prophecies. Not only would they be brought into bondage, but they would have *burdens lashed upon their backs* and be driven like a *dumb ass*. Because of their afflictions, they would *howl all the day long*. They would be slain, and vultures and wild animals would devour their flesh. The life of King Noah would be valued *even as a garment in a hot furnace.* Unless they repented, the Lord would *utterly destroy them from off the face of the earth.*

The people were again angry with Abinadi, but this time they were able to bind him and carry him before King Noah. They repeated to the king all that he had said.

> *And now, O king, what great evil hast thou done, or what great sins have thy people committed, that we should be condemned of God or judged of this man?*
>
> *And now, O king, behold, we are guiltless, and thou, O king, hast not sinned; therefore, this man has lied concerning you, and he has prophesied in vain.*
>
> *And behold, we are strong, we shall not come into bondage.* (Mosiah 12:13–15)

King Noah had Abinadi cast into prison, and then he and his priests held a council to decide what to do with him. They decided to question him, being sure that Abinadi would say something contrary to their laws, which would give them reason to accuse him. To their astonishment, Abinadi withstood all their questions and confounded them in all their words. Then one of the priests asked him what a certain passage of Isaiah's writings meant. Abinadi replied,

> *Are you priests, and pretend to teach this people, . . . and yet desire to know of me what these things mean?* (Mosiah 12:25)

Abinadi went on to reprimand the priests for not living the law of Moses, then rehearsed some of the Ten Commandments to them. Again Abinadi chided the priests for not teaching these laws.

King Noah was not going to listen to any more of this, so he ordered his priests to slay Abinadi, calling him *mad.* As they attempted to lay their hands on him, Abinadi withstood them, saying:

> *Touch me not, for God shall smite you if ye lay your hands upon me, for I have not delivered the message which the Lord sent me to deliver; . . . therefore, God will not suffer that I shall be destroyed at this time.* (Mosiah 13:3)

No one dared touch Abinadi because the Spirit of the Lord was upon him *and his face shone with exceeding luster.* Speaking *with power and authority from God,* he told them that when he finished his message it would no longer matter what they did to him. He added this warning:

> *What you do with me . . . shall be as a type and a shadow of things which are to come.* (Mosiah 13:10)

Abinadi went on to teach the people the remainder of the Ten Commandments and many other points of doctrine. These things had not been taught by the priests because they had *studied and taught iniquity the most part of [their] lives.* Because the priests mistakenly believed that salvation came through living the law of Moses, Abinadi spent a considerable amount of time teaching them about the Atonement of Jesus Christ.

When Abinadi finished his sermon, he was thrown back into prison. After three days King Noah had him brought before him. He and his priests had concocted an accusation worthy of death: Abinadi had said that God himself would come down among the children of men. (Were the priests unaware of all the prophecies concerning the coming of Jesus Christ?) He was given one last chance to free himself—he simply had to recant all the prophecies he gave concerning Noah and his people. Abinadi would not comply, saying he would suffer death instead.

> *[My words] shall stand as a testimony against you. And if ye slay me ye will shed innocent blood, and this shall also stand as a testimony against you at the last day.* (Mosiah 17:10)

King Noah was very disturbed at Abinadi's words and was about to release him, fearing that the judgments of God would come upon him. However, the priests convinced him to carry out the execution, and Abinadi was bound and set on fire. As the flames began to scorch him, he told King Noah and his priests that they would be afflicted with all manner of diseases. They would be driven and scattered like a wild flock driven by wild beasts. They would be hunted by their enemies, and many would also suffer the pains of death by fire.

> *Thus God executeth vengeance upon those that destroy his people. O God, receive my soul.* (Mosiah 17:19)

·24·

IN HIDING WITH ALMA

MOSIAH 17–18, 23

One of the wicked priests of Noah was a young man named Alma. Alma's heart had been softened by Abinadi's teachings, and he believed all his words. He knew Abinadi spoke the truth about the iniquity of his people. When Abinadi was sentenced to die, Alma pleaded with the king not to be angry with Abinadi but to let him depart in peace. This made King Noah even angrier. He had Alma thrown out and sent his servants after him to kill him. Alma managed to elude the servants and find a hiding place, where he wrote down all the words that Abinadi had spoken. Alma repented of his many sins and went secretly among the people, teaching them the words of Abinadi.

In the border of the land was a place called Mormon, which during certain seasons had been infested with wild animals. In Mormon was a fountain of pure water, and close by was a thicket of small trees. It was here that Alma hid during the daytime from the searches of the king. The people who believed what Alma taught went to this place to hear him preach, and before long there was a large number of people coming to hear him. He taught them about repentance and faith on the Lord. The people desired *to come into the fold of God, and to be called his people.* They were willing to *bear one another's burdens, . . . to mourn with those that mourn, . . . and comfort those that stand in need of comfort, and to stand as witnesses of God at all times and in all things, and in all places* (see Mosiah 18:8–9). Alma's followers were ready for baptism. Alma took Helam, one of his first converts, and stood in the water and cried,

> *O Lord, pour out thy Spirit upon thy servant, that he may do this work with holiness of heart.* (Mosiah 18:12)

After Alma said these words, the Spirit of the Lord was upon him. A baptismal prayer was given, and then both Alma and Helam were buried in the water. They came forth out of the water rejoicing and filled with the Spirit. Alma baptized about 204 people who had gathered at the Waters of Mormon that day, and they called themselves the Church of Christ. Having authority from God, Alma ordained one priest for every fifty people. The priests were to teach the word of God, and Alma admonished them to labor with their own hands for their support. When it was possible, the people gathered together one day a week to worship God and to hear instruction.

> *And again Alma commanded that the people of the church should impart of their substance, every one according to that which he had; if he have more abundantly he should impart more abundantly; and of him that had but little, but little should be required; and to him that had not should be given.* (Mosiah 18:27)

All the activities of Alma and his followers were done in secret to keep King Noah and his priests from finding out. Somehow the king was apprised of their doings and had his servants watch them. He then accused Alma of stirring up the people to rebel against him and promptly sent his army to destroy all of them. Alma was warned by the Lord that the army of King Noah was coming. Alma's people, now numbering about 450, gathered their tents and provisions and their flocks and grain and departed into the wilderness. The Lord strengthened them so that King Noah's army could not overtake them. They journeyed for eight days and came to *a very beautiful and pleasant land, a land of pure water.* Here they settled and began to build a new life for themselves.

·25·

PROPHECIES FULFILLED
MOSIAH 19

King Noah's army returned, having had no success in finding Alma and his followers. Shortly after, there began to be a division among the people.

> *And the lesser part began to breathe out threatenings against the king, and there began to be a great contention among them.* (Mosiah 19:3)

One of the enemies of the king was a strong man named Gideon. He *swore in his wrath* that he would slay the king, and when the opportunity came he drew his sword and fought with him. The king could see that he was about to be overpowered, and so he fled to the tower near the temple. As Gideon started to climb the tower after him, King Noah saw the Lamanites in the borders of their land.

> *And now the king cried out in the anguish of his soul, saying: Gideon, spare me, for the Lamanites are upon us, and they will destroy us; yea, they will destroy my people.* (Mosiah 19:7)

King Noah was more concerned with saving his own life; nevertheless, Gideon spared him. The king ordered the people to flee before the Lamanites into the wilderness, he himself taking the lead. As the Lamanites began to overtake them, King Noah commanded the men to leave their women and children behind in order to have a better chance of outrunning the Lamanites! Many of the men chose to stay with their families and risk being killed, but the rest left their wives and children and fled. The men who stayed behind sent their *fair daughters* to meet the Lamanites and plead with them to spare the lives of the people.

And it came to pass that the Lamanites had compassion on them, for they were charmed with the beauty of their women. (Mosiah 19:14)

The Lamanites took them captive back to the land of Nephi. They allowed them to again possess the land under the following conditions: They would deliver up King Noah, and they would give one-half of all their gold, silver, and precious things, as well as one-half of their grain and one-half of the increase of their flocks and herds as tribute to the king of the Lamanites each year.

Gideon secretly sent men into the wilderness to search for King Noah and the men who had followed him. They found all but the king and his priests. The men who had deserted their families rejoiced upon hearing that their wives and children had not been slain. The story then unfolded about what had happened to King Noah and those who had followed him into the wilderness. The men, with the exception of the priests, had decided to return to their families, even at the cost of their lives. When King Noah commanded them to stay, they refused to obey him *and caused that he should suffer, even unto death by fire.* They were about to take the priests and put them to death also, but they escaped. It was shortly after this that Gideon's men met up with the returning husbands and fathers.

The people conferred the kingdom upon Limhi, a just man who was one of the sons of King Noah. He made an oath with the king of the Lamanites that they would pay tribute of one-half of all they owned. In return, the king of the Lamanites made an oath with Limhi that his people would not be slain. Even with the Lamanites guarding the land, Limhi had peace in his kingdom for the next two years.

·26·

THE LAMANITE DAUGHTERS AND THE PRIESTS OF NOAH
MOSIAH 20

The priests of Noah were hiding in the wilderness—too ashamed and afraid to return to their families in the city of Nephi.

Now there was a place in Shemlon where the daughters of the Lamanites did gather themselves together to sing, and to dance, and to make themselves merry. (Mosiah 20:1)

One day when a small number of the Lamanite daughters had gathered at their special place, the priests discovered them. They watched until only twenty-four remained, then came out of hiding and carried them off into the wilderness. When the Lamanites found their daughters missing, they blamed the people of Limhi. King Laman himself led the army to destroy the Nephites. Limhi could see the advancing army from the tower, so he gathered his people together and lay in wait for them in the fields and forests. When the Lamanites got closer, the people of Limhi came upon them and began to slay them.

And it came to pass that the battle became exceedingly sore, for they fought like lions for their prey. (Mosiah 20:10)

The people of Limhi got the upper hand of the battle, even though their numbers were half those of the Lamanites.

But they fought for their lives, and for their wives, and for their children; therefore they exerted themselves and like dragons did they fight. (Mosiah 20:11)

They found the king of the Lamanites lying wounded among the dead, left behind during the swift retreat of his people. After binding up his wounds, they brought him before King Limhi, who asked,

> *What cause have ye to come up to war against my people?*
> *Behold, my people have not broken the oath that I made unto you;*
> *therefore, why should ye break the oath which ye made unto my*
> *people?* (Mosiah 20:14)

King Laman explained that he'd broken the oath because of the abduction of their daughters and had come to war in retaliation. King Limhi was unaware of this event and promised to search among his people and put to death those responsible. Gideon, who was now Limhi's chief captain, went before the king and asked him to call off the search. He knew that the perpetrators would not be found among their people. He reminded King Limhi that the wicked priests were still out in the wilderness and surely it was they who abducted the Lamanite daughters.

The Lamanite army was again preparing to come against the people of Limhi, who would likely be destroyed because of their small numbers. At Gideon's suggestion, King Limhi told the Lamanite king all about the priests hiding in the wilderness and blamed them for the abduction. This explanation pacified the king, and he said to them,

> *Let us go forth to meet my people, without arms; and I swear*
> *unto you with an oath that my people shall not slay thy people.*
> (Mosiah 20:24)

When they met the approaching army, the king of the Lamanites bowed down before his people and pleaded in behalf of the people of Limhi. The Lamanites saw that they were carrying no weapons and had compassion on them and allowed them to return in peace to their own land.

·27·

THE DELIVERANCE OF KING LIMHI'S PEOPLE

MOSIAH 21–22

L imhi and his people returned home and began to dwell peacefully again, but the peace was short-lived. The Lamanites started to come into the borders of their land and harass them.

> *Now they durst not slay them, because of the oath which their king had made unto Limhi; but they would smite them on their cheeks, and exercise authority over them; and began to put heavy burdens upon their backs, and drive them as they would a dumb ass.* (Mosiah 21:3)

All of this had been prophesied by Abinadi to the exact detail. The afflictions of the Nephites were so great that they begged their king to allow them to go to battle against the Lamanites. Three times they gathered their people and went to battle. Each time they were beaten and driven back, losing many lives and leaving a great number of widows in the land.

If the people of Limhi wanted to remain alive, their only choice was to *humble themselves even to the dust, and subject themselves to the yoke of bondage.* They cried continually to the Lord for deliverance, but he was slow to hear their cries because of their past wickedness. The Lord did soften the hearts of the Lamanites, who began to ease the burdens they placed on their captives, *yet the Lord did not see fit to deliver [the Nephites] out of bondage.* Limhi's people gradually prospered in the land, raising enough grain and animals so that they did not suffer from hunger. Every man was commanded to help support the great number of widows and their children.

The people secured their flocks and grain and kept together as much as possible. Even King Limhi would not go outside the walls of the city without the protection of his guards.

The people were anxious to capture the priests of King Noah who were still hiding in the wilderness. Their abduction of the Lamanite daughters had caused the loss of many lives. Now they were coming into their city by night and carrying off their grain and many of their valuables.

It was during this period of time that the king and his guards came upon Ammon and his men outside the gates of the city (see chapter 20 herein). They immediately took them captive because the king assumed they were the priests of Noah. When they found out they were their brethren from Zarahemla, there was great rejoicing, for now they had reason to hope for deliverance from the Lamanites.

(The discovery of the land of the Jaredites is covered in chapter 20 herein.)

Since the coming of Ammon, King Limhi and many of his people had entered into a covenant with God to serve him and keep his commandments. They were desirous to be baptized, but no one in the land had the proper authority. Ammon considered himself to be an unworthy servant, and so the church was not organized at that time. Alma had the authority but had fled earlier with his people.

> *Yea, they did mourn for their departure, for they knew not whither they had fled. Now they would have gladly joined with them.* (Mosiah 21:31)

All the people were gathered so they might come up with a plan for deliverance. They all agreed that it would be impossible to fight the Lamanites. Gideon, the king's chief captain, was held in high esteem and had advised the king many times before when dealing with the Lamanites. He presented a plan to King Limhi: There was a pass through the back wall of the city, and at night the Lamanites who guarded there were always drunk. The people would be waiting with their possessions and their flocks and herds while Gideon paid the last tribute of wine to the Lamanites. (This had to do with paying one-half of all they owned or produced in exchange for their lives.) Then, as the guards slept, all the people and animals would leave the city through that pass.

King Limhi agreed to Gideon's plan and sent a proclamation to all his people instructing them to prepare for the departure. The king sent the tribute of wine to the Lamanites, and then sent even more wine as a present to them, of which they drank freely. As the guards slept, the people departed by night into the wilderness with their flocks and provisions and what they could carry of their gold and silver and precious things. Ammon and his men led them around the land of Shilom and headed toward the land of Zarahemla. After traveling many days in the wilderness, they arrived in Zarahemla, where King Mosiah and his people received them with joy. King Limhi's people gratefully became Mosiah's subjects.

> *And now it came to pass when the Lamanites had found that the people of Limhi had departed out of the land by night, that they sent an army into the wilderness to pursue them;*
>
> *And after they had pursued them two days, they could no longer follow their tracks; therefore they were lost in the wilderness.* (Mosiah 22:15–16)

·28·

ALMA AND HIS PEOPLE ARE LED TO ZARAHEMLA
MOSIAH 23–25

I n chapter 24 of *And It Came to Pass*, we learned that Alma and his people had eluded King Noah's army and had settled into a new land, which they called Helam. They were an industrious people and immediately began to plant crops and construct buildings. Because Alma was so loved by his people, they wanted him to be their king. Alma refused because not all of their future kings would be righteous and just. He reminded them of how wicked King Noah had been.

Being the high priest and having authority from God, Alma consecrated other priests and teachers. He taught his people *that every man should love his neighbor as himself, that there should be no contention among them.*

> *And it came to pass that they did multiply and prosper exceedingly in the land of Helam. . .*
> *Nevertheless the Lord seeth fit to chasten his people; yea, he trieth their patience and their faith.* (Mosiah 23:20–21)

As the people were working in their fields, an army of Lamanites came into the borders of the land. The people fled from their fields and gathered in the city of Helam. Alma calmed them and told them not to be frightened, but to remember the Lord, who would deliver them. They prayed that the Lord would soften the hearts of the Lamanites so their lives would be spared. Alma and his brethren then went before the Lamanites and delivered themselves into their hands. The Lamanites spared their lives but took possession of the land of Helam.

The Lamanite army had found Alma and his people completely by accident. While searching for the people of Limhi who had escaped, they ended up lost in the wilderness. During their wanderings, the army stumbled onto the priests of Noah. The priests had settled into a land they named after their leader, Amulon. The priests feared the Lamanites, and with good reason, since they had abducted twenty-four of their daughters. Amulon and the Lamanite daughters went before the Lamanites and pleaded with them to spare their lives. The Lamanites had compassion on them because their daughters were now married to the priests, and they were allowed to join with them. They were all traveling in the wilderness in search of their home in the land of Nephi when they came upon Alma and his people.

Even though the Lamanites, who now included the priests, had taken possession of the land of Helam, they promised Alma they would free his people if they would show them the way back to the land of Nephi. After being shown the way home, the Lamanites did not keep their promise. Instead, they posted guards throughout the land and made Amulon the king and ruler over Alma and his people. *Amulon did gain favor in the eyes of the king of the Lamanites,* and he and his other priests were appointed teachers over every land possessed by the Lamanites.

> *And thus the language of Nephi began to be taught among all the people of the Lamanites.*
> *And they were a friendly people one with another; nevertheless they knew not God. . . .*
> *But they taught them that they . . . might write one to another.*
> *And thus the Lamanites began to increase in riches, and began to trade one with another . . . and began to be a cunning and a wise people, as to the wisdom of the world, . . . delighting in all manner of wickedness and plunder, except it were among their own brethren.* (Mosiah 24:4–7)

To have Amulon appointed king over the captured city made the situation even more difficult for Alma. They had both served together as priests under wicked King Noah, but because Alma tried to defend Abinadi, and was even converted by his teachings, he was especially hated by Amulon. Now Amulon was in a position to inflict great persecution upon Alma and even ordered his children to persecute the other children. He put taskmasters over the people and forced them to carry heavy burdens.

Their afflictions were so difficult to bear *that they began to cry mightily to God.* Amulon ordered them to stop praying, and whoever was found doing so was to be put to death. They continued to cry unto God in their hearts. The voice of the Lord came to them with words of comfort, saying he would deliver them out of bondage. The Lord also promised to ease the burdens that were put upon their shoulders so that *ye may know of a surety that I, the Lord God, do visit my people in their afflictions.*

> *And now it came to pass that the burdens which were laid upon Alma and his brethren were made light; yea, the Lord did strengthen them that they could bear up their burdens with ease, and they did submit cheerfully and with patience to all the will of the Lord.* (Mosiah 24:14–15)

Their faith was so great that the voice of the Lord came again to them and told them that on the following day they would be delivered out of bondage. During all that night the people gathered their flocks and their grain. *In the morning the Lord caused a deep sleep to come upon the Lamanites,* and Alma and his people escaped into the wilderness. They traveled all day and then pitched their tents in a valley and poured out their thanks to God.

> *And now the Lord said unto Alma: Haste thee and get . . . out of this land, for the Lamanites have awakened and do pursue thee; therefore get thee out of this land, and I will stop the Lamanites in this valley that they come no further in pursuit of this people.* (Mosiah 24:23)

After they journeyed for twelve more days, they arrived in the land of Zarahemla, where they were received with great joy. King Mosiah had all the people assemble into two groups—the Nephites and the Mulekites. The Mulekites had the largest group since their people were the original inhabitants of Zarahemla. Mosiah had the record of Zeniff read, starting from the time they left Zarahemla until their recent return. Then he had the account of Alma and his people read. After hearing the records, the people *were struck with wonder and amazement.* They were overcome with joy at how the people had been delivered, but also filled with sorrow when they thought of their brethren who had been slain by the Lamanites.

The children of the priests of King Noah *were displeased with the conduct of their fathers.* They would no longer be called by the names of their fathers and instead called themselves the children of Nephi.

While the people were still assembled, Alma went from one group to another preaching repentance and faith on the Lord. After Alma finished speaking, King Limhi and his people were baptized. Alma was granted permission by King Mosiah to establish the church throughout the land of Zarahemla. There were seven congregations formed, and Alma ordained priests and teachers over each one.

> *And they were called the people of God. And the Lord did pour out his Spirit upon them, and they were blessed, and prospered in the land.* (Mosiah 25:24)

·29·

A Recapping of Events

1. Zeniff and his group leave the main body of Nephites in Zarahemla and return to live in the land of Nephi, which is now inhabited by Lamanites.
2. Noah, the wicked son of Zeniff, becomes king.
3. Abinadi, the prophet sent to call the people to repentance, is killed.
4. Alma, one of the wicked priests of King Noah, is converted by Abinadi's teachings. Alma repents and converts hundreds of people.
5. King Noah sends his army after Alma and his people to destroy them, but they escape into the wilderness and build their own city, named Helam.
6. The Lamanites attack King Noah's people.
7. King Noah, the priests, and some of the men leave their women and children behind in order to outrun the pursuing Lamanite army.
8. The remaining people of King Noah are captured by the Lamanites.
9. Limhi, the son of King Noah, becomes king. He makes an oath with the Lamanites to pay half of all they own from that time forward in exchange for their lives. They live in bondage to the Lamanites.
10. There is an uprising in the wilderness. King Noah is burned to death, the priests escape, and the other men return home.
11. While hiding in the wilderness, the priests of Noah abduct 24 of the Lamanite daughters. King Limhi's people are blamed, causing bloodshed.
12. King Mosiah appoints Ammon to lead a search party for the people of Zeniff who left Zarahemla several decades before.
13. Ammon and three of his men are captured by King Limhi and his guards, who think they are the priests of Noah.

14. Ammon and his men help King Limhi's people escape. They get the guards drunk and leave the city by night and travel to Zarahemla.

15. The Lamanite army pursues King Limhi's people but ends up lost in the wilderness.

16. While lost and wandering in the wilderness, the Lamanite army runs into two groups of people: First they find the priests of Noah, who have married the Lamanite daughters they abducted. They join together. The Lamanites and priests then run into Alma and his people and take over their city.

17. Alma's people suffer terrible persecution at the hands of the Lamanites and the wicked priests.

18. The Lord delivers Alma and his people by causing a deep sleep to come upon the Lamanites. Alma's people make their home in Zarahemla too.

·30·

ALMA THE YOUNGER AND THE SONS OF MOSIAH

MOSIAH 26–27; ALMA 36

Now it came to pass that there were many of the rising generation that could not understand the words of king Benjamin, being little children at the time he spake unto his people; and they did not believe the tradition of their fathers. (Mosiah 26:1)

Because of their hardened hearts, many of this younger generation would not be baptized. They became *a separate people as to their faith* and remained *in their carnal and sinful state.* They deceived many of the members of the church with their *flattering words* and caused them to commit many sins.

Because Alma was the high priest over all the church, the unrepentant members were brought before him to be judged. Alma was greatly troubled by these events because nothing like this had happened before. Fearing that he might do the wrong thing, Alma poured out his soul to the Lord and was told to judge the people according to the sins they had committed. If they sincerely repented they were to be forgiven, but those who did not repent were not to be numbered among his people. Alma did as the Lord commanded, and they again began to have peace in the church, baptizing many.

The persecutions inflicted upon the members of the church by the unbelievers continued, however. It became so unbearable that King Mosiah made a law against the persecution. The sons of Mosiah and one of the sons of Alma, whose name was also Alma, were numbered among the unbelievers.

[Alma] became a very wicked and an idolatrous man. And he was a man of many words, and did speak much flattery to the people;

therefore he led many of the people to do after the manner of his iniquities.

And he became a great hinderment to the prosperity of the church of God; stealing away the hearts of the people; causing much dissension among the people; giving a chance for the enemy of God to exercise his power over them. (Mosiah 27:8–9)

Alma and the sons of Mosiah went about secretly trying to destroy the church and to lead the people of the Lord astray. This was against the law that King Mosiah had just established.

One day as they were traveling, an angel of the Lord appeared to them, speaking with a voice of thunder that caused the ground to shake!

And so great was their astonishment, that they fell to the earth, and understood not the words which he spake unto them.

Nevertheless he cried again, saying: Alma, arise and stand forth, for why persecuteth thou the church of God? For the Lord hath said: This is my church, and I will establish it; and nothing shall overthrow it, save it is the transgression of my people. (Mosiah 27:12–13)

The angel told Alma that the Lord had heard the prayers of his people, especially those of his father, who had prayed with great faith that Alma might be brought to the knowledge of the truth. The angel had been sent in answer to the tremendous faith of his father and others. After lecturing Alma further about the power of God, he told him to *go [his] way and seek to destroy the church no more.* Then the angel departed.

Alma and the sons of Mosiah again fell to the earth because their astonishment was so great. With their own eyes they had seen an angel of the Lord whose voice of thunder had shaken the earth as *though it would part asunder.* They knew that only through the power of God could such an event take place.

Alma was so overwhelmed by this experience that he was left unable to speak and too weak to even move. The sons of Mosiah carried him to his father and related all that had happened to them. Knowing that it was the power of God, his father rejoiced. He invited a multitude of people to come and witness what the Lord had done for his son and the sons of Mosiah. The priests also assembled together to fast and pray that Alma would regain his strength and be able to speak. After they had fasted and prayed for two days and nights, Alma stood up and began to speak.

He told them to be of *good comfort* because he had repented of his sins and had been redeemed of the Lord. He was *in the darkest abyss,* but now beheld *the marvelous light of God.*

In Alma 36:6–23, Alma shares this same conversion story with his son, Helaman. In this account he gives more detail about his experience. He tells his son that the angel told him to seek no more to destroy the church of God **or else he himself would be destroyed**. After hearing this, Alma was *struck with such great fear and amazement* that he fell to the earth and heard no more of what the angel had to say.

> But I was racked with eternal torment, for my soul was har-rowed up to the greatest degree and racked with all my sins.
>
> Yea, I did remember all my sins and iniquities, for which I was tormented with the pains of hell; yea, I saw that I had rebelled against my God, and that I had not kept his holy commandments.
>
> Yea, and I had murdered many of his children, or rather led them away unto destruction; yea, and in fine so great had been my iniquities, that the very thought of coming into the presence of my God did rack my soul with inexpressible horror.
>
> Oh, thought I, that I could be banished and become extinct both soul and body, that I might not be brought to stand in the presence of my God, to be judged of my deeds.
>
> And now, for three days and for three nights was I racked, even with the pains of a damned soul. (Alma 36:12–16)

Then Alma remembered his father's teachings of how the Savior would atone for the sins of the world. He cried in his heart for Jesus to have mercy on him, and suddenly he was no longer pained by the memory of his sins.

> And oh, what joy, and what marvelous light I did behold; yea, my soul was filled with joy as exceeding as was my pain! (Alma 36:20)

Like Lehi and other prophets, Alma saw God sitting upon his throne, surrounded by throngs of angels singing praises to him, *and [his] soul did long to be there.*

For three days and three nights Alma had been unable to speak or use his limbs. Now he stood upon his feet and told the people that he had been *born of God.* From this time forward, Alma and the sons of Mosiah—Ammon, Aaron, Omner, and Himni—began to teach the people.

> *And they traveled throughout all the land of Zarahemla . . .*
> *zealously striving to repair all the injuries which they had done to the*
> *church, confessing all their sins, and publishing all the things which*
> *they had seen, and explaining the prophecies and scriptures to all*
> *who desired to hear them.*
>
> *And thus they were instruments in the hands of God in bringing*
> *many to the knowledge of the truth.* (Mosiah 27:35–36)

·31·

THE REIGN OF THE JUDGES BEGINS
MOSIAH 28–29

The sons of Mosiah and a small group of men whom they had selected asked King Mosiah for permission to go on a mission to the Lamanites. They hoped that by teaching them of God and convincing them that the traditions of their fathers were incorrect, they could *cure them of their hatred towards the Nephites.* They envisioned a land free of contention as the two peoples were friendly to each other.

Because of the bloodthirsty nature of the Lamanites, King Mosiah was very opposed to the idea. After many days of listening to their pleadings, he inquired of the Lord whether he should let them go.

> *And the Lord said unto Mosiah: Let them go up, for many shall believe on their words, and they shall have eternal life; and I will deliver thy sons out of the hands of the Lamanites.* (Mosiah 28:7)

King Mosiah granted their request, and the group departed. (Their experiences are found in chapters 40–45 of *And It Came to Pass.*)

King Mosiah translated the gold plates that were found by the people of King Limhi. It was the record of the Jaredite civilization, which is found in the book of Ether. All the records and other sacred possessions that Mosiah had been keeping were conferred upon Alma the Younger.

It was King Mosiah's desire to pass the kingdom on to one of his sons, but each had chosen to go on a mission to the Lamanites instead. The time seemed right to change the system of government. King Mosiah proposed to the people that they appoint judges instead of having a king. He explained that if they could be guaranteed righteous kings who would establish the laws of God, then a king would be preferred. But he reminded them of King Noah and how much destruction can be brought upon the people by a wicked ruler. Also, a wicked king cannot be dethroned without much bloodshed.

The system that King Mosiah proposed consisted of three levels of judges—higher judges, lower judges, and a "chief judge" over all. If the lower judges did not follow the laws that had been given, they would be judged by the higher judges. If the higher judges did not give *righteous judgments*, a small number of the lower judges could judge the higher judges. With this system it would be difficult for a corrupt judge to remain in office. Since the people elected the judges, this system of government was *by the voice of the people.*

Throughout all the land the people cast their votes and appointed judges to rule over them. Alma the Younger was appointed to be the first chief judge, at the same time serving as the high priest over all the church. Alma was a righteous judge and there was continual peace in the land.

Alma's father, Alma, died at the age of eighty-two. He had been converted by Abinadi's teachings many years earlier and was later responsible for establishing the church throughout all of Zarahemla. King Mosiah also died, in the thirty-third year of his reign, at the age of sixty-three. The people had greatly loved him and did *esteem him more than any other man.*

> *Five hundred and nine years [had passed] from the time Lehi left Jerusalem.*
> *And thus ended the reign of the kings over the people of Nephi.*
> (Mosiah 29:46–47)

NOTE: "The change in government instituted through King Mosiah was viewed as so significant that from that point on the Nephites recorded their time from the beginning of the reign of the judges. Until this point the Nephites had kept track of time from the year Lehi left Jerusalem" (*The Book of Mormon Student Manual for Religion 121 and 122* [Salt Lake City, Utah: The Church of Jesus Christ of Latter-day Saints, 1989], 70).

·32·

NEHOR INTRODUCES PRIESTCRAFT
ALMA 1

In the first year of Alma's reign as chief judge, a man named Nehor was brought before him. He was a large man, *noted for his much strength.* He had been preaching his version of the word of God among the people, which was contrary to the teachings of the church. He taught that the teachers and priests should be supported by the people instead of laboring with their own hands. He also taught that since everyone would be *saved at the last day,* they should be rejoicing instead of living in fear of the Lord. Many people believed in Nehor's words and even supported him with their money.

> *And he began to be lifted up in the pride of his heart, and to wear very costly apparel, yea, and even began to establish a church after the manner of his preaching.* (Alma 1:6)

One day as Nehor was on his way to preach to his followers, he met Gideon, one of the teachers of the church of God. Gideon was well loved and respected, having helped deliver the people of Limhi out of bondage. Nehor got into a verbal confrontation with Gideon over the doctrines of the church, hoping to lead him and others from their beliefs. Gideon *withstood him, admonishing him with the words of God.* This made Nehor angry, and he drew his sword and began to fight him.

> *Now Gideon being stricken with many years . . . was not able to withstand his blows, therefore he was slain by the sword.* (Alma 1:9)

Nehor was brought before Alma to be judged of his crimes. He *stood before Alma and pleaded for himself with much boldness.* Alma told Nehor that this was the first time priestcraft had been introduced, which would bring about the entire destruction of his people if not stopped. (2 Nephi 26:29 tells us that *priestcrafts are that men preach and set themselves up for a light unto the world, that they may get gain and praise of the world; but they seek not the welfare of Zion.* Verse 31 plainly states that *the laborer in Zion shall labor for Zion; for if they labor for money they shall perish.*)

Nehor was not only guilty of this wicked practice but had also tried to enforce it with the sword.

> *And thou hast shed the blood of a righteous man, yea, a man who has done much good among this people; and were we to spare thee his blood would come upon us for vengeance.* (Alma 1:13)

Nehor was condemned to die and was carried to the top of a hill called Manti. After admitting that his teachings were contrary to the word of God, he was put to death. But this did not stop priestcraft from spreading throughout the land, because the practice brought riches and honor to those who preached the false doctrines. The nonmembers began to persecute those who belonged to the church of God, and the contention between the two groups even came to blows—*yea, they would smite one another with their fists.*

All of this was happening during the second year of Alma's reign, causing *much affliction to the church.* Succumbing to false teachings, many members hardened their hearts and left the church.

> *Those that did stand fast in the faith . . . were steadfast and immovable in keeping the commandments of God, and they bore with patience the persecution which was heaped upon them.* (Alma 1:25)

As the priests worked to support themselves, they would take a break from their labors to teach the word of God. The people would leave their work to listen to them, and then all would return to their tasks. With this system they were all considered equal, the teacher no better than the learner.

> *And they did impart of their substance . . . to the poor, and the needy, and the sick, and the afflicted; and they did not wear costly apparel, yet they were neat and comely.* (Alma 1:27)

The members of the church gave freely to anyone who was in need, whether they belonged to their church or not. Even though they continued to be persecuted, those within the church had peace. They began to be *exceedingly rich,* becoming far wealthier than those outside the church who indulged in wicked practices. The Nephites enjoyed peace until the fifth year of the reign of the judges.

·33·

AMLICI SEEKS TO BECOME KING
ALMA 2–3

I n the beginning of the fifth year of the reign of the judges, contention again arose. Another wise and cunning man, who adhered to
the teachings of Nehor, had drawn followers. His name was Amlici,
and it was the intention of his supporters to establish him as king. The rest
of the people became alarmed as they watched his power grow.

> *If it were possible that Amlici should gain the voice of the people,*
> *he, being a wicked man, would deprive them of their rights and*
> *privileges of the church; for it was his intent to destroy the church of*
> *God.* (Alma 2:4)

After having many discussions and *wonderful contentions* on the issue,
the people throughout the land finally put it to a vote. The voice of the
people came against Amlici, causing great joy for those who supported
the government and the freedom it granted. However, Amlici's followers consecrated him king anyway. The first thing he did as king was to
command the *Amlicites,* as they were now called, to take up arms against
the Nephites. Aware of this threat, the Nephites too took up arms. Alma
himself went at the head of his army to battle the Amlicites upon the
hill Amnihu, east of the river Sidon. The Amlicites fought with great
strength, slaying many of the Nephites. Nevertheless, the Lord blessed
the Nephites and the tables turned. There was such a slaughter among
the Amlicites that they began to flee. All that day the Nephites pursued
them; then Alma's people pitched their tents for the night in the valley
of Gideon. (The valley had been named after that Gideon who had been
killed by Nehor.) By the end of this first day of battle, 12,532 Amlicites
and 6,562 Nephites had been slain!

Alma sent spies to watch the camp of the Amlicites, and they returned
the next day in *great haste* with terrible news. The Amlicites had joined

with the Lamanites. At that very moment their large combined army was upon the people in the land of Minon, which was near the land of Zarahemla. Alma's army immediately gathered their tents and headed towards Zarahemla to defend their people.

> *And behold, as they were crossing the river Sidon, the Lamanites and the Amlicites, being as numerous almost . . . as the sands of the sea, came upon them to destroy them.* (Alma 2:27)

Because the Nephites had prayed mightily for deliverance, the Lord gave them strength and the Lamanites and Amlicites began to fall before them. As Alma fought with Amlici in a mighty duel with the sword, he cried to the Lord, asking that his life might be spared so he could be an instrument in the Lord's hands in preserving his people. He was then given the strength to slay Amlici. He also fought with the king of the Lamanites, but the king fled and sent his guards to fight instead. The king's guards were either slain or driven back at the hands of the Nephites. Then Alma ordered the bodies of the Lamanite dead to be thrown into the waters of Sidon, *that thereby his people might have room to cross and contend with the Lamanites and Amlicites on the west of the river Sidon* (Alma 2:34).

The dead of the Amlicites were distinguishable from those of the Nephites by a red mark they painted on their foreheads.

After both armies crossed the river Sidon, the huge Lamanite and Amlicite armies began to flee toward the wilderness. As the Nephites pursued them, the Lamanites and Amlicites were scattered and slain. Others were driven into a wilderness called Hermounts, a place infested with *wild and ravenous beasts.*

> *And it came to pass that many died in the wilderness of their wounds, and were devoured by those beasts and also the vultures of the air; and their bones have been found, and have been heaped up on the earth.* (Alma 2:38)

The Nephites buried their dead and then returned to their lands. There had been so many slain, including women and children, that they could not number them. Many of their flocks and herds had been killed, and their fields of grain had been trodden down by the contending armies.

The Nephites scarcely had time to rest from this horrendous battle before another army of Lamanites came upon them! Alma had been wounded in the last battle and had to stay behind, but he sent a large army to meet the Lamanites. The Nephites slew many of them and drove the remainder out of the borders of their land. They again established peace in their land—for a time. All this contention and warfaring had begun and ended in the fifth year of the reign of the judges.

And in one year were thousands and tens of thousands of souls sent to the eternal world . . . to reap eternal happiness or eternal misery, according to the spirit which they listed to obey. (Alma 3:26)

·34·

ALMA RESIGNS AS CHIEF JUDGE
ALMA 4–8

During the sixth and seventh years of the reign of the judges, there were no contentions or wars in the land of Zarahemla. However, the last terrible war with the Lamanites had left the Nephites severely afflicted. They mourned for the loss of the many thousands of their people who had been killed. They had also lost a substantial number of their flocks and herds, and their fields of grain had been trampled by the Lamanites.

> *And so great were their afflictions that every soul had cause to mourn; and they believed that it was the judgments of God sent upon them because of their wickedness and their abominations; therefore they were awakened to a remembrance of their duty.* (Alma 4:3)

With the Nephites in this humbled state, the church began to grow, and during the seventh year 3,500 people were baptized. Amazingly, the people soon turned from their righteousness.

> *In the eighth year of the reign of the judges . . . the people of the church began to wax proud, because of their exceeding riches, and their fine silks, and their fine-twined linen, and because of their many flocks and herds, and their gold and their silver, and all manner of precious things . . . ; and in all these things were they lifted up in the pride of their eyes, for they began to wear very costly apparel.* (Alma 4:6)

For Alma and many of the teachers, priests, and elders, this was the cause of much affliction. They grieved for the wickedness of their people.

> *For they saw and beheld with great sorrow that the people of the church . . . began to be scornful, one towards another, and they began*

92

to persecute those that did not believe according to their own will and pleasure. (Alma 4:8)

During the eighth year contentions arose among the members of the church, which caused the church to *fail in its progress.* In the beginning of the ninth year, Alma could see that the wickedness of his people was going to bring on their destruction. They were turning their backs upon those who were hungry, sick, and afflicted. Still, there remained the humble followers of God, who shared what they had with the poor. Alma resigned as chief judge in order to devote all his time to preaching to the people. A vote was taken and a wise man named Nephihah was chosen to succeed him as chief judge. Alma retained the office of high priest. He planned to go among the people and *preach the word of God unto them, to stir them up in remembrance of their duty.*

> *[He saw] no way that he might reclaim them save it were in bearing down in pure testimony against them.* (Alma 4:19)

Alma first preached to the people in Zarahemla, and there he ordained priests and elders to preside and watch over the church. Many people were baptized, but members who remained unrepentant were taken off the rolls of the church.

After the church in Zarahemla was cleansed and set in order, Alma went to the city of Gideon. He found to his great joy that the people there were not in the same *awful dilemma* as the people in Zarahemla had been. The people of Gideon were more diligent in keeping the commandments of God. After preaching to the people and leaving his blessings with them, he returned to his own house in Zarahemla to rest.

In the beginning of the tenth year of the reign of the judges, Alma journeyed to the land of Melek, where he had great success. The people came to Alma throughout all the borders of the land to be baptized. When Alma finished his work at Melek, he traveled to the city of Ammonihah, a three-day journey. In Ammonihah, Alma would have one of his most trying yet greatest experiences.

·35·

REJECTION IN AMMONIHAH
ALMA 8–10

W hen Alma arrived in the city of Ammonihah, he began to preach the word of God to the people.

Now Satan had gotten great hold upon the hearts of the people . . . ; therefore they would not hearken unto the words of Alma. (Alma 8:9)

Determined to reach them, Alma *wrestl[ed] with God in mighty prayer.* He asked the Lord to pour out his Spirit upon them so that they might have a desire to be baptized. Still, their hearts remained hardened. They told Alma that they knew who he was—high priest over the church—but they were not members of his church and did not believe in such *foolish traditions.* They also reminded Alma that because he had delivered up the judgment-seat to Nephihah, he had no power over them.

After suffering more verbal abuse and even being spit upon, Alma was cast out of the city. He was on his way to a different city, *being weighed down with sorrow . . . and anguish of soul,* when an angel of the Lord appeared to him!

*Blessed art thou, Alma . . . , for thou hast great cause to rejoice; for thou hast been faithful in keeping the commandments of God from the time which thou receivedst thy first message from him. Behold, **I am he that delivered it unto you**.*

. . . I am sent to command thee that thou return to the city of Ammonihah, and preach again unto the people. . . . Yea, say unto them, except they repent the Lord God will destroy them. (Alma 8:15–16)

Alma was told that the people of Ammonihah were plotting to destroy the liberty of the people.

After receiving the message from the angel, Alma *returned speedily to the land of Ammonihah.* This time he entered the city from a different direction. Being very hungry, he asked a man if he would give something to eat to a humble servant of God. The man, whose name was Amulek, replied that he had been told by an angel to expect a prophet of God. He took Alma to his home and fed him bread and meat until he was filled.

At a later time, Amulek described to the people of Ammonihah who he was and how it happened that he met Alma:

> *I am also a man of no small reputation among all those who know me; . . . I have many kindreds and friends, and I have also acquired much riches by the hand of my industry.* (Alma 10:4)

He explained to the people that he knew the teachings of the church but had hardened his heart.

> *For I was called many times and I would not hear; . . . therefore I went on rebelling against God.* (Alma 10:6)

Then one day as Amulek was journeying to see a close relative, an angel appeared to him and said:

> *Amulek, return to thine own house, for thou shalt feed a prophet of the Lord; . . . for he has fasted many days because of the sins of this people, and he is an hungered, . . . and he shall bless thee and thy house.* (Alma 10:7)

Alma stayed several days with Amulek, and just as the angel had promised, Alma blessed him and all of his household. Then the Lord commanded both men to preach to the people of Ammonihah. They went forth and began to teach the people with the Spirit and power that the Lord had given them.

·36·

CONTENDING WITH ZEEZROM
ALMA 9–14

A s Alma began once again to preach to the people of Ammonihah, the spirit of contention was immediately present.

> *Who is God, that he sendeth no more authority than one man among this people, to declare unto them the truth of such great and marvelous things?* (Alma 9:6)

The people were ready to lay their hands on Alma, and yet he boldly stood before them and testified of their wickedness.

> *But behold, I say unto you that if ye persist in your wickedness that your days shall not be prolonged in the land, for the Lamanites shall be sent upon you; and if ye repent not they shall come in a time when you know not, and ye shall be visited with utter destruction.* (Alma 9:18)

(In Alma 16:9 we learn that Alma's prophecy came true—Ammonihah was destroyed in **one** day by the Lamanites!)

Alma reminded them that when the Nephites were wicked in the past, the Lord sometimes sent an angel or a prophet to give warning. Alma had been sent to the people of Ammonihah to try to prevent their destruction.

> *And now, my beloved brethren, for ye are my brethren, and ye ought to be beloved, and ye ought to [repent], seeing that your hearts have been grossly hardened against the word of God, and seeing that ye are a lost and a fallen people.* (Alma 9:30)

The people were so angry with Alma's last comment that they attempted to take him and put him into prison, but the Lord did not allow this just yet.

Amulek then went forth and preached to the people. He began by telling them who he was and how he met Alma and that the angel who had
visited him had said that Alma was a holy man. He related to them how
the Lord's blessings had been upon his whole household while Alma stayed
with him. Amulek testified to the people that what Alma spoke was true.

The people were quite astonished to find there was now a second witness supporting Alma's teachings.

Alma and Amulek were beginning to turn the hearts of the people
and might have been able to save the city from destruction—if it had not
been for the lawyers and judges.

> Now these lawyers were learned in all the arts and cunning of
> the people; and this was to enable them that they might be skillful in
> their profession. (Alma 10:15)
>
> Because they received their wages according to their employ,
> therefore, they did stir up the people to riotings, and all manner
> of disturbances and wickedness, that they might have more employ,
> that they might get money according to the suits which were brought
> before them; therefore they did stir up the people against Alma and
> Amulek. (Alma 11:20)

The lawyers contended with Alma and Amulek, with the intent of trick-
ing them into crossing or contradicting themselves. Then they could be
judged according to the law and cast into prison or slain. Perceiving their
thoughts, Amulek cried out with righteous indignation:

> O ye wicked and perverse generation, ye lawyers and hypocrites,
> for ye are laying the foundations of the devil; for ye are laying traps
> and snares to catch the holy ones of God. . . .
>
> . . . If it were not for the prayers of the righteous, who are now in
> the land, . . . ye would even now be visited with utter destruction. . . .
>
> But it is by the prayers of the righteous that ye are spared; now
> therefore, if ye will cast out the righteous from among you then . . . the
> Lord [will not] stay his hand; . . . then ye shall be smitten by famine,
> and by pestilence, and by the sword. (Alma 10:17, 22–23)

The people lashed out against Amulek, saying that he spoke against their *just*
laws and their *wise* lawyers. After Amulek told the people that their destruction was being laid by the unrighteousness of their lawyers and judges, the

people called him a *child of the devil*. The most outspoken of the lawyers and the *foremost* to accuse Alma and Amulek was a man named Zeezrom. He was one of the more prominent lawyers in Ammonihah.

> *Now Zeezrom was a man who was expert in the devices of the devil, that he might destroy that which was good.* (Alma 11:21)

Zeezrom offered Amulek a sizable sum of money if he would deny the existence of a Supreme Being. Amulek responded to this bribe by calling him a *child of hell* and by unfolding Zeezrom's plan in front of everyone—that he never intended to give him the money once he had denied God. Zeezrom went on to contend with Amulek about other points of doctrine, frantically trying to trap him in his own words. The people were astonished at how well Amulek was able to defend the gospel.

Alma could see that Amulek's preaching had actually *silenced* Zeerom, and that *he began to tremble under a consciousness of his own guilt,* so he took his turn to speak to him. He explained to Zeezrom that he had lied not only to men but also to God and that he and Amulek had been able to discern his thoughts through the Spirit. Zeezrom was shown how he had allowed himself to be part of Satan's plan to bring all of the people under Satan's power. He again trembled as he became more and more convinced of the power of God. Zeezrom continued with his questioning, but this time he displayed a sincere desire to learn the truth. The conversion of this wicked lawyer was taking root! Alma spoke for a long time, expounding on the principles of the gospel. He especially wanted to impress upon Zeezrom what it would be like to appear before God after this life in our unrepentant state:

> *And in this awful state we shall not dare to look up to our God; and we would fain be glad if we could command the rocks and the mountains to fall upon us to hide us from his presence.* (Alma 12:14)

Alma went on to teach the people many things, but the most important part of his discourse was to call the people to repentance. He told his listeners that he wished *from the inmost part of [his] heart, yea, with great anxiety even unto pain* that they would take to heart what he had said and *not procrastinate the day of [their] repentance.*

After Alma finished speaking, many of the people were converted and *began to repent, and to search the scriptures.*

·37·

ALMA AND AMULEK
ARE IMPRISONED
ALMA 14–15

Even though Alma and Amulek had made many converts in Ammonihah, the majority of the people wanted to see them killed *because they had testified so plainly against their wickedness*. They were bound and taken before the chief judge of the land. Witnesses testified that the two missionaries had spoken against their laws and against their lawyers and judges as well. The witnesses also twisted the doctrines they had been preaching. Zeezrom was appalled at what the people were doing to Alma and Amulek and knew that he was greatly responsible for their blindness because of his *lying words*.

> *And his soul began to be harrowed up under a consciousness of his own guilt; yea, he began to be encircled about by the pains of hell.* (Alma 14:6)

In desperation, Zeezrom cried out that *he* was the guilty one and that Alma and Amulek were *spotless before God*. He continued to plead with the people, but they only reviled him, asking, *art thou also possessed with the devil?* They spat on him and cast him out of the city, along with others who believed in the teachings of the two brethren. Then they sent men to cast stones at them. The next action they took demonstrates why they were ripe for destruction.

> *And they brought the wives and children together [of the men who had been cast out of the city], and whosoever believed . . . in the word of God they caused that they should be cast into the fire; and they also brought forth . . . the holy scriptures, and cast them into the fire also.* (Alma 14:8)

Alma and Amulek were forced to witness this diabolical scene. Amulek, pained by the horror of seeing the suffering of the women and children as they were consumed by the fire, said to Alma,

> *How can we witness this awful scene? Therefore let us stretch forth our hands, and exercise the power of God which is in us, and save them from the flames.* (Alma 14:10)

Alma responded that he was constrained by the Spirit not to do so and that God was receiving these people in glory. God was allowing this to happen so that *the blood of the innocent [would] stand as a witness against them.* Amulek thought that perhaps they would be burned also, but Alma told him they would be spared because their work was not yet finished.

When the fires died down, the chief judge of Ammonihah came to Alma and Amulek and *smote* their faces.

> *After what ye have seen, will ye preach again unto this people, that they shall be cast into a lake of fire and brimstone?* (Alma 14:14)

The chief judge smugly told them that they hadn't the power to save these people and neither had God chosen to save them. He struck them again and asked them what they had to say for themselves. Alma and Amulek said nothing. They were struck again, then delivered to the officers and cast into prison.

After Alma and Amulek had been in prison for three days, many lawyers, judges, priests, and teachers came and questioned them. Again, Alma and Amulek said nothing. The chief judge asked them why they refused to answer their questions and reminded them that he had the power to put them to death. He commanded them to speak, but still they answered nothing. The people left but came again the next day. Again the judge *smote* the faces of Alma and Amulek. Many of the others came forward, also striking them and taunting them to deliver themselves if they had such great power.

> *And many such things did they say unto them, gnashing their teeth upon them, and spitting upon them, and saying: How shall we look when we are damned?* (Alma 14:21)

For many days the people mocked them, all the while depriving them of food and water. They also stripped them of their clothing and kept them bound with strong cords. After Alma and Amulek had suffered for many days, the chief judge of Ammonihah, as well as many of their teachers and lawyers, again came to the beleaguered missionaries. Once again the chief judge struck them and said:

> *If ye have the power of God deliver yourselves from these bands, and then we will believe that the Lord will destroy this people according to your words.* (Alma 14:24)

One by one they came forth and struck Alma and Amulek, each repeating the same challenge.

> *And when the last had spoken unto them the power of God was upon Alma and Amulek, and they rose and stood upon their feet.*
> *And Alma cried, saying: How long shall we suffer these great afflictions, O Lord? O Lord, give us strength according to our faith which is in Christ, even unto deliverance. And they broke the cords with which they were bound; and when the people saw this, they began to flee, for the fear of destruction had come upon them.* (Alma 14:25–26)

The people were in such a great state of fear that they fell to the ground, not even making it to the outer door of the prison. Then *the earth shook mightily and the walls of the prison were rent in twain.* Every soul within the walls of the prison was killed, except for Alma and Amulek, who walked out unharmed.

Upon hearing the great noise, a multitude of people ran from the city to the scene of the calamity. When they saw Alma and Amulek walking away from the pile of rubble that moments before had been the prison, *they were struck with great fear.*

> *And [they] fled from the presence of Alma and Amulek even as a goat fleeth with her young from two lions.* (Alma 14:29)

Alma and Amulek were commanded to depart the city of Ammonihah. They went to the land of Sidom, where they found all the believers who had been stoned and cast out of Ammonihah. Alma and Amulek sadly related to these men how their wives and children had been burned to death and how they themselves had been miraculously delivered from the prison. Alma's prophecy concerning the wicked city of Ammonihah was soon to be fulfilled.

·38·

ZEEZROM IS BAPTIZED
ALMA 15

Zeezrom lay sick with a burning fever in Sidom. He had been one of the more prominent lawyers of Ammonihah who had contended with Alma and Amulek—until he started believing in their words! When he tried to defend them, he was stoned and cast out of the city along with other believers. Now Zeezrom mistakenly thought that Alma and Amulek were dead and that he was responsible. His guilt brought on his serious illness. Then he got word that the two missionaries were in Sidom, and *his heart began to take courage.* He immediately sent a message asking them to come to him.

Alma and Amulek went directly to see Zeezrom and found him gravely ill. Zeezrom asked them to heal him. Alma asked him if he believed in the power of Christ, and Zeezrom replied that he believed all the words that Alma had taught. Then Alma cried unto the Lord, asking for Zeezrom to be healed *according to his faith which is in Christ.*

> *And when Alma had said these words, Zeezrom leaped upon his feet, and began to walk; and this was done to the great astonishment of all the people; and the knowledge of this went forth throughout all the land of Sidom.*
>
> *And Alma baptized Zeezrom unto the Lord; and he began from that time forth to preach unto the people.* (Alma 15:11–12)

Alma established the church in the land of Sidom. He consecrated priests to baptize the many people who were flocking in from all the regions around Sidom to join the church.

The people in Ammonihah *remained a hard-hearted and a stiffnecked people,* attributing the miraculous power of Alma and Amulek to the devil. They were followers of Nehor (see chapter 32 herein) and did not believe in repenting of their sins.

Now that the church in Sidom was doing well, Alma felt free to return to his own land. Amulek had been rejected by his friends and family after joining with Alma to preach the word of God. He had also *forsaken all his gold and silver and precious things* for the gospel's sake. He could no longer call Ammonihah his home.

> *[Alma] took Amulek and came over to the land of Zarahemla, and took him to his own house, and did administer unto him in his tribulations, and strengthened him in the Lord.* (Alma 15:18)

·39·

THE DESTRUCTION
OF AMMONIHAH
ALMA 16

In the early part of the eleventh year, *there was a cry of war heard throughout the land.* The Lamanites had come into Ammonihah to destroy the city (see Alma 25:1–2 for related information). Before the Nephites could raise a sufficient army, the people of Ammonihah had been completely annihilated. The Lamanites also killed many people who lived near the city of Noah and took others captive.

> *Every living soul of the Ammonihahites was destroyed, and also their great city, which they said God could not destroy, because of its greatness.*
>
> *But behold, in one day it was left desolate; and the carcasses were mangled by dogs and wild beasts of the wilderness.*
>
> *Nevertheless, after many days their dead bodies were heaped up upon the face of the earth, and they were covered with a shallow covering. And now so great was the scent thereof that the people did not go in to possess the land of Ammonihah for many years.* (Alma 16:9–11)

A man named Zoram had been appointed chief captain over the Nephite army. His first order of business was to rescue the people who had been taken captive from the bordering areas when the city of Ammonihah was destroyed. Knowing that Alma, as high priest over the church, had the spirit of prophecy, he asked him where they should go in the wilderness to find their brethren. After taking the matter to the Lord, Alma returned and declared prophetically:

> *The Lamanites will cross the river Sidon in the south wilderness, away up beyond the borders of the land of Manti. . . . there shall ye*

meet them, on the east of the river Sidon, and there the Lord will deliver unto thee thy brethren who have been taken captive by the Lamanites. (Alma 16:6)

The Nephite army followed the Lord's instructions exactly and came upon the army of the Lamanites. They drove them into the wilderness, and all the captives were rescued—*not one soul of them had been lost.*

After its destruction, the land of Ammonihah was called *Desolation of Nehors: Desolation* because it remained unoccupied, and *Nehors* because the people of the city had believed in the teachings of Nehor.

The Nephites enjoyed peace for the next three years. The church was well established in the land because of the tireless efforts of Alma and Amulek and others ordained to the work.

And there was no inequality among them; the Lord did pour out his Spirit on all the face of the land. (Alma 16:16)

·40·

AMMON PROTECTS THE KING'S FLOCKS

ALMA 17

B ecause Alma had not seen his close friends in many years, he was filled with joy upon being reunited. When Alma and the sons of Mosiah were young, they were numbered among the *unbelievers* and went about trying to destroy the church. They were all converted after the Lord sent an angel to stop their destructive behavior. During the last fourteen years, while Alma served as high priest over the church, the sons of Mosiah had been on a mission to the Lamanites (see chapter 31 herein).

(The scripture account now goes back fourteen years to the time that the sons of Mosiah departed on their mission. Chapters 40 through 45 of *And It Came to Pass* tell of their miraculous experiences.)

Ammon, Aaron, Omner, and Himni left the land of Zarahemla to begin their mission, each one having refused to be the next king. The four brothers had selected a small group of men to accompany them. Weapons were taken, but only to provide food. As they headed toward the land of Nephi, they fasted and prayed that they might bring the Lamanites to the knowledge of the truth. The Spirit of the Lord visited them and gave them comfort. They were told to be patient in their afflictions and to be good examples to the Lamanites; if they followed this admonition they would be instruments in the Lord's hands in bringing salvation to many souls.

After reaching the borders of Lamanite land and receiving a blessing from Ammon, they parted ways (see Alma 17:17), trusting in the Lord that they would accomplish a great work and meet again.

> *And assuredly [the work] was great, for they had undertaken to preach the word of God to a wild and a hardened and a ferocious people; a people who delighted in murdering the Nephites, and robbing and plundering them.* (Alma 17:14)

When Ammon entered the land of Ishmael, he was immediately captured by the Lamanites. As was their custom, he was tied up and carried before the king, who would then decide whether to cast him out of the land, throw him into prison, or slay him. The king's name was Lamoni, and he asked his prisoner if it was his intention to live among his people. Ammon replied that he might just dwell among them for the rest of his life! King Lamoni was pleased to hear this and ordered his men to untie him. Then the king wanted Ammon to take one of his daughters for a wife. (The scriptural account is probably leaving out some details here!) Ammon declined, saying he just wanted to be his servant. So Ammon became a servant to the king and was assigned with other servants to watch the king's flocks.

Three days later, Ammon and the other servants were driving the flocks to be watered at a place called the waters of Sebus. Suddenly, a group of wicked Lamanites began scattering their flocks as a ploy to steal them. As the animals fled in all directions, the terrified servants began to weep. It was the king's policy to have his servants put to death if they allowed his flocks to be stolen.

> *Now when Ammon saw this his heart was swollen within him with joy; for, said he, I will show forth my power unto these my fellow-servants, or the power which is in me, in restoring these flocks unto the king, that I may win the hearts of these my fellow-servants, that I may lead them to believe in my words.* (Alma 17:29)

Addressing the other servants as *my brethren,* Ammon told them to *be of good cheer*—they would gather the flocks and bring them back to the watering hole. Ammon and the men *rushed forth with much swiftness* until the flocks were gathered. When the thieves reappeared, Ammon told his brethren to keep the flocks together and that he would contend with the marauders. As Ammon approached, they did not fear him, thinking that just one of their men could easily slay him. Using a sling, Ammon cast stones at them with such skill and *mighty power* that he killed six men. The other thieves were astonished at Ammon's power but were so enraged that they were determined to kill him. Since they could not hit him with their stones, they came after him with clubs. For each man who lifted his club to strike, Ammon cut off his arm with his sword! Soon the thieves fled. Ammon had killed six men with the sling and their leader with his sword, and he had cut off as many arms *as were lifted against him, and they were not a few.*

Ammon and his fellow servants finished watering the flocks and then returned them to the pasture. While Ammon was feeding the king's horses, the other servants went to the king, bearing all the arms that Ammon had cut off as a testimony of the day's events!

·41·

THE CONVERSION OF
KING LAMONI

ALMA 18–19

When King Lamoni learned of Ammon's faithfulness in preserving his flocks and of his miraculous power in doing so, *he was astonished exceedingly, and said: Surely, this is more than a man. Behold, is not this the Great Spirit who doth send such great punishments upon this people, because of their murders?* (Alma 18:2)

The servants answered that they did not know if he was the Great Spirit or a man. What they did know was that Ammon could not be slain by his enemies and that he was a friend to the king. But they added that they did not believe a man could have such power. King Lamoni was now convinced that Ammon was the Great Spirit who had come down to prevent him from killing more servants who would lose his flocks to thieves. The king *began to fear exceedingly . . . lest he had done wrong in slaying his servants.*

King Lamoni asked where Ammon was, and his servants told him that he was preparing the king's horses and chariots. This had been part of their orders for the day because Lamoni's father, who was king over all the Lamanites, was hosting a great feast in the land of Nephi. Ammon was part of the group assigned to accompany the king to the feast. Upon hearing what Ammon was doing, King Lamoni remarked that he had never had a servant as faithful as he and that he was sure Ammon was the Great Spirit. The king wanted to see Ammon but dared not send for him.

Ammon finished preparing the horses and chariots and went to report to the king, but when he saw him looking so troubled he changed his mind. One of the king's servants saw him leaving and called after him, *Rabbanah, the king desireth thee to stay. Rabbanah* was a title of honor that meant *powerful or great king.* Ammon returned to the king and asked what he could do for him. Lamoni, not knowing what to say, said nothing for one hour! Finally, Ammon broke the long silence and again asked what it was the king wanted. When the king gave no answer a second time, Ammon, being filled with the Spirit, perceived his thoughts. He mentioned the miraculous things he had done that day and asked if that was what caused him to marvel. He assured the king that he was only a man and that *whatsoever thou desirest which is right, that will I do.* The king was further surprised when he realized that Ammon could discern his thoughts. He asked Ammon if he was the Great Spirit *who knows all things.* Ammon answered that he was not. Then Lamoni asked him how he knew the thoughts of his heart and by what power he contended with the enemies of the king.

> *And now, if thou wilt tell me concerning these things, whatsoever thou desirest I will give unto thee; and if it were needed, I would guard thee with my armies; but I know that thou art more powerful than all they.* (Alma 18:21)

Ammon replied that he would tell him by what power he did those things if he would hearken to what he had to say. The king answered that he would believe all his words. Ammon began teaching Lamoni and his servants by explaining that God and the Great Spirit were the same person. He taught about heaven, since that had not been part of Lamoni's beliefs, and how God created all things. Then Ammon began at the creation of the world and laid before him the teachings of the scriptures, down to the time that Lehi left Jerusalem. He told them how Laman and Lemuel rebelled and how this rebellion related to the long-standing Lamanite tradition of hating the Nephites. He taught them that which was in the records from Lehi's time to the present. He discussed the coming of Christ and the plan of redemption.

After Ammon finished speaking, King Lamoni believed all his words and cried unto the Lord for mercy upon himself and his people.

> *And now, when he had said this, he fell unto the earth, as if he were dead.*
>
> *And . . . his servants took him and carried him in unto his wife, and laid him upon a bed; and he lay as if he were dead for the space of two days and two nights; and his wife, and his sons, and his daughters mourned over him, after the manner of the Lamanites, greatly lamenting his loss.* (Alma 18:42–43)

As the servants were preparing to bury the king, the queen, having heard of Ammon's fame, sent for him. She told him that she heard he was a prophet and that he had power to do mighty deeds. She asked Ammon to go and see her husband because she was not sure what to do. Some servants told her that he was still alive; others said that the body was beginning to stink and ought to be buried. Ammon knew that King Lamoni was under God's power and that *the dark veil of unbelief was being cast away from his mind.* Ammon told the queen that her husband was not dead but *sleepeth in God* and that he would awaken the next day. He asked her if she believed his words, and she replied that she knew it would happen just as he said.

> *And Ammon said unto her: Blessed art thou because of thy exceeding faith; I say unto thee, woman, there has not been such great faith among all the people of the Nephites.* (Alma 19:10)

The queen watched over the bed of her husband all that day and the next, until the time Nephi had appointed for him to awake. The king arose just as Ammon had promised and began to praise God, relating how he had seen Jesus Christ. His *heart was swollen within him, and he sunk again with joy.* The queen was also overpowered by the Spirit, and she too fell unconscious. Ammon was so overcome with gratitude to the Lord for answering his prayers and pouring out his Spirit upon the Lamanites that he also fell unconscious. When the king's servants saw the three of them lying there, they began to cry mightily to God until all but one of them had fallen to the earth. Her name was Abish. She had been converted to the Lord many years before because of an extraordinary vision that her father had, but she had kept it a secret. As she looked upon all these people lying unconscious, she knew it was the power of God. She believed that if other Lamanites could witness this amazing scene it would cause them also to believe in the power of God.

> *Therefore she ran forth from house to house, making it known unto the people.*
> *And they began to assemble themselves together unto the house of the king. And there came a multitude, and to their astonishment, they beheld the king, and the queen, and their servants prostrate upon the earth, and they all lay there as if they were dead.* (Alma 19:17–18)

Then their eyes fell upon Ammon and they saw that he was a Nephite. The people began to murmur among themselves, speculating on what had happened to those lying before them. Some said that because King Lamoni had allowed a Nephite to remain in the land, this great evil had come upon his household. Others said the king had brought this evil upon himself for slaying the servants when their flocks were stolen at the waters of Sebus.

Standing in the multitude were the very men who had been stealing the king's flocks, and they were angry with Ammon for having killed so many of their brethren. One of them, whose brother had been slain by Ammon's sword, was especially angry with Ammon. He drew his sword, but before he could kill Ammon, he fell dead! (The Lord had promised Mosiah that he would protect his sons. See Mosiah 28:7.) A great fear fell upon the multitude, and they dared not touch anyone but marveled at what the cause of this great power could be.

> *And it came to pass that there were many among them who said that Ammon was the Great Spirit, and others said he was sent by the Great Spirit;*
> *But others rebuked them all, saying that he was a monster, who had been sent from the Nephites to torment them.* (Alma 19:25–26)

The contention heated further as some said that Ammon had been sent by the Great Spirit to punish them for their unrighteousness. They even suggested that it was the Great Spirit who had been attending the Nephites, delivering them out of their hands and helping to kill so many of the Lamanites! (See Alma 19:27.)

Abish could see that bringing the people to the king's house had only caused contention, and *she was exceedingly sorrowful, even unto tears.* She took the queen by the hand in hopes of raising her from the ground. Just as she touched her, the queen arose and stood upon her feet, praising God. The queen then took the king by the hand and he too arose. The king rebuked the people for their contention and then began teaching them the things he had learned from Ammon.

By this time Ammon and the other servants had also risen and were administering to the people. The king and queen and their servants all had the same message to bear—their hearts had been changed and they had no more desire to do evil. They told of seeing angels, who taught them the things of God. Many people believed and were converted, but others refused to listen and went their way.

And as many as did believe were baptized; and they became a righteous people, and they did establish a church among them.

And thus the work of the Lord did commence among the Lamanites. (Alma 19:35–36)

·42·

ON THE WAY TO MIDDONI
ALMA 20–21

King Lamoni decided that the time had come for Ammon to meet his father, who lived in the land of Nephi and was king over all the Lamanites. (Lamoni's father had given his son and others jurisdiction over parts of his kingdom, but he retained ultimate power over all the land.)

> *[But] the voice of the Lord came to Ammon, saying: Thou shalt not go up to the land of Nephi, for behold, the king will seek thy life; but thou shalt go to the land of Middoni; for behold, thy brother Aaron, and also Muloki and Ammah are in prison.* (Alma 20:2)

Ammon told the king that he needed to go to Middoni to free his brethren from prison. King Lamoni suggested that he would also come because the king of Middoni was a personal friend and he could persuade him to release the three men. When the king asked Ammon who had told him his brethren were in prison, Ammon replied, *No one hath told me, save it be God.* King Lamoni ordered his servants to make ready his horses and chariots.

As they were traveling to Middoni, by coincidence they met Lamoni's father, who said to his son:

> *Why did ye not come to the feast on that great day when I made a feast unto my sons, and unto my people?*
>
> *And he also said: Whither art thou going with this Nephite, who is one of the children of a liar?* (Alma 20:9–10)

Fearing to offend his father, Lamoni explained what had happened at home that prevented him from attending the feast and where he and Ammon were now going. Lamoni's father was even angrier after hearing this. He told his son that these Nephites had come among them to deceive them and ordered him to return home. He also commanded him to slay Ammon!

> *But Lamoni said unto him: I will not slay Ammon, neither will I return to the land of Ishmael, but I go to the land of Middoni that I may release the brethren of Ammon, for I know that they are just men and holy prophets of the true God.* (Alma 20:15)

These words so enraged the old king that he drew his sword to kill Lamoni. Ammon came forward and told him not to slay his son, though it would be better for his son to die rather than him because Lamoni had repented of his sins. Ammon fearlessly explained to the old king that if he died now, in his anger, his *soul could not be saved.* If he were to kill his son he would be killing an innocent man and *his blood would cry from the ground . . . for vengeance.* The old king replied that he knew his son was innocent, that it was Ammon who was trying to destroy his son. With that he came after Ammon with his sword, *but Ammon withstood his blows, and also smote his arm that he could not use it.* When the king saw that Ammon could slay him, he began to plead with him to spare his life. Ammon raised his sword and threatened to kill him unless he promised to release his brethren from prison.

> *Now the king, fearing he should lose his life, said: If thou wilt spare me I will grant unto thee whatsoever thou wilt ask, even to half of the kingdom.* (Alma 20:23)

Ammon could see that he was now in a good position to bargain, so he added more to his terms for sparing the old king's life: Lamoni was to remain as king and have the freedom to govern his people as he wished. The old king was surprised that Ammon wanted no part of his kingdom and that he would so readily spare his life. He was also *astonished exceedingly* when he saw the great love Ammon had for his son. He agreed to all the conditions asked of him. Ammon's brethren were to be freed from prison, and Lamoni would retain his kingdom and would no longer be under his father's rule. The old king *greatly desired* that they would come to his land and teach him after they had freed Ammon's brethren.

Ammon and King Lamoni proceeded on their journey to Middoni, where Ammon's brethren were brought out of prison.

And when Ammon did meet them he was exceedingly sorrowful, for behold they were naked, and their skins were worn exceedingly because of being bound with strong cords. And they also had suffered hunger, thirst, and all kinds of afflictions; nevertheless they were patient in all their sufferings. (Alma 20:29)

Aaron and his companions had *fallen into the hands of a more hardened and a more stiffnecked people.* Among the Lamanite people in that area were Amalekites and Amulonites, descendants of apostate Nephites who had earlier joined with the Lamanites. Their beliefs were of the order of Nehor, which taught that there was no need for repentance, because everyone would be guaranteed eternal life. In one synagogue where Aaron had preached, an Amalekite contended with him:

Hast thou seen an angel? Why do not angels appear unto us? Behold are not this people as good as thy people?

Thou also sayest, except we repent we shall perish. . . . How knowest thou that we have cause to repent? How knowest thou that we are not a righteous people? Behold, we have built sanctuaries, and we do assemble ourselves together to worship God. . . .

. . . We do not believe in [your] foolish traditions. We do not believe that thou knowest of things to come. (Alma 21:5–6, 8)

The Lamanites cast them out, driving them from house to house and place to place. Finally they arrived in the land of Middoni, where they were thrown into prison. There they remained for many days until Ammon and Lamoni came to free them. Once out of prison, Aaron and his companions went back to preach in the synagogues of the Amalekites and any other assemblies of the Lamanites where they were admitted. They were led by the Spirit and brought many to the knowledge of the truth.

Ammon and King Lamoni returned home to the land of Ishmael. Lamoni had synagogues built throughout the land so his people could assemble to worship. He announced to all those under his reign that they were a free people—free from the oppressions of his father. Ammon diligently spent his time preaching the gospel. The people listened to him and *were zealous for keeping the commandments of God.*

·43·

TEACHING LAMONI'S FATHER
ALMA 22–23

After Aaron and his brethren left Middoni, they were led by the Spirit to the land of Nephi to the palace of the old king. Bowing before him, they introduced themselves as the brethren he had delivered out of prison. Aaron told the king that if he would spare their lives they would be his servants. The king told them to arise and said he would not allow them to be his servants. He insisted that they *administer* to him instead because he had been troubled over the *generosity and greatness* of the words of Ammon. The king wanted to know why Ammon had not come with them. Aaron explained that the Spirit had called Ammon to the land of Ishmael to teach the people of Lamoni.

The king had two questions for the missionaries: what was meant by *the Spirit of the Lord,* and what Ammon meant when he said, *If ye will repent ye shall be saved, and if ye will not repent, ye shall be cast off at the last day.* Aaron asked the king if he believed there was a God. The king replied that the Amalekites said there was a God, and he had allowed them to build sanctuaries to worship in. Then he stated,

> *And if now thou sayest there is a God, behold I will believe.*
> (Alma 22:7)

Aaron's heart rejoiced and he assured the king that there was a God.

> *And the king said: Is God that Great Spirit that brought our fathers out of the land of Jerusalem?* (Alma 22:9)

Aaron answered that he was the same God and that he created all things both in heaven and in earth. Aaron began reading the scriptures to him, starting with the creation of Adam. He explained to the king about the fall of man. He laid before him the plan of redemption and how the

117

suffering and death of Christ would atone for their sins through their faith and repentance.

> *[Then] the king said: What shall I do that I may have this eternal life of which thou hast spoken? Yea, what shall I do that I may be born of God, having this wicked spirit rooted out of my breast, and receive his Spirit, that I may be filled with joy. . . . I will give up all that I possess, yea, I will forsake my kingdom, that I may receive this great joy.* (Alma 22:15)

Aaron explained to the king that in order to receive the joy he was seeking, he needed to repent of all his sins and call on God in faith, believing that he would receive an answer to his prayers. The king did as Aaron had instructed and bowed down upon his knees and cried mightily to the Lord, saying:

> *O God, Aaron hath told me that there is a God; and if there is a God, and if thou art God, wilt thou make thyself known unto me, and I will give away all my sins to know thee, and that I may be raised from the dead, and be saved at the last day. And now when the king had said these words, he was struck as if he were dead.* (Alma 22:18)

The servants ran and told the queen all they had just seen. When she saw the king looking as if he were dead and Aaron and his brethren standing over him as though they were the cause, she ordered the servants to slay them! The servants had witnessed the events leading to the king's fall and dared not touch Aaron and his brethren. They told the queen that *one of them is mightier than us all.* The fear of the servants made the queen afraid, so she ordered them to call the people to come and slay them. Aaron could see *the determination of the queen,* so he took the king by his hand and commanded him to stand. When the queen and the servants saw this, they *greatly marveled and began to fear,* but then the king *did minister unto them* and the entire household was converted.

A multitude of people had gathered because of the queen's earlier orders and were having a heated discussion about the Nephites among them. After the king spoke to them, they were pacified toward Aaron and his brethren and listened to their preaching.

The king sent a proclamation among all his people that Ammon, Aaron, Omner, Himni, and their brethren should have *free access to their houses, and also their temples, and their sanctuaries* and not be harmed. It was the king's desire that the word of God be taught throughout all the land so that his people might turn away from their wickedness. He wanted them to know that the traditions of their fathers were incorrect and that the Nephites and Lamanites were all brethren.

·44·

THE ANTI-NEPHI-LEHIES
ALMA 23-26

Aaron and his brethren traveled throughout the land establishing churches and consecrating priests and teachers to minister to the people. They had great success as thousands of Lamanites were brought to the knowledge of the truth. Unlike some missionary efforts, their success was long lasting.

> *As many of the Lamanites as believed in their preaching, and were converted unto the Lord, **never did fall away**.* (Alma 23:6)

They became a righteous people and put down their weapons of war and fought no more against God or any of their brethren. Whole cities were converted unto the Lord: Ishmael, Middoni, Nephi, Shilom, Shemlon, Lemuel, and Shimnilom. But of the Amalekites and Amulonites who lived among them, only one person was converted! (Remember, these two groups of people descended from apostate Nephites.)

The king and all his people who were converted wanted to be called by a different name in order to be distinguished from the rest of the Lamanites. They chose the name *Anti-Nephi-Lehies* and were no longer called Lamanites.

> *And they began to be a very industrious people; yea, and they were friendly with the Nephites; therefore, they did open a correspondence with them, and the curse of God did no more follow them.* (Alma 23:18)

The king conferred the kingdom upon his son, who was the brother of Lamoni, and the new king changed his name to *Anti-Nephi-Lehi*. Soon after, the old king died.

In that same year the Amalekites and Amulonites began to stir up the remainder of the Lamanites to make preparations for war against the people of God. Upon hearing this, Ammon and his brethren traveled to the land of Ishmael to hold a council with Lamoni and his brother, Anti-Nephi-Lehi. They had to decide how to defend themselves against the Lamanites.

> *Now there was not one soul among all the people who had been converted unto the Lord that would take up arms against their brethren; nay, they would not even make any preparations for war.* (Alma 24:6)

The new king had come before the people and made an impassioned plea with them not to take up arms against the Lamanites.

> *And now behold, my brethren, since it has been all that we could do, (as we were the most lost of all mankind) to repent of all our sins and the many murders which we have committed, and to get God to take them away from our hearts, . . . then let us stain our swords no more with the blood of our brethren.* (Alma 24:11–12)

The king was afraid that if they used their swords again, after having been forgiven of the terrible sins of their past, perhaps they would not be forgiven a second time. He suggested that they bury their swords deep in the earth and added that if they died defenseless at the hands of their brethren they would be taken home to God and be saved.

When the king finished speaking, the people took all their weapons of war and buried them deep in the ground. This was their way of covenanting with God that they would never use weapons again for the shedding of man's blood. Instead of taking the life of another, they would risk giving up their own lives instead. They also covenanted to labor abundantly with their hands rather than spend their days in idleness.

Soon after the people buried their weapons, the Lamanites arrived in the land of Nephi, bent on destroying the king and all the people of Anti-Nephi-Lehi. The people ran out to meet the approaching army, threw themselves on the ground, and began to call upon God. Without meeting any resistance, the Lamanites killed a thousand and five of them.

> *The Lamanites saw that their brethren would not flee from the sword, neither would they turn aside to the right hand or to the left, but that they would lie down and perish, and praised God even in the very act of perishing under the sword.* (Alma 24:23)

As the Lamanites continued the slaughter, many were *stung for the murders which they had committed.* They threw down their swords and joined their brethren. On that day there were more Lamanites that repented and joined the Anti-Nephi-Lehies than the number of men slain.

The Amalekites and Amulonites had done most of the killing, and the majority of them were of the order of Nehor. Of all the Lamanites who deserted the army to join with the Anti-Nephi-Lehies, none were Amalekites or Amulonites.

> *And thus we can plainly discern, that after a people have been once enlightened by the Spirit of God, and have had great knowledge of things pertaining to righteousness, and then have fallen away into sin and transgression, they become more hardened, and thus their state becomes worse than though they had never known these things.* (Alma 24:30)

Having killed their own brethren, the Lamanites were now angrier than before. This time they directed their anger at the Nephites. Their army went over into the borders of Zarahemla and destroyed the people of Ammonihah (see chapter 39 herein). After the Lamanite army left Ammonihah, they were pursued by the Nephite army. They had many battles with the Nephites but ended up being driven and slain.

Among the Lamanites who were slain were almost all the descendants of the wicked priests of King Noah. As the Lamanites fled into the east wilderness, the few remaining descendants of the priests of Noah seized leadership of the army. By this time, because of the great suffering the Lamanites had endured, many of them remembered the teachings of Aaron and his brethren. They began to disbelieve the traditions of their fathers and to believe in the Lord. The new leaders (the descendants of the priests) had the converts put to death by fire because of their beliefs. This martyrdom caused a great contention among the Lamanites, and they turned on the rulers to slay them. Those who were not slain fled into the east wilderness and were hunted for years to come, directly fulfilling a prophecy spoken by Abinadi to the priests of Noah (see Mosiah 17:15–18).

The Lamanites returned to their own land when they saw that they could not overpower the Nephites. Those that had been converted in the wilderness left the Lamanites and joined with the Anti-Nephi-Lehies. They too buried their weapons of war and became a righteous people.

The sons of Mosiah and their missionary companions *did rejoice exceedingly* for the success they had had among the Lamanites. Ammon reminded his brothers that the people in Zarahemla had *laughed [them] to scorn* when they told them of their plans to preach to the Lamanites. They had said the Lamanites were too wicked to ever accept the gospel. Not only that, but they thought the best course of action was to simply destroy the Lamanites before they destroyed the Nephites.

Through the Lord's help, the sons of Mosiah had brought thousands of the Lamanites to love not only the Lord, but the Nephites as well! In one way, the Anti-Nephi-Lehies were even more righteous than the Nephites—they would rather suffer death than take up arms against their enemy. Ammon gives us the formula behind the success of the sons of Mosiah:

> *Yea, he that repenteth and exerciseth faith, and bringeth forth good works, and prayeth continually without ceasing—unto such it is given to know the mysteries of God . . . and it shall be given unto such to bring thousands of souls to repentance.* (Alma 26:22)

·45·

A NEW HOME IN JERSHON
ALMA 27–28

When the Lamanites found that they could not overpower the Nephites, they returned home to their own land. The Amalekites among them were especially angry that they had not been successful in getting revenge against the Nephites. They stirred up the Lamanites and once again went after the Anti-Nephi-Lehies to destroy them. Just as before, the new converts refused to fight back.

> *Now when Ammon and his brethren saw this work of destruction among those whom they so dearly beloved, and among those who had so dearly beloved them—for they were treated as though they were angels sent from God to save them from everlasting destruction— . . . they were moved with compassion.* (Alma 27:4)

Ammon and his brethren suggested to the king that they gather the people and flee to the land of Zarahemla and join the Nephites. The king was against this, fearing that the Nephites would destroy them *because of the many murders and sins [they had] committed against them.* Ammon asked the king if he would allow the people to go if the Lord told them to go. The king replied that if that were the case, they would go and become slaves to the Nephites until they paid them back for the many atrocities that they had committed against them. Otherwise, they would stay and perish in the land. Ammon assured the king that their laws did not allow slavery. He then prayed to the Lord for direction in the matter, and the Lord said unto him:

> *Get this people out of this land, that they perish not; for Satan has great hold on the hearts of the Amalekites, who do stir up the Lamanites to anger against their brethren to slay them; . . . and blessed are this people, . . . for I will preserve them.* (Alma 27:12)

The people gathered together their flocks and herds and departed out of the land. They traveled to Zarahemla and stopped outside the borders of the city. Ammon and his brethren traveled alone into the city to make sure the Nephites were willing to take in the refugees.

As they traveled into the city, Ammon and his brethren met Alma and had a very joyful reunion. It had been over fourteen years since Alma and the sons of Mosiah had been visited by the angel. Shortly after this visitation, Ammon and his brothers left on their mission to the Lamanites and they had not seen Alma in all this time. Ammon's meeting with Alma and the culmination of their successful missionary labors caused him such joy that he fell into an unconscious state.

> *Now was not this exceeding joy? Behold, this is joy which none receiveth save it be the truly penitent and humble seeker of happiness.*
> (Alma 27:18)

Alma took the sons of Mosiah back to his own home. Soon after, they met with Nephihah, the chief judge, and gave him a report of all that had happened to Ammon and his brothers in the land of the Lamanites. Nephihah sent a proclamation throughout all the land asking the people if they would allow the Anti-Nephi-Lehies to join them. Not only did they agree to this, but they generously gave up a portion of their land for these people to make their new home. The land was called Jershon, and it was on the east by the sea, which joined the land of Bountiful. Knowing that the Anti-Nephi-Lehies would not defend themselves, they also chose to protect them by setting up an army between Jershon and the land of the Lamanites. In order to support the army, the Nephites would ask for a portion of what they produced.

Alma and the sons of Mosiah went back into the wilderness with the news of the overwhelming generosity of the Nephites. Alma also shared the story of his conversion with the Anti-Nephi-Lehies. Then the people were brought down into Jershon, where they took possession of the land. From that time forward they were called the people of Ammon, or Ammonites.

> *And they were also distinguished for their zeal towards God, and also towards men; for they were perfectly honest and upright in all things; and they were firm in the faith of Christ, even unto the end.*
> *And they did look upon shedding the blood of their brethren with the greatest abhorrence. . . .*

> *Therefore, they would suffer death in the most aggravating and distressing manner which could be inflicted by their brethren, before they would take the sword or cimeter to smite them.*
>
> *And thus they were . . . a highly favored people of the Lord.* (Alma 27:27–30)

The people of Ammon settled into their new home and established the church, while the Nephite army guarded all the borders of their land. Peace was not to be enjoyed, however, because the Lamanite army had followed the people of Ammon to the land of Jershon and was waiting in the wilderness. Before long they attacked.

> *And thus there was a tremendous battle; yea, even such an one as never had been known among all the people in the land from the time Lehi left Jerusalem; yea, and tens of thousands of the Lamanites were slain and scattered abroad.* (Alma 28:2)

Even though the Nephites had driven the Lamanites out of their land, it was a time of great mourning because they had also suffered a tremendous slaughter. Husbands, fathers, sons, and brothers had been slain.

> *And now surely this was a sorrowful day; . . . a time of much fasting and prayer.* (Alma 28:6)

·46·

KORIHOR, THE ANTICHRIST
ALMA 30

During the sixteenth year of the reign of the judges, peace once again settled over the land. Most of the following year also passed away in peace because the people had been strict in keeping the commandments of the Lord.

Toward the end of the seventeenth year, a man named Korihor came into Zarahemla and began preaching that there would be no Christ. There was no law against a man's beliefs, so the law had no hold on him. This *Anti-Christ* told the people that it was *a foolish and a vain hope* to believe that Christ would come, *for no man can know of anything which is to come.* He said their prophecies were only foolish traditions of their fathers.

> *Ye . . . say that ye see a remission of your sins. But behold, it is the effect of a frenzied mind; and this derangement of your minds comes because of the traditions of your fathers, which lead you away into a belief of things which are not so.* (Alma 30:16)

He preached many more things unto them, such as *every man prospered according to his genius, every man conquered according to his strength, whatsoever a man did was no crime,* and *when a man was dead, that was the end thereof.* He led away the hearts of many men and women to do wickedness.

Korihor went over to Jershon to preach to the people of Ammon (the Anti-Nephi-Lehies), but they were wiser than the Nephites. They took him to Ammon, who cast him out of their land. Korihor went to the land of Gideon, where he again found no success. He was bound and taken before their high priest, Giddonah, to whom he spewed out his false doctrine. After listening to him revile against God, Giddonah sent him to the land of Zarahemla, where he was brought before Alma and the chief judge, Nephihah.

> *And he did rise up in great swelling words before Alma, . . . accusing [the priests and teachers] of leading away the people after the silly traditions of their fathers, for the sake of glutting on the labors of the people.* (Alma 30:31)

Alma took great offense at Korihor's words because he had always labored with his own hands for his support.

> *And notwithstanding the many labors which I have performed in the church, I have never received so much as even one senine for my labor.* (Alma 30:33)

Since the priests and teachers received no wages either, Alma asked Korihor what he thought their motive was for preaching, if not for the joy they received in declaring the truth. Then Alma asked him if he believed in God, and he replied that he did not. Alma said unto him:

> *And now what evidence have ye that there is no God, or that Christ cometh not? . . . Ye have none, save it be your word only.*
> *But behold, I have all things as a testimony that these things are true.* (Alma 30:40–41)

Korihor said that he would be convinced that there was a God if Alma would show him a sign. Alma chastised him for tempting God and said that he had had signs enough.

> *All things denote there is a God; yea, even the earth, and all things that are upon the face of it, yea, and its motion, yea, and also all the planets which move in their regular form do witness that there is a Supreme Creator.* (Alma 30:44)

Alma was grieved because of the hardness of Korihor's heart but decided it was better that one man's soul be lost rather than allow him to bring *many souls down to destruction*. Alma warned him that if he denied the existence of God again, he would be struck dumb, and that would be the sign. Korihor promptly proclaimed that not only did he not believe in God, but he knew *Alma* did not know there was a God either! He insisted that without a sign he would not believe, so in the name of God, Alma struck him dumb. When the chief judge saw this, he wrote a note to Korihor:

Art thou convinced of the power of God? In whom did ye desire that Alma should show forth his sign? Would ye that he should afflict others, to show unto thee a sign? (Alma 30:51)

Korihor wrote back that he knew that only the power of God could bring this affliction on him. He said that he always knew there was a God but that the devil had deceived him—

For he appeared unto me in the form of an angel, and said unto me: Go and reclaim this people, for they have all gone astray after an unknown God. And he said unto me: There is no God; yea, and he taught me that which I should say. (Alma 30:53)

Korihor said that he taught these words because *they were pleasing unto the carnal mind,* and that after convincing so many others of his lies, he began to believe his own words. He pleaded with Alma to take away the curse. Alma would not because he knew that Korihor would again lead the hearts of the people astray.

After being cast out, Korihor went from house to house begging for his food. The chief judge sent a proclamation throughout all the land informing the people of what had happened to this wicked man. Korihor's followers were warned to repent or the same judgments would come upon them. This put an end to his false doctrine.

Korihor went over to the land of the Zoramites, a group of people who had dissented from the Nephites.

As he went forth amongst them, behold, he was run upon and trodden down, even until he was dead.

And thus we see the end of him who perverteth the ways of the Lord; and thus we see that the devil will not support his children at the last day, but doth speedily drag them down to hell. (Alma 30:59–60)

·47·

A MISSION TO THE ZORAMITES

ALMA 31–35

The Zoramites were dissenters from the Nephites and had developed their own religious beliefs. Alma received word that Zoram was leading his people to pervert the ways of the Lord and bow down to idols. Alma's *heart again began to sicken because of the iniquity of the people.*

The Zoramites were living in a land called Antionum, which was east of Zarahemla and south of Jershon. It also bordered on the wilderness that was occupied by the Lamanites, causing the Nephites to fear that the Zoramites might join in an alliance with the Lamanites.

Since history had proven that preaching the word of God changed people more than the sword, Alma decided to take a group of brethren on a mission to the Zoramites. Those who went were Ammon, Aaron, and Omner (three of the four sons of Mosiah who had just spent fourteen years on a mission to the Lamanites!), Amulek, Zeezrom, and Alma's two younger sons, Shiblon and Corianton.

When the missionaries arrived in the land, they were surprised to find the Zoramites worshipping in a manner they had never seen before. The people gathered together in their synagogues on one day of the week, which they called their sabbath. In the center of the synagogue, high above the head, was a platform that would admit only one person. They called this platform the *Rameumptom,* which interpreted means *the holy stand.* Whoever desired to worship would stand on the top, stretch forth his hands to heaven, and cry with a loud voice:

> *Holy, holy God; we believe that thou . . . art a spirit, and that thou wilt be a spirit forever.*
> *Holy God, we believe that thou hast separated us from our brethren; and we do not believe in the tradition of our brethren, which*

> *was handed down to them by the childishness of their fathers; but we*
> *believe that thou hast elected us to be thy holy children, and also that*
> *thou hast made it known unto us that there shall be no Christ.*
>
> *. . . And thou hast elected us that we shall be saved, whilst all*
> *around us are elected to be cast by thy wrath down to hell. . . .*
>
> *And again we thank thee, O God, that we are a chosen and a*
> *holy people. Amen.* (Alma 31:15–18)

As Alma and the other missionaries heard this same prayer being offered each time, *they were astonished beyond all measure.* After these people had taken turns on the stand repeating this prayer, they would return to their homes, never speaking of their God again until the following week when they returned to the Rameumptom.

Alma was filled with sorrow to see the *wicked and perverse* ways of the people. Not only had they changed the doctrines of the church, but their hearts were set upon riches. They wore costly apparel and gold ringlets and bracelets, and their *hearts were lifted up unto great boasting.* Alma prayed that he and his fellow missionaries would have success in their labors among them. Their souls were precious to him, and he asked for power and wisdom to bring them back to God. The missionaries separated from each other, trusting that the Lord would provide for all their needs and give them strength to perform their labors.

Alma and his brethren went forth among the people, preaching in their synagogues, in their homes, and in the streets. After a time they began to have success, but only among the poor. These people had been cast out of the synagogues, after laboring to build them, because of the *coarseness of their apparel.* Alma told them that it was just as well they were cast out because it had made them humble, and this sometimes led people to repentance.

Alma said that there are many who say *show unto us a sign from heaven . . . [and] then we shall believe.*

> *Now I ask, is this faith? . . . Nay; for if a man knoweth a thing*
> *he hath no cause to believe, for he knoweth it.*
>
> *Faith is not to have a perfect knowledge of things; therefore if*
> *ye have faith ye hope for things which are not seen, which are true.*
> (Alma 32:18, 21)

Alma explained that at first they could not know for certain that what he spoke was true, *any more than faith is a perfect knowledge.* He asked them to experiment upon his words and exercise just a *particle of faith.* They had to start with at least a *desire* to believe. Then, if they would let this desire work in them, they could come to believe in a *portion* of his words. He compared this process to planting a seed in our hearts. If it is a true seed it will begin to swell within us; otherwise, we will cast it away.

> *And when you feel these swelling motions, ye will begin to say within yourselves—It must needs be that this is a good seed, or that the word is good, for it beginneth to enlarge my soul; yea, it beginneth to enlighten my understanding, yea, it beginneth to be delicious to me.* (Alma 32:28)

He explained that at this point our faith still hasn't grown into a perfect knowledge. But because the seed is swelling and sprouting and growing inside us, we can know that the seed (or doctrine taught to us) is good. This will strengthen our faith, and our faith will eventually grow into a perfect knowledge of that particular principle.

Alma added a warning as he continued with his analogy. As the seed sprouts and grows into a tree, we must nourish the tree with great care (or put into practice the new principles we are learning) so that it will become strong and bring forth good fruit. If the tree is neglected it will not take root, and when the heat of the sun comes, it will be scorched and will wither away.

Since the Zoramites did not believe in Christ, Alma went on to tell about prophets of old who testified of him and added his own testimony that the Son of God was coming to redeem his people and atone for their sins.

Then Amulek took his turn preaching to the people and taught them about the atonement of Christ. He also delivered one of the great discourses on prayer. He admonished them to pray morning, midday, and evening, over all their household and for protection from their enemies. They were to pray over their crops and the flocks of their fields that they may prosper in them.

> *But this is not all; ye must pour out your souls in your closets, and your secret places, and in your wilderness.*
> *Yea, and when you do not cry unto the Lord, let your hearts be full, drawn out in prayer unto him continually for your welfare, and also for the welfare of those who are around you.* (Alma 34:26–27)

Amulek added that their prayers would be in vain if they did not help the needy or visit the sick.

When their mission was completed, all the brethren left Antionum, the land of the Zoramites, and returned to the land of Jershon. They had been instruments in the hands of God in bringing many of the Zoramites to the truth.

The rulers and priests of Antionum were angry that the missionaries had come because it opened the eyes of many to their priestcraft. They secretly found out which people believed in the teachings of Alma and his brethren and had them cast out of the land. The new converts, *and they were many,* found a new home in the land of Jershon. They were given food and clothing and *lands for their inheritance.*

Zoram, the chief ruler of the Zoramites, was a very wicked man. He sent a message to the people of Ammon (the Anti-Nephi-Lehies), who lived in Jershon, insisting that they cast out all the Zoramite refugees who had just settled there. Because they received no response to their threat, the Zoramites convinced the Lamanites to join with them and go to war against the Nephites. When the Nephites discovered their plans, all the inhabitants of Jershon were temporarily moved to Melek to protect them. The Nephite army then gathered in the land of Jershon to make preparations for war.

·48·

ALMA COUNSELS HIS SONS
ALMA 35–42

The iniquity of the people and their continual wars and contentions brought great sorrow to Alma. In spite of all his missionary endeavors, he saw that *the people began to wax hard, and that they began to be offended because of the strictness of the word.*

Alma counseled with each of his sons, perhaps because he knew his remaining time on earth was short. He first spoke to his oldest son, Helaman. Knowing firsthand the follies of youth, Alma recounted to his son the experiences he himself had as a young man with the sons of Mosiah— how they tried to destroy the church, the visit by the angel, Alma's subsequent vision, and his unshakable testimony because of it. Helaman was entrusted with all the sacred records, and Alma commanded him to continue the record of the people. Then Alma added that it had been prophesied that these records would be handed down from one generation to another and preserved by the hand of the Lord, *until they should go forth unto every nation, kindred, tongue, and people.* He also promised Helaman that if he kept the commandments and did as the Lord directed him concerning the plates, *no power of earth or hell* could take them from him.

Among the records given to Helaman were the twenty-four gold plates that King Mosiah had translated, which was the history of the Jaredites. This record was important to the people as a witness that the Jaredite nation had been destroyed because of its wickedness. In the record, the Jaredites had written their secret oaths, signs, and covenants of darkness. Helaman was commanded to keep these particular details from his people to prevent them too from falling into darkness.

Alma ended his counsel to Helaman with a lesson about the Liahona (see chapter 7 herein). It was given to Lehi's family to show them the course to follow in the wilderness. The spindles on the ball worked according to their faith. Whenever Lehi's family took the Liahona for granted and became slothful in keeping the commandments, it stopped working and they did not progress in their journey. Alma compared the Liahona to the word of Christ:

> *For behold, it is as easy to give heed to the word of Christ, which will point to you a straight course to eternal bliss, as it was for our fathers to give heed to this compass, which would point unto them a straight course to the promised land.* (Alma 37:44)

Alma's counsel to his son Shiblon was relatively brief. He commended him for being faithful from the time of his youth and told him that he had had great joy in him already because of his faithfulness and diligence as a missionary to the Zoramites. On that mission he had been put in shackles and even stoned, yet he endured these trials with patience because of his trust in the Lord. Included in Alma's counsel was the admonition to be humble and *not boast in [his] own wisdom, nor of [his] much strength, . . . [and to] use boldness, but not overbearance.*

Alma had much more to say to his son Corianton. Unlike his brothers, Corianton had caused his father much grief. He had not served with honor while on his mission to the Zoramites. He was boastful about his accomplishments and did not heed his father's counsel, but far worse, he forsook the ministry and went over into the land of Siron after the harlot Isabel.

> *Know ye not, my son, that these things are an abomination in the sight of the Lord; yea, most abominable above all sins save it be the shedding of innocent blood or denying the Holy Ghost?* (Alma 39:5)

Corianton had hurt not only himself with his actions but the missionary effort as well. When the Zoramites saw his conduct, they would not believe the words taught them. Alma implored his son to repent of his sins and *turn to the Lord with all [his] might, mind and strength.*

Alma went on to give a lengthy discourse to Corianton in answer to three questions that had been troubling his son. First, Corianton wondered why Christ's coming should be known so long beforehand. (It was currently about seventy-three years before Christ would be born.) In answer to his question, his father replied:

> *Behold, I say unto you, is not a soul at this time as precious unto God as a soul will be at the time of his coming?* (Alma 39:17)

He further explained that the plan of redemption needed to be made known to the people who lived before Christ as well as to those who would live after Christ's coming.

Corianton was also troubled concerning the resurrection of the dead. Two chapters record Alma's teachings about the resurrection to his son. In Alma chapter 40 we learn what happens to us between the time of death and the time of resurrection.

> *The spirits of all men, as soon as they are departed from this mortal body, . . . whether they be good or evil, are taken home to that God who gave them life.*
>
> *. . . The spirits of those who are righteous are received into a state of happiness, which is called paradise, . . . where they shall rest from all their troubles and from all care, and sorrow.* (Alma 40:11–12)

The spirits of the wicked will dwell in a state of misery until the resurrection. These are they who had *no part nor portion of the Spirit of the Lord . . . [and] chose evil works rather than good.* They had allowed themselves to be *led captive by the will of the devil.*

Alma further details how complete the restoration of the body will be at the time of the resurrection. *Every limb and joint shall be restored to its body,* and not even a hair of the head shall be lost.

Alma chapter 41 explains how we will be judged according to our works, or deeds, and the desires of our hearts while we lived on earth.

The third question bothering Corianton concerned God's punishment of the sinner. Corianton thought it unjust *that the sinner should be consigned to a state of misery.* Alma gives a long discourse in chapter 42 in answer to him. In summary, Jesus Christ took our sins upon himself through the Atonement, on the condition of our repentance. If we do not repent, his suffering in our behalf is of no benefit to us; mercy can have no claim on us and we must suffer the punishment according to the laws of God. If there was not a consequence for sin, Alma explains, justice could not be satisfied.

Alma counseled his son not to let these questions trouble him, but instead to let his sins trouble him enough to lead him to repentance. Corianton was called back to the ministry.

·49·

MORONI LEADS THE NEPHITE ARMY

ALMA 43–44

In chapter 47 of *And It Came to Pass* we learned that the Zoramites had joined with the Lamanites and were preparing to come to war against the Nephites. The leader of the Lamanites was a man named Zerahemnah. He cunningly appointed Amalekites and Zoramites, who were of a *more wicked and murderous disposition* than his own men, to be his chief captains.

The leader appointed to be the commander over all the Nephite armies was a young man named Moroni, who was only twenty-five years old. He protected his men with breastplates, arm-shields, head plates, and thick clothing, and armed them with all types of weapons.

Moroni and his army met the Lamanites in the borders of Jershon. When the Lamanites saw the well-armored Nephites they were very afraid, even though they greatly outnumbered them. The Lamanites had an impressive array of weapons but were only wearing a loin cloth. They dared not fight the Nephites in Jershon and instead headed to the land of Manti, supposing that it was not well protected. They assumed that if they took a roundabout journey the Nephites would not know where they were headed.

As soon as the Lamanites retreated, Moroni sent spies into the wilderness to watch their camp. He also petitioned Alma to ask the Lord where the Nephite army should go in order to defend themselves. The answer came back that the Lamanites planned to attack the city of Manti. Moroni left part of his army to guard Jershon, and then led the remainder of the army to Manti, arriving ahead of the Lamanites. He had all the people in that quarter of the land gather together to fight the Lamanites.

Moroni's spies told him which course the Lamanites were taking. He divided his army and concealed part of them in the valley south of the hill Riplah, which was east of the river Sidon. This army was led by a man named Lehi. Moroni concealed the rest of his army in the valley west of the river Sidon. The Lamanites came up north of the hill Riplah and into the valley, marching right past Moroni's hidden army. As the Lamanites began to cross the river Sidon, Lehi's army came upon them from behind. The Lamanite army turned around and began to fight them.

> *And the work of death commenced on both sides, but it was more dreadful on the part of the Lamanites, for their nakedness was exposed to the heavy blows of the Nephites with their swords and their cimeters, which brought death almost at every stroke.* (Alma 43:37)

The Nephites were so well protected with their armor that only now and then did one fall. The Lamanites became frightened because of the great destruction among them and began running toward the river Sidon. They were driven into the river by Lehi's men, who then remained on the bank. As the Lamanites crossed the river into the valley on the other side, they ran right into Moroni's army, who began to fall upon them and slay them. The Lamanites then fled from Moroni's army and headed toward the land of Manti. Here they were met by additional men Moroni had positioned along the route to Manti.

> *Now in this case the Lamanites did fight exceedingly; yea, never had the Lamanites been known to fight with such exceedingly great strength and courage, no, not even from the beginning.*
> *. . . They did fight like dragons, and many of the Nephites were slain by their hands, yea, for they did smite in two many of their head-plates, and they did pierce many of their breastplates, and they did smite off many of their arms; and thus the Lamanites did smite in their fierce anger.* (Alma 43:43–44)

When Moroni's men saw the ferociousness of the Lamanites, they were about to flee. Knowing their thoughts, Moroni sent a message of inspiration to his men. He reminded them that the Lamanites were fighting for monarchy and power, whereas the Nephites were fighting only to defend their families and their lands, their rights, their religion, and their freedom from bondage. Moroni's men then turned on the Lamanites and cried with one voice unto the Lord for their freedom. They now fought with power, and within the hour the Lamanites began fleeing to the river Sidon. Even though the Lamanite army was twice the size of the Nephite army, it was driven into one body on the riverbank. When Zerahemnah and his army saw that they were surrounded by Nephites, they were *struck with terror.* Seeing their fear, Moroni commanded his men to stop fighting and retreat a pace from them.

Moroni came forward and told Zarahemnah that they had no desire to kill his people, because the Nephites were not men of blood. They were only fighting to maintain their liberty. It was the Lord who had delivered the Lamanites into their hands because of their faith in Christ. Then he commanded Zerahemnah to have his men surrender their weapons. If they promised to go their way and not come again to war, their lives would be spared. If they did not agree to this, the fighting would resume until their whole army was destroyed.

Zerahemnah came forward and delivered up his sword, his cimeter, and his bow. He told Moroni that they would give up their weapons but would not take the oath to never come to war again, because they would only break it. Zerahemnah also retorted that it was not the Nephite God who caused them to be victorious but their cunning strategies and their breastplates and shields. He asked Moroni to take their weapons and let them go.

When Zerahemnah finished speaking, Moroni returned his weapons to him, saying:

> Behold, we will end the conflict.
> . . . Ye shall not depart except ye depart with an oath that ye will not return again against us to war. Now as ye are in our hands we will spill your blood upon the ground, or ye shall submit to the conditions which I have proposed. (Alma 44:10–11)

Suddenly, Zerahemnah rushed forward with his sword to slay Moroni. As he raised his sword, one of Moroni's soldiers struck the sword out of Zerahemnah's hand, breaking it at the hilt. Then he sliced off Zerahemnah's scalp and it fell to the ground! Raising the scalp high with the point of his sword, the soldier said:

> Even as this scalp has fallen to the earth, which is the scalp of your chief, so shall ye fall to the earth except ye will deliver up your weapons of war and depart with a covenant of peace. (Alma 44:14)

Many of the Lamanites were struck with fear and came forward and threw down their weapons at the feet of Moroni. After entering into a covenant of peace, they were allowed to depart into the wilderness.

Even though Zerahemnah had been seriously wounded, he managed to withdraw back into the midst of his soldiers. Being guided by anger instead of reason, he stirred up the remaining Lamanites to fight more powerfully against the Nephites. Moroni was angry with the stubbornness of the Lamanites and ordered his men to slay them. The Lamanites fought with all their might, but still they *[fell] exceedingly fast before the swords of the Nephites.*

When Zerahemnah saw that his army was about to be destroyed, he cried out to Moroni, promising to make the covenant if they would spare the remainder of their lives. The fighting ceased and the weapons were gathered from the Lamanites. After they entered into a covenant of peace, the Lamanites were allowed to depart into the wilderness.

The number of men slain on both sides was so tremendous that they were not numbered. The bodies were thrown into the waters of Sidon and from there were washed out to the depths of the sea. The Nephite soldiers returned to their land, and the eighteenth year of the reign of the judges came to an end.

·50·

THE TITLE OF LIBERTY
ALMA 45–46

I
t was a time of great rejoicing for the Nephites because the Lord had
again delivered them from the hands of their enemies. They fasted
and prayed and worshipped God with *exceedingly great joy.*

There was a prophecy known to Nephite prophets that foretold the
ultimate destruction of the Nephite civilization. Alma revealed it to Helaman with instructions to record the prophecy but to conceal it from the
people.

> *In four hundred years from the time that Jesus Christ shall man-
> ifest himself unto them, [the Nephites] shall dwindle in unbelief.*
> *Yea, and then shall they see wars and pestilences, yea, famines
> and bloodshed, even until the people of Nephi shall become extinct.*
> (Alma 45:10–11)

Alma explained that this would happen because the Nephites would
fall into works of darkness and all kinds of iniquities, and also because
they would sin against the great light and knowledge they had received.
After Alma finished prophesying, he blessed each of his sons and then
blessed the church and *all those who should stand fast in the faith.* He gave
a stern warning to any people who might inhabit the American continent—if they were wicked, the Lord would destroy them when they were
fully ripe in iniquity.

Alma departed out of the land of Zarahemla as if on his way to Melek,
but he was never heard of again. The people speculated that he was either
taken up by the Spirit or buried by the hand of the Lord because he was
such a righteous man.

On account of the previous wars with the Lamanites, and other
dissensions and disturbances among the people, Helaman felt that the
Nephites needed to be taught the word of God. He and his brethren went

throughout the land establishing the church and appointing priests and teachers. Even so, there arose a dissension among the people, and a group of them would not obey the counsel given to them. Instead, they grew proud in their hearts because of their *exceedingly great riches* and banded together against the believers of the church. Their leader was a large and strong man named Amalickiah, who wanted to be king. His supporters were, for the most part, the lower judges of the land, who were also seeking power. They were promised that they would be made rulers over the people if they helped Amalickiah to become king.

There were many members who believed *the flattering words* of Amalickiah and left the church. This dissension among the Nephites caused the situation to become *exceedingly precarious and dangerous*, even though they had just won a great victory over the Lamanites. The very foundation of their liberty was being destroyed.

> *Thus we see how quick the children of men do forget the Lord their God, yea, how quick to do iniquity, and to be led away by the evil one.*
>
> *Yea, and we also see the great wickedness one very wicked man can cause to take place among the children of men.* (Alma 46:8–9)

When Moroni, the chief commander of the Nephite army, heard of the discord among his people, he was angry with Amalickiah. He *rent* his coat and on a piece of the material wrote:

> *In memory of our God, our religion, and freedom, and our peace, our wives, and our children.* (Alma 46:12)

He fastened the banner upon the end of a pole and called it *the title of liberty.* He then put on his head plate and breastplate, his shields and his weapons, and bowed down to the earth. He prayed mightily to God, asking that he preserve the liberty of his people *so long as there should a band of Christians remain to possess the land.* (The true believers were called Christians because of their belief in Christ, who was to come.) Moroni had faith that God would not allow those who were despised because they had taken upon themselves the name of Christ to *be trodden down and destroyed* unless they brought it on by their own transgressions.

Moroni went among the people, waving the *title of liberty* high in the air for all to see. He invited those who valued their freedom to join with him and enter into a covenant with God to help defend that liberty. The people came running to Moroni, *rending their garments . . . as a covenant.* They promised that they would not forsake the Lord and fall into transgression. Otherwise, *the Lord should rend them even as they had rent their garments* and allow them to be destroyed by their enemies.

The people who desired to maintain their freedom gathered from all parts of the land. They were ready to stand against Amalickiah and his followers, who were now called Amalickiahites.

Amalickiah saw that Moroni's army was far greater than his, but even more troubling to him was the fact that many of his people had begun to doubt the justice of the cause they were fighting for. Fearing he would not be victorious under these conditions, he took his most ardent supporters and fled. Knowing that Amalickiah's plan was to join with the Lamanites, Moroni marched his army after them and succeeded in heading them off before they reached the Lamanites. Amalickiah managed to flee with a small number of his men, but the remainder were delivered up into the hands of Moroni and taken back to Zarahemla.

Most of the captured Amalickiahites entered into a covenant to support the cause of freedom and were set free. A few refused to make the covenant, so Moroni had them put to death.

> *And it came to pass . . . that he caused the title of liberty to be hoisted upon every tower which was in all the land, which was possessed by the Nephites; and thus Moroni planted the standard of liberty among the Nephites.* (Alma 46:36)

They began again to have peace, but that peace would be shattered by the Lamanites before the end of the year.

·51·

AMALICKIAH BECOMES KING
OF THE LAMANITES
ALMA 47

A fter escaping into the wilderness with a small group of his men, Amalickiah went directly to the Lamanites—just as Moroni had predicted. He succeeded in persuading the king to go to war against the Nephites. The king sent a proclamation throughout the land ordering his people to gather together in preparation for war. This news was not well received by the Lamanites. Although they were afraid to displease the king, they were more afraid to go to battle against the Nephites. It had been less than a year since their last terrible battle, when they had been soundly defeated and thousands of their people had been slain. To end that war, Zerahemnah stood scalpless before Moroni and made a covenant that his people would not come to war against the Nephites ever again. Now with this new order to prepare for war, the better part of the Lamanite army refused to obey the king.

> And now it came to pass that the king was wroth because of their disobedience; therefore he gave Amalickiah the command of that part of his army which was obedient unto his commands, and commanded him that he should go forth and compel them to arms. (Alma 47:3)

The dissenting soldiers appointed their own king and fled to a place called Onidah. They were determined not to be forced to go to war against the Nephites. Having found out that Amalickiah and his army were coming after them, they gathered on top of a mount called Antipas in preparation for battle.

> Now it was not Amalickiah's intention to give them battle according to the commandments of the king; but behold, it was his

intention to gain favor with the armies of the Lamanites, that he might place himself at their head and dethrone the king and take possession of the kingdom. (Alma 47:8)

Amalickiah ordered his army to camp at the base of Antipas. That night he sent a secret embassy to the top of the mount with a message for Lehonti, the leader of the other army. Lehonti was asked to come down to the foot of the mount to meet with Amalickiah, but he refused. The embassy was sent a second and a third time, still with no success. Finally, Amalickiah himself climbed the mount, nearly to Lehonti's camp. A fourth message was sent asking for the meeting, this time suggesting that Lehonti bring his guards with him. Lehonti was persuaded. When he came down from the mount, this plan was presented to him: He was to bring his army down in the night and surround Amalickiah's men. Amalickiah would then deliver up the king's army into Lehonti's hands. The armies would combine and Lehonti would make Amalickiah second in command of the whole army. Lehonti agreed to the plan, and when the king's army awoke at dawn they were surrounded by Lehonti's men. Amalickiah's men begged him to allow them to join Lehonti's army so their lives would be spared, which was, of course, all according to Amalickiah's plan.

> *Now it was the custom among the Lamanites, if their chief leader was killed, to appoint the second leader to be their chief leader.*
> *And it came to pass that Amalickiah caused that one of his servants should administer poison by degrees to Lehonti, that he died.* (Alma 47:17–18)

As the chief commander of the newly combined armies, Amalickiah marched them back to the city of Nephi, where the king of the Lamanites resided. The king came out with his guards to meet the army, having assumed that Amalickiah had overpowered the dissenters. He was pleased at the sight of the great army that had been gathered to go against the Nephites to battle. Amalickiah sent his servants to meet the king, and they bowed in reverence before him. The king held out his hand to raise them as a token of peace. The first servant he raised stabbed the king to the heart, and he fell dead. The king's own servants fled, providing the perfect scapegoats to blame the murder on. Amalickiah ordered his army to march forward to see what had happened to the king.

> *And [when they] found the king lying in his gore, Amalickiah*
> *pretended to be wroth, and said: Whosoever loved the king, let him go*
> *forth, and pursue his servants that they may be slain.* (Alma 47:27)

Upon seeing a whole army coming after them, the innocent guards fled into the wilderness. They went to the land of Zarahemla and joined the people of Ammon.

Amalickiah's army returned after being unsuccessful in capturing the guards. The next day they entered the city of Nephi, which was the Lamanite headquarters, and took possession of the city. Amalickiah sent an embassy to the queen informing her of how the king had been slain by his own guards. The queen sent back a message asking Amalickiah to spare the people of the city and meet with her and bring witnesses of the king's murder. Amalickiah took the same servant who had stabbed the king, along with the other servants who had witnessed it. The queen believed their false testimonies, especially since the king's own servants had fled.

In yet another triumph, Amalickiah won the heart of the queen and took her to be his wife.

> *And thus by his fraud, and by the assistance of his cunning*
> *servants, he obtained the kingdom; yea, he was acknowledged king*
> *throughout all the land, among all the people of the Lamanites.*
> (Alma 47:35)

·52·

AMALICKIAH'S PLANS
ARE THWARTED

ALMA 48–49

Near the end of the nineteenth year of the reign of the judges, Amalickiah had accomplished most of his grand plan. By treachery and fraud he, a Nephite by birth, had become king over all the Lamanites.

> *And now it came to pass that as soon as Amalickiah had obtained the kingdom he began to inspire the hearts of the Lamanites against the people of Nephi; yea, he did appoint men to speak unto the Lamanites from their towers, against the Nephites.* (Alma 48:1)

By means of such propaganda, Amalickiah *hardened the hearts of the Lamanites and blinded their minds, and stirred them up to anger.* With the people in this state of mind, he was able to raise a considerably large army to go to war against the Nephites. Amalickiah was now ready to accomplish the rest of his plan, which was to conquer the Nephites and bring them into bondage.

Amalickiah appointed Zoramites to be chief captains over his armies, supposing they knew which Nephite cities were strong and which were weak. This time the Lamanites protected themselves with shields, breastplates, and even thick clothing made from animal hides. Because of the enormous size of his army and the extent of its preparations, Amalickiah believed victory to be certain.

> *They supposed that they should easily overpower and subject their brethren to the yoke of bondage, or slay and massacre them according to their pleasure.* (Alma 49:7)

Feeling very confident, the mighty Lamanite army headed toward the land of Zarahemla. Little did they know that Moroni had a surprise waiting for them! During these months when Amalickiah was rising in power among the Lamanites, Moroni was busily engaged with a plan of his own. He had been fortifying all the Nephite cities in a manner never before undertaken among the descendants of Lehi.

> *Yea, he had been . . . erecting small forts, or places of resort; throwing up banks of earth round about to enclose his armies, and also building walls of stone to encircle them about, round about their cities and the borders of their lands.* (Alma 48:8)

In the weaker cities Moroni placed the greater number of men. Even more important than fortifying the cities, he fortified the hearts of his people by teaching them to be faithful to God. Moroni is one of the great leaders in the Book of Mormon, and the prophet Mormon pays this stirring tribute to him:

> *And Moroni was a strong and a mighty man; he was a man of a perfect understanding; yea, a man that did not delight in bloodshed . . . .*
>
> *Yea, a man whose heart did swell with thanksgiving to his God, . . . a man who did labor exceedingly for the welfare and safety of his people.*
>
> *Yea, and he was a man who was firm in the faith of Christ, and he had sworn with an oath to defend his people, his rights, and his country, and his religion, even to the loss of his blood.*
>
> *Yea, . . . **if all men had been, and were, and ever would be, like unto Moroni, behold, the very powers of hell would have been shaken forever; yea, the devil would never have power over the hearts of the children of men.*** (Alma 48:11–13, 17)

(We learn about a different Moroni later in the Book of Mormon. He was a great prophet who buried the gold plates and centuries later, as a resurrected being, appeared to Joseph Smith with instructions about translating them.)

Alma chapter 48 gives insight into the Nephite philosophy of war. The Nephites *were taught to defend themselves against their enemies, even to the shedding of blood if it were necessary.* But it was critical to their receiving protection from God that they took a defensive stand only, never the offensive. In other words, they had to wait to be attacked by the Lamanites before they could fight. They could never raise the sword against their enemy unless it was to preserve their lives. By so conducting themselves, the Lord would tell them when to prepare for war, reveal the whereabouts of their enemy, guide them in their strategies, or warn them to flee.

Because they were living in a righteous state at this period of time, the Nephites were sorry to be forced to take up arms against the Lamanites. They were especially sorry to send them to their death, *unprepared to meet their God*. With the Lamanites marching toward their land, they had no choice but to defend their wives and children against the *barbarous cruelty of those who were once their brethren*.

The first city the Lamanites planned to attack was Ammonihah. Because they had destroyed it once, they assumed it would again be an *easy prey*. As they came to the city, *to their uttermost astonishment* and great disappointment, they found the city to be impregnable. The ridge of earth that the Nephites had dug up around the city was too high for their arrows and stones to have any effect. The only way to fight them was to go through the entrance, or pass. Here the Nephites had placed a group of their strongest men, armed with swords and slings, ready to strike down all who attempted to come through.

> *Now, if king Amalickiah had come down out of the land of Nephi, at the head of his army, perhaps he would have caused the Lamanites to have attacked the Nephites at the city of Ammonihah; for behold, he did not care for the blood of his people.* (Alma 49:10)

But Amalickiah was *not* there, and his chief captains could see the futility of attacking the city, so they retreated. Instead they headed toward the land of Noah, figuring it to be the second-best place to attack. (Moroni assumed they would do this.) They had no idea that every city in the land had been fortified the same way. As they marched toward the land of Noah, *their chief captains came forward and took an oath that they would destroy the people of that city* (Alma 49:13).

They were astonished again as they discovered that the city of Noah exceeded the strength of Ammonihah! Moroni had appointed Lehi to be the chief captain over the men in Noah. When the Lamanites discovered this, it was yet another blow to them because *they feared Lehi exceedingly*. Even though logic should have told the Lamanite captains to retreat a second time, they had sworn with an oath to attack, so they readied their men to fight. Since the entrance was the only way of getting in, the Lamanites made several attempts to force through it, but they were driven back each time. This resulted in an immense slaughter of the Lamanites. They gave up trying to get in by the pass and began to dig down the banks of earth instead.

> But behold, in these attempts they were swept off by the stones
> and arrows which were thrown at them; and instead of filling up
> their ditches by pulling down the banks of earth, they were filled up
> in a measure with their dead and wounded bodies. (Alma 49:22)

As soon as the Lamanites realized that all their chief captains had been slain, they fled into the wilderness. In all, more than a thousand Lamanites lost their lives, whereas not a single Nephite was killed. About fifty Nephites who had been guarding the pass were wounded on their legs, some very severely, but their armor had protected the rest of their bodies.

The Lamanites returned to the land of Nephi to inform King Amalickiah of their great loss. He, of course, was very angry with his people for not carrying out his plan.

> Yea, he was exceedingly wroth, and he did curse God, and also
> Moroni, swearing with an oath that he would drink his blood.
> (Alma 49:27)

As the nineteenth year of the reign of the judges ended, the people of Nephi gave thanks unto God for delivering them from the hands of their enemies. There was a season of peace among the Nephites and great prosperity in the church because of the diligence of the people in keeping the commandments.

·53·

MORIANTON DISRUPTS THE PEACE
ALMA 50

During the twentieth year of the reign of the judges, Moroni continued to prepare his people against an attack from the Lamanites. The work of building up the banks of earth around the cities resumed. On top of these ridges of earth Moroni had *works of timbers built up to the height of a man.* Upon the works of timbers he had *a frame of pickets built . . . and they were strong and high.*

> *And he caused towers to be erected that overlooked those works of pickets, and he caused places of security to be built upon those towers, that the stones and the arrows of the Lamanites could not hurt them.* (Alma 50:4)

At this time there were Lamanites living in the east wilderness, which was Nephite territory. Moroni had his army drive them back to their own lands south of Zarahemla, and Nephites were sent to occupy the east wilderness. On the southernmost border that separated the Nephite and Lamanite lands, Moroni placed armies and had fortifications built. By driving the remaining Lamanites out of Nephite lands and fortifying the border, Moroni was able to cut off all the strongholds of the Lamanites. Moroni's armies increased daily because of the *assurance of protection which his works did bring forth unto them.* The Nephites began the foundation for several new cities, three of which were named Moroni, Nephihah, and Lehi.

The twenty-first year found the Nephites in very prosperous circumstances.

> *And they became exceedingly rich; yea, and they did multiply and wax strong in the land.*
> *[And] behold there never was a happier time among the people of Nephi, since the days of Nephi, than in the days of Moroni.* (Alma 50:18, 23)

The twenty-second and twenty-third years also ended in peace. In the twenty-fourth year, a border dispute arose between the people of Lehi and the people of Morianton. Those in Morianton claimed part of the land of Lehi and went so far as to take up arms against their brethren. The residents of Lehi fled to the camp of Moroni for assistance, for *they were not in the wrong.* When the people of Morianton found out where the people of Lehi had gone, they were afraid that Moroni's army would come and destroy them. Their leader, Morianton, came up with a plan. He convinced his followers to flee northward to a land that was covered with large bodies of water and take possession of it. (This was the land they called Desolation, the land of the extinct Jaredite civilization.)

> *And behold, they would have carried this plan into effect, (which would have been a cause to have been lamented) but behold, Morianton being a man of much passion, therefore he was angry with one of his maid servants, and he fell upon her and beat her much.* (Alma 50:30)

The maid servant fled to Moroni's camp and told Moroni about Morianton's plans to flee northward. Moroni did not want Morianton to take possession of that land, because it could ultimately lead to the overthrow of their liberty. To head them off, he sent his army under the leadership of a man named Teancum. Teancum and his men caught up with them at the borders of the land Desolation, *by the narrow pass which led by the sea into the land northward.* Here a battle erupted in which Morianton was slain by Teancum and his army was defeated.

Teancum and his army returned with the prisoners to Moroni's camp. Upon covenanting to keep the peace, the people of Morianton were restored to their land. A union then took place between the people of Lehi and the people of Morianton.

At the end of the twenty-fourth year of the reign of the judges, Nephihah, the second chief judge, died. He had filled the judgment-seat *with perfect uprightness before God.* Nephihah's son, Pahoran, was appointed in his stead.

·54·

THE RISE OF THE KING-MEN
ALMA 51

The twenty-fifth year of the reign of the judges began with peace. The border dispute between the people of Morianton and the people of Lehi had been settled, but peace was short-lived because another contention arose. Some of the people wanted the chief judge, Pahoran, to alter *a few particular points of the law*. They had even sent in petitions to that effect, but Pahoran would not change the law. Those who were in favor of the changes were angry with Pahoran and wanted him dethroned from the judgment-seat. They were called king-men because the changes they were seeking would allow the overthrow of the free government and the establishment of a king.

> *Now those who were in favor of kings were those of high birth, and they sought to be kings; and they were supported by those who sought power and authority over the people.* (Alma 51:8)

Those who wanted Pahoran to remain chief judge called themselves freemen and a *warm dispute* arose over the matter. A vote was taken to see what type of government the majority of the people desired. The results favored the freemen, so there was much rejoicing among Pahoran's supporters. This silenced the king-men temporarily because they dared not oppose the voice of the people.

The contention between the king-men and the freemen had come at a critical time for the Nephites. While their focus had been diverted to this internal conflict, Amalickiah, the Lamanite king, had again stirred up his people against the Nephites. He had been recruiting men from all parts of his land and preparing them for war *with all diligence*. Even though many thousands of his people had been slain by the Nephites in the last battle, he gathered together a *wonderfully great army*.

At about the time the contention was being settled concerning the chief judge, Amalickiah was leading his army to the land of Zarahemla.

> *And it came to pass that when the men who were called king-men had heard that the Lamanites were coming down to battle against them, they were glad in their hearts; and they refused to take up arms . . . to defend their country.* (Alma 51:13)

With the Lamanites already within the borders of their land, Moroni was extremely angry with the stubbornness of the king-men. After all, these were people for whom *he had labored with so much diligence to preserve.* Moroni sent a petition to the governor asking for the power to put the dissenters to death if they would not defend their country. His request was granted *according to the voice of the people,* and he sent his army against the king-men.

> *And they did pull down their pride and their nobility, insomuch that as they did lift their weapons of war to fight against the men of Moroni they were hewn down and leveled to the earth.* (Alma 51:18)

Four thousand of the dissenters were killed. The leaders of the king-men still alive were cast into prison until a later time when they could be tried. The remainder of the dissenters chose to hoist the title of liberty upon their towers and defend their country rather than be slain.

> *And thus Moroni put an end to those king-men . . . ; [and] they were brought down to humble themselves like unto their brethren, and to fight valiantly for their freedom from bondage.* (Alma 51:21)

·55·

AMALICKIAH IS SLAIN
ALMA 51–52

Behold, it came to pass that while Moroni was thus breaking down the wars and contentions among his own people . . . the Lamanites had come into the land of Moroni. (Alma 51:22)

Because the city of Moroni was not well fortified, the Lamanites were able to take possession of it. The Nephites were driven out and many were slain. Then Amalickiah swept his army along the east border by the seashore, capturing the cities of Nephihah, Lehi, Morianton, Omner, Gid, and Mulek! They continued their march to the borders of the land of Bountiful, leaving men in each conquered city to maintain and defend it. The immense fortifications of each city, which had previously been the Nephites' strong point, now worked to their disadvantage. The cities were almost impossible to retake from the Lamanites.

As Amalickiah and his army reached the borders of the land of Bountiful, they were greatly disappointed to find Teancum and his men waiting for them.

For they were great warriors; for every man of Teancum did exceed the Lamanites in their strength and in their skill of war. (Alma 51:31)

During the ensuing battle, Teancum and his men gained the advantage. When it was dark, the Nephites pitched their tents in the borders of Bountiful and Amalickiah's army camped on the beach by the seashore, where they had been driven. That night Teancum and his servant stole into Amalickiah's camp. The entire Lamanite army was fast asleep *because of their much fatigue, which was caused by the labors and heat of the day.*

> *And it came to pass that Teancum stole privily into the tent of*
> *the king; and put a javelin to his heart; and he did cause the death*
> *of the king immediately that he did not awake his servants.* (Alma
> 51:34)

Teancum quickly returned to his own camp and awoke his men to stand in readiness should the Lamanites awake and come upon them.

The following morning, which was the first morning of the new year (the twenty-sixth year of the reign of the judges), the Lamanites awoke to find their leader dead in his own tent and Teancum ready with his men to battle. This frightened the Lamanites, and they abandoned their design to march farther north. They retreated back to the city of Mulek instead, where the fortifications gave them protection. Ammoron, the brother of Amalickiah, was appointed to be the new Lamanite king.

During the following year, no progress was made by the Nephites in retaking the cities lost to the Lamanites. Because of the enormity of their numbers, the Lamanites were able to maintain those cities, and Teancum felt it unwise to attack. During this year Teancum kept his men busy erecting more walls and other fortifications around the cities still in their possession. He had received orders from Moroni to retain all the Lamanite prisoners to be used as a ransom for the Nephite prisoners. He was also instructed to fortify the land Bountiful and secure the narrow pass leading into the land northward. This would prevent the Lamanites from spreading north, which would have given them power to harass the Nephites on every side. Moroni was unable to come with his army to the aid of Teancum at this time because the Lamanites were *upon [them] in the borders of the land by the west sea.* (Ammoron, the Lamanite king, had taken part of his army out of Zarahemla to fight Moroni in the west.) The Nephites were now in *dangerous circumstances,* with the Lamanites harassing them on both sides of the Nephite territory.

In the twenty-seventh year, Teancum received orders from Moroni to attack the city of Mulek and retake it if possible. After marching with his men to the city, he decided not to. It would have been impossible to overpower the Lamanites because of the fortifications that protected them. Teancum and his army returned to the city of Bountiful to await the coming of Moroni.

·56·

THE CITY OF MULEK IS RETAKEN

ALMA 52–53

During the latter end of the twenty-seventh year, Moroni and his army finally arrived in the land of Bountiful to join forces with Teancum. He had left armies behind to protect the south and the west borders of the land.

In the beginning of the twenty-eighth year, Moroni, Teancum, and many of the other chief captains held a council of war. Their problem was a difficult one: how to lure the Lamanites out of their cities so they could fight them on equal ground. An embassy was sent to meet with Jacob, the leader of the Lamanite army that occupied the city of Mulek. They asked him to come with his army to meet them upon the plains between the two cities. Jacob knew this would not be good strategy and refused.

> *And it came to pass that Moroni, having no hopes of meeting them upon fair grounds, therefore, he resolved upon a plan that he might decoy the Lamanites out of their strongholds.* (Alma 52:21)

Teancum was ordered to take a small number of men and march down near the seashore. During the night, Moroni and his army secretly made their way in the wilderness to the west of the city of Mulek. The next morning the Lamanite guards discovered Teancum and his little band and ran with the news to their leader, Jacob. The Lamanites promptly marched against Teancum's men, assuming that their large numbers could easily overpower them. When Teancum saw the Lamanites coming, he retreated northward to the seashore.

> *And it came to pass that when the Lamanites saw that he began to flee, they took courage and pursued them with vigor.* (Alma 52:24)

While the Lamanites were in pursuit of Teancum, Moroni ordered part of his army to take possession of the city of Mulek. They were met by the guards left to protect the city, and all who would not surrender were killed. The city of Mulek was retaken with just a small portion of Moroni's army. Meanwhile, Moroni was marching with the remainder of his army to assist Teancum.

The Lamanites pursued Teancum until they came near the city of Bountiful. Here they were met by Lehi and a small army that had been left to protect that city.

> And now behold, when the chief captains of the Lamanites had beheld Lehi with his army coming against them, they fled in much confusion, lest perhaps they should not obtain the city Mulek before Lehi should overtake them; for they were wearied because of their march, and the men of Lehi were fresh. (Alma 52:28)

What the Lamanites did not know was that Moroni's army was directly in their path of retreat. Lehi paced his pursuit so that his men would not overtake the Lamanites until they were met by Moroni coming from the opposite direction. The wearied Lamanites were soon surrounded by Nephites on every side—*all of whom were fresh and full of strength.*

Jacob's only hope, or so he thought, was to get his men back to the protection that Mulek afforded. (He was unaware that the city was now in the hands of the Nephites.) Moroni and his army stood in his way, but Jacob *was determined to slay them and cut his way through to the city of Mulek.*

> Jacob, being their leader, being also a Zoramite, and having an unconquerable spirit, . . . led the Lamanites forth to battle with exceeding fury against Moroni. (Alma 52:33)

As the Lamanites engaged in battle with Moroni's army in the front, Lehi and his men began fighting them at the rear. Lehi's army fought with such fury that those Lamanites fighting them delivered up their weapons of war. The Lamanites contending with Moroni's men became so confused that they *knew not whither to go or to strike.* Seeing their confusion, Moroni sent word to the Lamanites that if they would deliver up their weapons of war, the bloodshed would stop. The chief captains came forth immediately and threw down their weapons at Moroni's feet and commanded their men to do the same.

Moroni was wounded during the battle. Many were slain on both sides, including Jacob, but the number of prisoners taken was more than those killed. Moroni set guards over the prisoners and compelled them to bury all the Nephite and Lamanite dead.

Moroni and Lehi traveled back to Mulek, where Lehi was given command of the city.

> *Lehi was a man who had been with Moroni in the more part of all his battles; and he was a man like unto Moroni, and they rejoiced in each other's safety; yea, they were beloved by each other and also beloved by all the people of Nephi.* (Alma 53:2)

After all the dead had been buried, Teancum marched the prisoners back to the land of Bountiful. The Nephites now had thousands of prisoners on their hands and needed to keep them occupied for security reasons. By orders of Moroni, Teancum had the prisoners dig a ditch around the city of Bountiful.

> *And he caused that they should build a breastwork of timbers upon the inner bank of the ditch; and they cast up dirt out of the ditch against the breastwork of timbers; and thus they did cause the Lamanites to labor until they had encircled the city of Bountiful round about with a strong wall of timbers and earth, to an exceeding height.* (Alma 53:4)

The city of Bountiful was now one of the most fortified of the Nephite cities. It was here that the Lamanite prisoners were guarded—within walls they had built with their own hands.

Moroni spent the remainder of the year preparing his men for war and making other fortifications. Time was also spent in *delivering their women and children from famine and affliction, and providing food for their armies.*

It had been over a year since Moroni had come with his army from the land by the west sea to assist Teancum in the east. In Moroni's absence, the Nephites in the west began to have dissensions among themselves, which allowed the Lamanites to capture a number of their cities. Now as the year came to an end, the Nephites were once again in very precarious circumstances. In the east they were trying to guard thousands of prisoners, as well as retake cities lost to the Lamanites. In the west the Nephite cities were being overtaken by the Lamanites.

·57·

RESCUING THE NEPHITE PRISONERS
ALMA 54–55

In the beginning of the twenty-ninth year, Ammoron, the king of the Lamanites, sent a message to Moroni asking for an exchange of prisoners. This was good news for Moroni because it required a lot of food to feed the Lamanite prisoners—food that his own people sorely needed. Also, the returning Nephite prisoners would enlarge his army.

The Lamanites had many Nephite women and children among their prisoners, whereas the Nephites had not taken a single woman or child. Moroni devised a plan to obtain as many of their people from the Lamanites as possible. He sent a letter back to Ammoron stating his conditions: for every Lamanite prisoner returned, Moroni wanted one Nephite man plus his wife and children. Included in the letter was a bitter rebuke against Ammoron and his people. Moroni told him that God's *almighty wrath* hung over the Lamanites unless they repented and withdrew their armies back to their own land. He told him of the *awful hell* that was waiting to receive such murderers as he and his brother had been. (Ammoron's brother was Amalickiah, who had been slain when Teancum stole into his tent and stabbed him with a javelin.) Moroni also called him *a child of hell.* He ended his letter by warning Ammoron what would happen if he did not agree to his terms for exchanging prisoners:

> *I will come against you with my armies; yea, even I will arm my women and my children, . . . and I will follow you even into your own land, . . . and it shall be blood for blood, yea, life for life; and I will give you battle even until you are destroyed from off the face of the earth.* (Alma 54:12)

Not surprisingly, Ammoron was angry after receiving this letter. He fired back an equally long, scathing letter to Moroni. He told him that he did not fear his threats and that he would avenge the murder of his brother. Then he brought up the centuries-old argument that the Lamanite people had been wronged from the time Lehi brought his family out of Jerusalem. He told Moroni that if his people would surrender and be *governed by those to whom the government doth rightly belong,* they would no longer be at war. If they did not surrender, he was willing to wage a war that would either subject the Nephites to bondage or cause their *eternal extinction.*

> *And as concerning that God whom ye say we have rejected, behold, we know not such a being; neither do ye; but if it so be that there is such a being, we know not but that he hath made us as well as you.*
>
> *And if it so be that there is a devil and a hell, behold will he not send you there to dwell with my brother whom ye have murdered, whom ye have hinted that he hath gone to such a place?* (Alma 54:21–22)

Ammoron also said he was a descendant of Zoram, *whom your fathers pressed and brought out of Jerusalem.* (This was another false belief passed down through the generations by the Lamanites. Zoram was Laban's servant who willingly followed Nephi and his brothers back to the wilderness, and when the Nephites separated themselves from the Lamanites, Zoram and his family chose to go with Nephi.)

In the middle of his rantings, Ammoron mentioned that he was still gladly willing to exchange prisoners so that he too could preserve his food for his own men.

> *And behold now, I am a bold Lamanite; . . . this war hath been waged to avenge their wrongs, and to . . . obtain their rights to the government; and I close my epistle to Moroni.* (Alma 54:24)

After receiving Ammoron's letter, Moroni was even angrier. *He knew that Ammoron had a perfect knowledge of his fraud* and that this was not a just cause to wage a war over. Since it was clear that Ammoron would continue to fight even after the prisoners were exchanged, Moroni decided against it. He knew where the Lamanites kept their prisoners and came up with a plan to rescue them. A search was made among Moroni's men for a man of Lamanite descent. A man was found by the name of Laman, who had been one of the servants accused of killing the Lamanite king. He had fled and joined the people of Ammon. Moroni sent Laman and a small group of his men to the city of Gid, where the prisoners were being kept. That evening as he and his men approached the guards, Laman told them not to fear, that he was a Lamanite and had escaped from the Nephites while they slept. He also mentioned that he had stolen some of their wine and had taken it with him. Upon hearing this, the Lamanites *received him with joy.* They wanted to drink the wine right then because they were weary. Laman suggested that they wait until after they fought the Nephites, but this made them desire it all the more. They told Laman that the wine would help strengthen them in their fight against the Nephites.

> *And it came to pass that they did take of the wine freely; and it was pleasant to their taste, therefore they took of it more freely; and it was strong, having been prepared in its strength.* (Alma 55:13)

First the Lamanites became merry, then drunk, and then they eventually fell into a deep sleep. Laman and his men returned to Moroni, who immediately took men back to the city of Gid. While the guards slept, Moroni and his men slipped weapons to the prisoners so that they were all armed—including those women and children who could handle a weapon. *All [these] things were done in a profound silence.* Moroni did not kill the guards in their drunken condition because *he did not delight in murder or bloodshed.* Moroni ordered his men to move back and surround the city.

> *Now behold this was done in the night-time, so that when the Lamanites awoke in the morning they beheld that they were surrounded by the Nephites without, and that their prisoners were armed within.* (Alma 55:22)

Realizing they were in an impossible situation, the Lamanites cast their weapons at the feet of the Nephites, pleading for mercy. The Lamanites were taken captive, and Moroni now had possession of the city. All the Nephites who had been held as prisoners joined with Moroni's men, becoming a great strength to his army.

Before leaving the city of Gid, Moroni had the Lamanite prisoners strengthen the fortifications around the city. They were then taken to the city of Bountiful, which was guarded with *an exceedingly strong force.* In spite of all the scheming of the Lamanites, the Nephites managed to control the enormous number of prisoners.

> *And many times did they attempt to administer of their wine to the Nephites, that they might destroy them with poison or with drunkenness.*
>
> *But behold, the Nephites . . . could not be taken in their snares; yea, they would not partake of their wine, save they had first given to some of the Lamanite prisoners.*
>
> *. . . For if their wine would poison a Lamanite it would also poison a Nephite.* (Alma 55:30–32)

Moroni now turned his attention back to reclaiming those cities taken by the Lamanites. Of particular concern to Moroni was the city of Morianton, which the Lamanites had fortified until it had become *an exceeding strong-hold.* Also, they were continually bringing new forces and fresh supplies into that city. Moroni made preparations to attack Morianton as the twenty-ninth year of the reign of the judges came to a close.

·58·

HELAMAN'S TWO THOUSAND
ALMA 53, 56

During the time that Moroni was retaking cities and rescuing prisoners in the east, major warfare was also taking place in the west. Remember, Moroni and part of his army left the west earlier to come to the aid of Teancum in the east. It was on the south end of the west territory that Helaman, the great spiritual leader and son of Alma the Younger, became the leader of the most famous army in Book of Mormon history. His army came about in an unusual way.

For many years, the people of Ammon (the converted Lamanites who were first called the Anti-Nephi-Lehies) had been living in Jershon under the protection of the Nephites. At the time of their conversion they had made a covenant not to use their weapons of war ever again. To seal this promise, they had buried their weapons deep in the earth.

> *But it came to pass that when they saw the danger, and the many afflictions and tribulations which the Nephites bore for them, they were moved with compassion and were desirous to take up arms in the defence of their country.* (Alma 53:13)

If it hadn't been for the persuasive powers of Helaman and his brethren, the people of Ammon would have broken their oath. Instead, they *were compelled to behold their brethren wade through their afflictions.*

But the Ammonites had many sons who had not made this promise! Two thousand of these young men took up arms and assembled together and called themselves Nephites. They each entered into a covenant to fight for the liberty of the Nephites, even if it meant laying down their own lives.

> *And they were all young men, and they were exceedingly valiant for courage, and also for strength and activity; but behold, this was not all—they were men who were true at all times in whatsoever thing they were entrusted.*

> *Yea, they were men of truth and soberness, for they had been taught to keep the commandments of God and to walk uprightly before him.* (Alma 53:20–21)

Having been asked by these young men to be their leader, Helaman took command during the twenty-sixth year of the reign of the judges. This little band of warriors became a great support to the Nephite army.

At the beginning of the thirtieth year, Moroni received a letter from Helaman in which he gave an account of their experiences at war. The entire story of these warriors comes from this letter.

Helaman told Moroni how the two thousand sons of the Ammonites had come to the defense of the Nephites, allowing the covenant of their fathers to remain unbroken. He explained that about four years prior to writing this letter, in the twenty-sixth year, he had marched at the head of his two thousand stripling soldiers to the land on the south by the west sea. They went to the city of Judea and joined with Antipus, whose army had been reduced significantly by the Lamanites. At this time the Lamanites had many Nephite prisoners, all of whom were chief captains, *for none other have they spared alive.* The Lamanites also had possession of four Nephite cities—Manti, Zeezrom, Cumeni, and Antiparah. Antipus and his men had been *toiling with their might* to fortify Judea in hopes of preventing it too from falling into Lamanite hands.

> *Yea, and they were depressed in body as well as in spirit, for they had fought valiantly by day and toiled by night to maintain their cities; and thus they had suffered great afflictions of every kind.*
> *And now they were determined to conquer in this place or die.*
> (Alma 56:16–17)

The arrival of Helaman and his two thousand *gave them great hopes and much joy.* The Lamanites were given orders not to attack Judea after seeing the additional forces arrive. This bought the much-needed time for the Nephites to better prepare their city and their men.

As the twenty-seventh year began, the Nephites were ready to go to battle against the Lamanites. Since they could not attack them in their well-fortified cities, they were hoping the Lamanites would attack them.

In the second month of the year, Helaman received many provisions from the fathers of his two thousand *sons.* (Helaman lovingly referred to them as sons, and they in turn called him father.) Two thousand men had also been sent from Zarahemla, giving them a total of ten thousand men. Now they had provisions for their whole army *and also for their wives and their children.*

> *And the Lamanites, thus seeing our forces increase daily, and provisions arrive for our support, they began to be fearful, and began to sally forth, if it were possible to put an end to our receiving provisions and strength.* (Alma 56:29)

The time had come to lure the Lamanites out to battle by using some strategy. Antipus ordered Helaman to march forth with his *little sons* to a neighboring city, as if they were transporting provisions. They purposely traveled close to the city of Antiparah, where the largest of the Lamanite armies was stationed. After allowing Helaman and his men some lead time, Antipus followed at a distance with part of his army, leaving the remainder to maintain the city of Judea.

When the Lamanite spies discovered Helaman and his small army, the Lamanite army stationed in Antiparah took off after them. Helaman and his men took off running to the north, leading away *the most powerful army of the Lamanites.* After the Lamanites had followed Helaman a considerable distance, they discovered the army of Antipus pursuing them from behind! Trying to avoid being surrounded by Nephites, the Lamanites attempted to overtake Helaman's men and slay them before Antipus caught up with them.

Antipus knew the danger that Helaman's army was in and speeded up the march of his army. As of nightfall, no army had overtaken the next, so everyone camped for the night. Before dawn the Lamanites were again in pursuit of Helaman's army. Helaman knew that they would not stand a chance if they were overtaken by the Lamanites, so all that day they marched in a straight course into the wilderness. The Lamanites knew that their only chance lay in getting to Helaman before Antipus overtook them, so they were speedily marching in a straight course after Helaman. And, of course, Antipus and his army were trying to overtake the Lamanites. Again at nightfall, all three armies camped for the night.

Before daybreak the Lamanites were once again in pursuit of Helaman's army, but after a short distance they stopped. Helaman held a council with his men to decide what to do. The Lamanites might have stopped because Antipus overtook them, in which case their help would be sorely needed. On the other hand, the Lamanites might be setting a trap. Helaman asked his men if they would go back, not knowing for sure what was awaiting them. Their answer demonstrated more courage than Helaman had ever witnessed among all the Nephites:

> For as I had ever called them my sons (for they were all of them very young) even so they said unto me: Father, behold our God is with us, and he will not suffer that we should fall; then let us go forth . . . lest they should overpower the army of Antipus.
>
> Now they never had fought, yet they did not fear death; and they did think more upon the liberty of their fathers than they did upon their lives; yea, they had been taught by their mothers, that if they did not doubt, God would deliver them. (Alma 56:46–47)

Helaman returned with his two thousand men to discover that Antipus had overtaken the Lamanites and a terrible battle was raging. Not only were Antipus's men weary from their speedy march, but Antipus and many of his leaders had been slain, causing confusion among the men. They would have fallen into the hands of the Lamanites had Helaman and his men not returned.

When Helaman and his army came upon their rear, the whole Lamanite army halted and turned upon them. This gave the men of Antipus courage to gather their forces and renew the fight. Being surrounded, the Lamanites were compelled to deliver up their weapons of war and surrender. Now Helaman had the dreaded task of counting the dead among his beloved sons.

> But behold, to my great joy, there had not one soul of them fallen to the earth; yea, and they had fought as if with the strength of God; yea, never were men known to have fought with such miraculous strength; and with such mighty power did they fall upon the Lamanites, that they did frighten them; and for this cause did the Lamanites deliver themselves up as prisoners of war. (Alma 56:56)

There was no place to keep the prisoners, so they were sent to Zarahemla under guard while the remainder of the army of Antipus joined with Helaman's two thousand and returned to the city of Judea.

·59·

THE TWO THOUSAND ARE
SPARED AGAIN
ALMA 57

Helaman received a letter from Ammoron, the king of the Lamanites, stating that he wanted the prisoners that the Nephites were holding. In return, he would deliver up the city of Antiparah. Helaman sent back a letter declining the offer. He was sure he could take the city by force and would only release the prisoners in exchange for Nephite prisoners. Ammoron refused to trade prisoners, so the Nephite army began to make preparations to seize the city of Antiparah. The city ended up falling into their hands without any bloodshed because the inhabitants fled the city. This took place at the close of the twenty-eighth year of the reign of the judges.

At the beginning of the twenty-ninth year, provisions were received from Zarahemla, as well as an additional 6,060 men. Sixty of these men were sons of the Ammonites who had come to join their brothers in Helaman's army. With the additional men and provisions, Helaman felt sufficiently prepared. Their next plan was to wage a battle with the Lamanite army that was protecting the city of Cumeni. The Nephites surrounded the city and camped there for many nights. They slept upon their swords and stationed guards to watch the Lamanites. The Lamanites attempted many times to come upon the Nephites and slay them by night, *but as many times as they attempted this their blood was spilt.*

One night when soldiers arrived with provisions for the Lamanites in Cumeni, the Nephites captured them as they were about to enter the city. They sent the provisions to Judea and the prisoners to Zarahemla. The Lamanites were determined to maintain the city anyway, but before too many days passed they gave up hope and surrendered. The Nephites once again had possession of Cumeni.

The Nephites now faced a critical situation. The number of prisoners was so great that it took the entire Nephite force to watch them.

For behold, they would break out in great numbers, and would fight with stones, and with clubs, or whatsoever thing they could get into their hands, insomuch that we did slay upwards of two thousand of them after they had surrendered themselves prisoners of war. (Alma 57:14)

With provisions getting low, it was decided to send the prisoners to Zarahemla under the guard of the chief captain, Gid, and his men. They had barely begun their march to Zarahemla when they met up with the Nephite spies who had been watching the camp of the Lamanites. The spies cried out that other Lamanite armies were at that moment marching toward Cumeni, and they feared that all the Nephites would be destroyed. Upon hearing this, the prisoners took courage and rose up in rebellion against their captors.

We did cause that our swords should come upon them. And it came to pass that they did in a body run upon our swords, in the which, the greater number of them were slain; and the remainder of them broke through and fled from us. (Alma 57:33)

Being unable to overtake the prisoners, Gid and his men headed back to Cumeni with great speed. Meanwhile, the other Lamanite armies had already arrived and had engaged the Nephites in battle. After having been gone but one day, Gid's army arrived back in time to save the Nephites just as the Lamanites were about to overpower them.

In those last desperate moments before Gid and his army arrived, Helaman's band of 2,060 remained *firm and undaunted.* They *did administer death unto all those who opposed them.*

Yea, and they did obey and observe to perform every word of command with exactness; yea, and even according to their faith it was done unto them; and I did remember the words which they said unto me that their mothers had taught them. (Alma 57:21)

The credit for their great victory was given jointly to Helaman's courageous young men and to Gid's army for its timely return. The Lamanites were driven back to the city of Manti, and the city of Cumeni was retained.

The Nephites had suffered a great loss of men in the battle. Helaman gave orders to have the injured taken from among the dead so their wounds could be dressed. Out of his 2,060 men, there were two hundred who had fainted because of the loss of blood.

> *Nevertheless, according to the goodness of God, and to our great astonishment, and also the joy of our whole army, there was not one soul of them who did perish; yea, and neither was there one soul among them who had not received many wounds.* (Alma 57:25)

It was amazing to all that not one life had been lost among Helaman's men, and yet a thousand of their Nephite brethren had been slain. They knew these young men had been spared because of their tremendous faith in God.

·60·

RETAKING THE CITY OF MANTI
ALMA 58

Helaman's next objective was to retake the city of Manti, but for the time being it seemed an impossible task. He was sure the Lamanites could not be fooled a third time into leaving their strongholds and chasing after a small band of Nephites. They had paid heavily for such a mistake. The Nephites could not attack them at Manti because the Lamanites far outnumbered them. There were only enough men in the Nephite army to maintain the cities they currently held in their possession. It was decided to wait until more men and provisions arrived from Zarahemla before they attempted to retake Manti. Helaman sent an embassy to the governor in Zarahemla to apprise him of their situation.

While the Nephites patiently waited for help, the Lamanite army grew stronger and stronger as men and provisions arrived on a regular basis. From time to time the Lamanites tried to lure the Nephites into battle, but without success. The Nephites dared not fight without reinforcements from Zarahemla.

> *And it came to pass that we did wait in these difficult circumstances for the space of many months, even until we were about to perish for the want of food.* (Alma 58:7)

At length they received men and provisions from Zarahemla—but only two thousand men!

> *And this is all the assistance which we did receive, to defend ourselves and our country from falling into the hands of our enemies, yea, to contend with an enemy which was innumerable.* (Alma 58:8)

It was a mystery to Helaman and his army why they had not received more help. The men were demoralized as they wondered if their entire nation was about to be overthrown because of the judgments of God. They poured out their souls in prayer, asking for strength and deliverance from their enemies.

> *Yea, and it came to pass that the Lord our God did visit us with assurances that he would deliver us; yea, insomuch that he did speak peace to our souls, and did grant unto us great faith, and did cause us that we should hope for our deliverance in him.* (Alma 58:11)

Helaman and his men took courage. Even though their numbers were small, they were determined to conquer their enemies and maintain their freedom. The strategy they devised was brilliant, yet almost humorous in its simplicity. It was the very strategy that Helaman said the Lamanites would never fall for a third time! (The first time was when Moroni's army took back the city of Mulek [see Alma 52:21]; the second time was when Helaman's two thousand were used as a decoy, [see Alma 56:30].)

Helaman's army marched to the city of Manti and pitched their tents nearby on the wilderness side. When the Lamanites discovered them the next day, they sent out their spies to calculate the size of the army. Fearing they might be cut off from their support, they prepared for battle, supposing they could easily destroy the small Nephite army.

Knowing his army would soon be attacked, Helaman ordered Gid to take a small number of men and hide in the wilderness to the right of the main group. Then he had Teomner hide with a small group of men in the wilderness to the left. Helaman and the rest of the army remained where they were and waited for the attack. When the Lamanites were nearly upon them, Helaman and his army took off into the wilderness. The Lamanites followed them with *great speed,* passing right between the small armies of Gid and Teomner. After the Lamanites had passed by, Gid and Teomner and their men *did rise up from their secret places* and cut off the Lamanite spies so they could not return to the city. Then Gid and Teomner's armies ran back to the city of Manti, killed the guards, and took possession of the city.

> *Now this was done because the Lamanites did suffer their whole army, save a few guards only, to be led away into the wilderness.* (Alma 58:22)

Helaman and his army continued on toward Zarahemla. Realizing that they were marching to the largest city in Nephite territory, the

Lamanites became *exceedingly afraid* that they were being led into a trap. They turned around and headed back to Manti, but when darkness overtook them they camped for the night. They assumed that Helaman's group was the entire Nephite army and that they would be tired and also camp for the night. Helaman's men did not sleep, but traveled back to the city of Manti by another route. By marching through the night, they arrived at the city before the Lamanites.

When the Lamanite army approached the city, they saw the Nephites waiting for them, prepared to battle! The Lamanites *were astonished exceedingly and struck with great fear* and fled into the wilderness.

> *And thus it came to pass, that by this stratagem we did take possession of the city of Manti without the shedding of blood.* (Alma 58:28)

The Lamanites fled out of this entire quarter of the land but, unfortunately, took many Nephite women and children with them. All the Nephite cities that had been taken by the Lamanites were now back in the possession of the Nephites, and the people returned to their homes.

> *But behold, our armies are small to maintain so great a number of cities and so great possessions.* (Alma 58:32)

It is now the latter part of the twenty-ninth year as Helaman ends his letter to Moroni. He tells him that the 2,060 sons of the Ammonites are with him in Manti. He does not know why more men have not been sent from Zarahemla but trusts that God will deliver them from their enemies. Once again he recounts how not one of his *sons* had been slain, even though they had received many wounds. They remained faithful, being strict to remember the commandments from day to day.

> *And now, my beloved brother, Moroni, may the Lord our God . . . keep you continually in his presence; yea, and may he favor this people, even that ye may have success in obtaining the possession of all that which the Lamanites have taken from us. . . . And now, behold, I close mine epistle. I am Helaman, the son of Alma.* (Alma 58:41)

·61·

MORONI'S SCATHING LETTER
ALMA 59–60

Moroni received Helaman's letter as the thirtieth year of the reign of the judges began. He rejoiced to hear about Helaman's great success in that quarter of the country and had the news spread throughout the land. He immediately sent a letter to Pahoran, the chief judge, asking for additional men to be sent to strengthen Helaman's army. Meanwhile, the Lamanites who fled that part of the land under Helaman's command came to Moroni's area. The Lamanites were becoming *exceedingly numerous* as more of their brethren joined them day by day.

The Lamanites had previously driven out the people who lived in the cities of Moroni, Lehi, and Morianton. The inhabitants of these cities were all living in Nephihah. While Moroni was making preparations to go to battle, Nephihah was attacked and there was *an exceedingly great slaughter* of the people. Moroni had assumed that men had been sent to help fortify Nephihah; therefore he had kept his men to maintain those cities that they had recovered.

> *And now, when Moroni saw that the city of Nephihah was lost he was exceedingly sorrowful, and began to doubt, because of the wickedness of the people, whether they should not fall into the hands of their brethren.*
>
> *And it came to pass that Moroni was angry with the government, because of their indifference concerning the freedom of their country.* (Alma 59:11, 13)

Moroni sent another letter to Zarahemla and directed it to Pahoran, the chief judge and governor of the land, and to any others who administered the affairs of the war. He announced at the beginning that his letter was coming *by way of condemnation*. He reminded them that they had been appointed to gather men and weapons and to send them against the Lamanites *in whatsoever parts they should come into our land*. Moroni recounted how he and Helaman and their armies had suffered greatly with hunger, thirst, fatigue, and afflictions of every kind. But if this were all they had suffered, they would not be complaining. They were outraged because of the great slaughter that was being inflicted upon their people. Because of the government's neglect, thousands of their people had fallen by the sword.

> *And now behold, we desire to know the cause of this exceedingly great neglect; yea, we desire to know the cause of your thoughtless state.*
> *Can you think to sit upon your thrones in a state of thoughtless stupor, while your enemies are spreading the work of death around you? Yea, while they are murdering thousands of your brethren.* (Alma 60:6–7)

Moroni also reminded them that they had withheld provisions as well as men. The men under his command had a strong desire to protect their people and their freedom but did so as they were about to perish with hunger. They *fought and bled out their lives* because of the indifference of the government. Moroni warned them that the blood of thousands would come upon their heads for vengeance.

> *Behold, could ye suppose that ye could sit upon your thrones, and because of the exceeding goodness of God ye could do nothing and he would deliver you?* (Alma 60:11)

Moroni mentioned the recent civil war that had been instigated by the king-men. If it had not been for their wickedness, the Lamanites never would have been able to gain power over them.

> *But why should I say much concerning this matter? For we know not but what ye yourselves are seeking for authority. We know not but what ye are also traitors to your country.* (Alma 60:18)

Full of righteous indignation, Moroni delivered an ultimatum to Pahoran: If men and provisions were not received soon, he would take a portion of his men, march back to Zarahemla, and destroy anyone blocking the cause of freedom!

> *Behold, I am Moroni, your chief captain. I seek not for power, but to pull it down. I seek not for honor of the world, but for the glory of my God, and the freedom and welfare of my country. And thus I close mine epistle.* (Alma 60:36)

·62·

PAHORAN'S HUMBLE REPLY
ALMA 61

Shortly after Moroni sent his letter to Pahoran, he received a reply. Pahoran detailed the events that had taken place in Zarahemla during Moroni's absence. The king-men had risen up in rebellion, and Pahoran and others had been forced to flee to the land of Gideon. The king-men had acquired a large group of supporters, had taken possession of Zarahemla, and had appointed a man named Pachus to be their king. Pachus had joined in an alliance with the king of the Lamanites. An agreement was made that when the Lamanites conquered all the Nephite land, Pachus would remain in power over the Nephites.

It was the king-men who were withholding provisions from Helaman's and Moroni's armies. They had also disheartened and intimidated the freemen to the point where they had chosen not to go to the aid of Moroni or Helaman. Pahoran had already sent a proclamation throughout the area asking those who supported the cause of freedom to join him.

> *And behold, they are flocking to us daily . . . in the defence of their country and their freedom, and to avenge our wrongs.* (Alma 61:6)

Because of the army gathering in Gideon, the king-men were afraid to come against them to battle. Pahoran then turned the subject back to Moroni's angry accusations.

> *And now, in your epistle you have censured me, but it mattereth not; I am not angry, but do rejoice in the greatness of your heart. I, Pahoran, do not seek for power, save only to retain my judgment-seat that I may preserve the rights and the liberty of my people. My soul standeth fast in that liberty in the which God hath made us free.* (Alma 61:9)

Pahoran asked Moroni to come to him *speedily* with a few of his men, leaving the remainder in the charge of Lehi and Teancum. Pahoran sent enough provisions to the remaining armies to sustain them during Moroni's absence. Moroni was to gather more men on his march back to the city of Gideon, where Pahoran's supporters had been gathering. The plan was to fight the dissenters and take back Zarahemla, putting an end to the uprising.

Before receiving Moroni's letter, Pahoran wasn't sure whether it was *just* to go against their own brethren. Moroni's words assured him that it was God's will to fight for their freedom.

> *And now I close mine epistle to my beloved brother, Moroni.*
> (Alma 61:21)

·63·

MORONI AIDS PAHORAN

ALMA 62

M oroni received Pahoran's letter with mixed feelings. He was *filled with exceedingly great joy* to know that Pahoran was still faithful to the cause of freedom, but *mourned exceedingly* for the iniquity that caused the rebellion. Moroni came as Pahoran had requested, marching toward the land of Gideon with a small number of men.

> *And he did raise the standard of liberty in whatsoever place he did enter. . . .*
> *And it came to pass that thousands did flock unto his standard, and did take up their swords in the defence of their freedom.* (Alma 62:4–5)

The closer Moroni came to his destination, the larger his army grew. After arriving in Gideon, he united with Pahoran's forces, creating a stronger army than that of the dissenters. Moroni and Pahoran marched their men to the land of Zarahemla and engaged in battle with the king-men. Pachus, the king of the dissenters, was slain, and his men were taken prisoners. Pahoran was restored to his judgment seat.

> *And the men of Pachus received their trial, according to the law, and also those king-men . . . ; and they were executed according to the law; yea, . . . whosoever would not take up arms in the defence of their country, but would fight against it, were put to death.* (Alma 62:9)

Peace was finally restored to Zarahemla as the thirtieth year of the reign of the judges ended. At the beginning of the next year, an army of six thousand men, plus provisions were immediately sent to Helaman to assist him in preserving that part of the land. The armies of Lehi and Teancum also received six thousand men and provisions.

The next order of business was to take back the city of Nephihah. Moroni and Pahoran divided their large army, leaving part to protect Zarahemla, and then marched toward Nephihah with the remaining men. On their way they came across a large army of Lamanites and a battle ensued. The Nephites slew many of them and took the remainder captive, then confiscated their provisions and weapons. True to Nephite tradition, the prisoners were granted their freedom *if* they covenanted not to take up arms against the Nephites again.

> *And when they had entered into this covenant they sent them to dwell with the people of Ammon, and they were in number about four thousand who had not been slain.* (Alma 62:17)

Moroni and Pahoran and their army continued their march to Nephihah to retake the city from the Lamanites. They pitched their tents nearby and hoped that the Lamanites would come out to battle them on the plains. This was not to be, for when the Lamanites saw the huge Nephite army, and knowing of their *exceedingly great courage,* they dared not leave the protection of their city.

That very night, Moroni crept in the darkness to the city and climbed to the top of the wall to see where the Lamanite army was camped. He found them by the entrance to the east, all asleep. Moroni returned to his army and had them hurriedly prepare strong cords and ladders. The men marched back to Nephihah, climbed the wall, and let themselves down into the city on the opposite side from where the Lamanite army was camped.

> *And now, when the Lamanites awoke and saw that the armies of Moroni were within the walls, they were affrighted exceedingly, insomuch that they did flee out by the pass.* (Alma 62:24)

Moroni ordered his men to pursue the fleeing army. Many Lamanites were slain, many were taken prisoner, and the rest fled into the land of Moroni. Moroni and Pahoran had succeeded in obtaining possession of the city of Nephihah without the loss of one of their own men. Again the prisoners taken chose to join the people of Ammon, relieving the Nephites of the great burden of guarding them.

·64·

THE VALIANT TEANCUM IS SLAIN
ALMA 62–63

Taking back the city of Nephihah had been advantageous for the Nephites for two reasons: Their army had been greatly strengthened with the addition of the men who had been freed from the Lamanites, and the size of the Lamanite army had been severely reduced. Thousands had been taken prisoner, and then were subsequently allowed to join with the people of Ammon.

Moroni's next objective was to retake the city of Lehi. When the Lamanites saw the army approaching, they again fled in fear. Moroni pursued them from city to city until they were met by the armies of Lehi and Teancum coming from the opposite direction. The Lamanites fled from them also, finally arriving in the land of Moroni. At this point all the Lamanite armies were in one group in the city of Moroni, along with Ammoron, their king. By nightfall, the armies of Moroni, Lehi, and Teancum had each made their camp, surrounding the city. The Nephites and the Lamanites were weary because of their long march and planned no further strategy for that night—except Teancum.

> *For he was exceedingly angry with Ammoron, insomuch that he considered that Ammoron, and Amalickiah his brother, had been the cause of this great and lasting war between them and the Lamanites, which had been the cause of so much war and bloodshed, yea, and so much famine. (Alma 62:35)*

Driven by his anger, Teancum went to the Lamanite camp and let himself down over the wall. He finally found Ammoron and threw his javelin, piercing Ammoron near his heart. Before the king died, he managed to awaken his servants, who pursued Teancum and slew him. (Alma 51:34 tells of how Teancum killed Amalickiah, Ammoron's brother, in almost identical circumstances about six years before.)

When Lehi and Moroni learned of Teancum's death, they were *exceedingly sorrowful.*

> *For behold, he had been a man who had fought valiantly for his country, yea, a true friend to liberty; and he had suffered very many exceedingly sore afflictions.* (Alma 62:37)

The next day, the Nephites marched upon the Lamanites and slew them with an immense slaughter, driving them out of the land. There would be no further wars with the Lamanites for more than eight years.

The thirty-first year of the reign of the judges ended. Moroni directed the affairs of the Nephite army until the land was sufficiently fortified against the Lamanites, then returned to Zarahemla. He turned the command of the armies over to his son, Moronihah.

> *And he retired to his own house that he might spend the remainder of his days in peace.* (Alma 62:43)

Pahoran returned to his judgment-seat. Helaman returned to the place of his inheritance and began preaching the word of God. The Nephites had been through many years of wars, famines, and afflictions, but these years had also been filled with contentions and *all manner of iniquity* among their own people. They had been spared only because of the prayers of the righteous. Helaman and his brethren once again established the church throughout the land. Because the people humbled themselves and turned their hearts to the Lord, they were blessed. They prospered in the land and *began to grow exceedingly rich,* but in spite of their prosperity they were not lifted up in pride. They remembered that it was God who had delivered them from their enemies.

Helaman died during the thirty-fifth year of the reign of the judges. In the beginning of the thirty-sixth year, Helaman's brother, Shiblon, took possession of the sacred records. He was a righteous man who kept the commandments of the Lord. By the end of the thirty-sixth year, Moroni had also died.

·65·

MIGRATIONS TO THE LAND NORTHWARD

ALMA 63

In the thirty-seventh year of the reign of the judges, a large company of Nephites departed out of the land of Zarahemla and traveled to the land in the far north. There were fifty-four hundred men *with their wives and their children.* The land northward was called Desolation, and it was here that the remnants of the Jaredite civilization had been found.

During this year the era of ship building began. It was started by a man named Hagoth, who was described as *exceedingly curious.* He built a very large ship on the borders of the land of Bountiful and launched it into the west sea by the narrow neck of land that led into the land northward. Many men, women, and children and a large supply of provisions were aboard this ship, which took a northward course.

During the thirty-eighth year, Hagoth built other ships. In this same year the first ship he built returned and was loaded with more people and provisions and again set out for the land northward.

> *And it came to pass that they were never heard of more. And we suppose that they were drowned in the depths of the sea. And . . . one other ship also did sail forth; and whither she did go we know not.* (Alma 63:8)

(In the third chapter of Helaman we are given information about other migrations to the north. It is also mentioned that timber was shipped to the north because it was so scarce in that land.)

In the thirty-ninth year, Shiblon died. His brother, Corianton, had gone to the land northward in a ship and was probably never heard from again. Before Shiblon died, he entrusted the sacred records to his nephew,

Helaman, who was the son of Helaman, the prophet and military commander. These records were copied and sent forth among the people throughout all the land.

In this same year there were some dissenters who joined the Lamanites and incited them to go to war. A large Lamanite army came to fight the army of Moronihah but was soundly beaten and driven back.

·66·

THE LAMANITES TAKE ZARAHEMLA
HELAMAN 1

In the beginning of the fortieth year of the reign of the judges, serious contentions arose as to who would be the next chief judge. Pahoran had died and three of his sons—Pahoran, Paanchi, and Pacumeni—were competing for the position, causing *three divisions among the people.* Pahoran was appointed by the voice of the people to be the next chief judge and governor. Pacumeni sustained his brother, but Paanchi and his supporters were greedy for power and did not.

Paanchi persuaded his band of followers *to rise up in rebellion against their brethren.* Before they had time to carry out their plans, Paanchi was taken, tried, and condemned to die for attempting to destroy the liberty of the people. This angered his supporters, and they retaliated by sending a man named Kishkumen to murder Pahoran as he sat upon his judgment-seat. After the evil deed was accomplished, Pahoran's servants pursued Kishkumen, but *so speedy was his flight* that he was not overtaken.

> *And he went unto those that sent him, and they all entered into a covenant, yea, swearing by their everlasting Maker, that they would tell no man that Kishkumen had murdered Pahoran.* (Helaman 1:11)

The king of the Lamanites was a man named Tubaloth, who was the son of Ammoron. (Ammoron had been slain by Teancum while sleeping in his tent; then Teancum was in turn killed by Ammoron's guards.) In the forty-first year, Tubaloth stirred up his people to go to war against the Nephites. He appointed a man named Coriantumr, who was a dissenter from the Nephites, to lead his army. Because Coriantumr was a *large and a mighty man* with *great wisdom,* Tubaloth was confident that he could overpower the Nephites.

The Lamanites gathered an *innumerable* army and equipped them with swords, cimeters, bows and arrows, and *all manner of shields of every kind.* Coriantumr and his army marched right into the center of Nephite territory to the city of Zarahemla, slaying anyone who opposed them and taking possession of the city. The huge army had come with such *exceedingly great speed* that the Nephites had no time to gather their men to fight.

> *And it came to pass that because of so much contention and so much difficulty in the government, that they had not kept sufficient guards in the land of Zarahemla; for they had supposed that the Lamanites durst not come into the heart of their lands to attack that great city Zarahemla.* (Helaman 1:18)

Pacumeni had become the next chief judge after his brother, Pahoran, had been murdered. Coriantumr found Pacumeni as he was fleeing the city and *did smite him against the wall,* where he died.

Taking possession of Zarahemla—*the strongest hold in all the land*—had given Coriantumr courage to conquer all the Nephite lands. He marched his large army towards Bountiful with the intention of obtaining the cities to the north. As Coriantumr's army plowed through the middle of the territory, the Nephites had only enough time to assemble in small groups and were therefore no match for their enemy. The Lamanites slaughtered men, women, and children and took possession of many cities as they moved north.

Coriantumr had wrongly assumed that the Nephites' strength lay in the center of their territory, where the great city of Zarahemla and other large cities were located. Coriantumr's strategy to march through the middle of the land had given Moronihah, the leader of the Nephite armies, somewhat of an advantage. Having assumed that the Lamanites would attack the borders of the land, Moronihah had placed his strongest armies there, and they could now close in on the Lamanite army.

Upon discovering that Coriantumr was marching toward Bountiful, Moronihah immediately sent Lehi with his army to head them off. When Lehi's army met up with the Lamanites a battle ensued, causing Coriantumr to head back towards the land of Zarahemla. In their retreat they ran into Moronihah's army, resulting in *an exceedingly bloody battle.* Many were slain, including Coriantumr.

> *And now, behold, the Lamanites could not retreat either way,*
> *neither on the north, nor on the south, nor on the east, nor on the*
> *west, for they were surrounded on every hand by the Nephites.*
> (Helaman 1:31)

Coriantumr had plunged the Lamanites right into the hands of the Nephites, where his army was forced to surrender. Moronihah took possession again of Zarahemla, and allowed the Lamanite prisoners to leave the land in peace.

·67·

GADIANTON'S SECRET BAND
HELAMAN 2

B y the beginning of the forty-second year of the reign of the judges, peace had been established between the Nephites and the Lamanites. The first order of business was to fill the judgment-seat, and once again a contention arose as to who that should be. The voice of the people chose Helaman, who was the son of Helaman and the grandson of Alma the Younger.

A man named Gadianton became the leader of the secret band that was responsible for the murder of the chief judge, Pahoran. Kishkumen had been the one sent to perform the deed.

> *Gadianton . . . was exceedingly expert in many words, and also in his craft. . . .*
> *Therefore he did flatter them, and also Kishkumen, that if they would place him in the judgment-seat he would grant unto those who belonged to his band that they should be placed in power and authority among the people; therefore Kishkumen sought to destroy Helaman.* (Helaman 2:4–5)

One of Helaman's servants had obtained *through disguise* a knowledge of this secret band and of their intentions *to murder, and to rob, and to gain power.* He also knew of Kishkumen's plans to murder Helaman. On the night that Kishkumen came, the servant was waiting for him *and gave unto him a sign.* Confident that he was with a fellow conspirator, Kishkumen told him of his plans and asked to be led to Helaman. On their way to the judgment-seat, the servant stabbed Kishkumen in the heart and *he fell dead without a groan.* The servant then ran and told Helaman he had killed Kishkumen and informed him about Gadianton's band. Helaman immediately sent men to find those who belonged to this band, but they were nowhere to be found. When Kishkumen did not return, Gadianton suspected his plans had been thwarted. He and his men quickly departed the land and went into the wilderness *by a secret way.*

> *And more of this Gadianton shall be spoken hereafter. . . .*
> *And behold, in the end of this book ye shall see that this Gadianton did prove the overthrow, yea, almost the entire destruction of the people of Nephi.*
> *Behold I do not mean the end of the book of Helaman, but I mean the end of the book of Nephi, from which I have taken all the account which I have written.* (Helaman 2:12–14)

[The above words were written by the prophet Mormon, who is the narrator for most of the Book of Mormon, having abridged the records. The book of Helaman came from the large plates of Nephi, so when Mormon refers to "the end of the book of Nephi," he means the end of the Book of Mormon.]

·68·

SETTLING THE LAND NORTHWARD
HELAMAN 3–4

For three years there had been peace in the land, but by the forty-sixth year of the reign of the judges *there was much contention and many dissensions.* Because of this, a great many people, including many of the people of Ammon, left the land of Zarahemla and traveled northward to settle the land called Desolation. The land received this name because of the great destruction of the Jaredites, although much of the land was without timber *because of the many inhabitants who had before inherited the land.*

Those people settling the land to the far north traveled a very long distance until they came to a land of *large bodies of water and many rivers.* They spread out upon the land, choosing the more fertile parts in which to live. Because of the shortage of timber, they became *expert in the working of cement,* with which they built their dwellings. Some of the people lived in tents.

> And it came to pass that they did multiply and spread . . . insomuch that they began to cover the face of the [land], from the sea south to the sea north, from the sea west to the sea east.
> . . . And they did suffer whatsoever tree should spring up upon the face of the land that it should grow up, that in time they might have timber to build their houses, yea, their cities, and their temples, and their synagogues . . . and all manner of their buildings. (Helaman 3:8–9)

Timber was later sent to this northland *by way of shipping,* which enabled the people to build many cities of wood and cement. It was only about nine years before this that the Nephites began building ships to carry people and provisions to the land in the north (see Alma 63:5–8).

The prophet Mormon, who is our narrator, mentions that extensive records were kept of the people all over the land—north and south. He was able to include only *a hundredth part of the proceedings of this people* in this work, meaning our present-day Book of Mormon.

In the forty-seventh and forty-eighth years there was still contention in the land of Zarahemla, even though Helaman reigned as chief judge with *justice and equity* and kept the commandments of God. (Helaman's father, also named Helaman, was the prophet and military commander who led the two thousand stripling soldiers.)

The wars and contentions slowly decreased by the forty-ninth year, when there was continual peace throughout the land *all save it were the secret combinations which Gadianton the robber had established in the more settled parts of the land, which at that time were not known unto those who were at the head of government; therefore they were not destroyed out of the land* (Helaman 3:23).

In this same year there was great prosperity in the church—tens of thousands of people were baptized! Even the high priests and teachers were *astonished beyond measure*. The remainder of the forty-ninth year and the fiftieth year was a time of peace and joy in all the lands of the Nephites. Sadly, in the fifty-first year, pride began to enter into the hearts of some *who professed to belong to the church of God.* The more humble part of the people suffered great persecution at their hands, but with much fasting and prayer they became stronger and stronger in their faith in Christ.

When Helaman died in the fifty-third year of the reign of the judges, his oldest son, Nephi, was appointed to reign in his stead. He was a righteous judge over the people *and did walk in the ways of his father.*

By the fifty-fourth year, the short era of peace had ended. A contention among the people caused much bloodshed, after which the *rebellious part* joined the Lamanites. In the fifty-sixth year more dissenters joined the Lamanites and succeeded in persuading them to go to war against the Nephites. All that year they prepared for war. The Lamanites came to battle in the fifty-seventh year, *and they did commence the work of death.* The next year they took possession of Zarahemla, driving the Nephites and the armies of Moronihah into the land of Bountiful. The Nephites fortified their boundary *from the west sea even unto the east* with their armies so they could defend their north country. Even so, the Nephites lost possession of almost all their lands by the fifty-ninth year.

And it was because of the pride of their hearts, because of their exceeding riches, yea, it was because of their oppression to the poor, withholding their food from the hungry, withholding their clothing from the naked, and smiting their humble brethren upon the cheek, making a mock of that which was sacred, denying the spirit of prophecy and of revelation, murdering, plundering, lying, stealing, committing adultery, rising up in great contentions, and deserting away into the land of Nephi, among the Lamanites. (Helaman 4:12)

Moronihah (the leader of the Nephite armies), Nephi (the chief judge), and Lehi (Nephi's brother), preached to the people and warned them what would happen if they remained wicked. The people repented and slowly began to prosper. Moronihah was encouraged by their repentance and led his army *from place to place, and from city to city* until they had regained half of their lands.

In the sixty-second year, Moronihah had to abandon his plans to regain the remainder of the Nephite lands because of the great number of the Lamanites. It took all of his armies just to maintain the cities they had retaken. The Nephites lived in great fear that the Lamanites would overpower them and destroy them. They now recognized that their wickedness had led to their present situation and that *the judgments of God did stare them in the face.*

·69·

ENCRICLED BY FIRE
HELAMAN 5

And it came to pass that Nephi had become weary because of their iniquity; and he yielded up the judgment-seat, and took it upon him to preach the word of God all the remainder of his days, and his brother Lehi also, all the remainder of his days. (Helaman 5:4)

The Nephites had corrupted their laws and were ripening for destruction. They were governed by the voice of the people, but *they who chose evil were more numerous than they who chose good.* Nephi and Lehi traveled from city to city and preached among the people. Then they went to the land of Zarahemla, which now belonged to the Lamanites who had taken it over a few years earlier. Their preaching was so powerful that many of the Nephite dissenters who lived in Zarahemla confessed their sins and were baptized. The reclaimed dissenters immediately returned home *to endeavor to repair unto them the wrongs which they had done.*

The two missionary companions had *great power and authority* given unto them to speak. Eight thousand Lamanites in the land of Zarahemla and the lands round about were baptized. They came to know that the traditions of their fathers had been based on falsehoods.

Next Nephi and Lehi journeyed to the land of Nephi, which had been Lamanite territory for nearly two hundred years. They were cast into prison and remained there many days without food until guards came to take them to their execution.

And it came to pass that Nephi and Lehi were encircled about as if by fire, even insomuch that [the guards] durst not lay their hands upon them for fear lest they should be burned. Nevertheless, Nephi and Lehi were not burned; and they were as standing in the midst of fire and were not burned. (Helaman 5:23)

Their hearts took courage at this manifestation of the Lord's power. Seeing that the Lamanites were *struck dumb with amazement,* they stood forth and began to speak to them. There were about three hundred people, Lamanites as well as Nephite dissenters, who witnessed this miracle. They were assured by Nephi and Lehi that it was God who had shown them this marvelous thing. Then the earth shook and the prison walls seemed ready to fall. A cloud of darkness overshadowed them *and an awful solemn fear came upon them.*

> *And it came to pass that there came a voice as if it were above the cloud of darkness, saying: Repent ye, repent ye, and seek no more to destroy my servants whom I have sent unto you to declare good tidings.*
>
> *And it came to pass when they heard this voice, and beheld that it was not a voice of thunder, neither was it a voice of great tumultuous noise, but behold, it was a still voice of perfect mildness, as if it had been a whisper, and it did pierce even to the very soul.* (Helaman 5:29–30)

Even though the voice was mild, the earth shook *exceedingly* and again the prison walls seemed about to collapse. The voice was heard a second time, repeating the same message as before, and the earth shook again. The voice was heard for the third time, but this time it spoke *marvelous words which cannot be uttered by man.* The walls began to tremble again as the earth shook violently. The Lamanites could not escape because of the great fear that gripped their hearts and the darkness that enveloped them.

A man named Aminadab was among them. He was a dissenter from the Nephites and had once belonged to the church of God. Through the cloud of darkness he could see that the faces of Nephi and Lehi were shining *exceedingly, even as the faces of angels.* Their eyes were lifted to heaven, and it looked as though they were talking to someone. Aminadab cried to the multitude to look upon the faces of Nephi and Lehi. The people asked him who he thought they were talking to, and Aminadab replied that they were talking to the angels of God. Then they asked him what they could do to get the cloud of darkness removed. Aminadab told them to repent and cry unto the voice until they had faith in Christ. The people cried unto the voice until the cloud of darkness dispersed. Suddenly they found themselves *encircled about, yea every soul, by a pillar of fire,* with Nephi and Lehi in the center of the multitude. They were not harmed by the fire, nor did the walls of the prison burn, *and they were filled with that joy which is unspeakable and full of glory.* The Spirit of God came down from heaven and entered into their hearts, *and they were filled as if with fire, and they could speak forth marvelous words.*

> *And it came to pass that there came a voice unto them, yea, a pleasant voice, as if it were a whisper, saying:*
> *Peace, peace be unto you, because of your faith in my Well Beloved, who was from the foundation of the world.* (Helaman 5:46–47)

As the people looked up to see where the voice was coming from *they saw the heavens open; and angels came down out of heaven and ministered unto them.*

Those who had witnessed this marvelous manifestation went throughout the entire region declaring the things that they had both seen and heard. Because there had been so many witnesses, the majority of the Lamanites were converted. They laid down their weapons of war and no longer believed in the traditions of their fathers.

> *And it came to pass that they did yield up unto the Nephites the lands of their possession.* (Helaman 5:52)

·70·

THE GADIANTON ROBBERS TAKE OVER
HELAMAN 6

B y the end of the sixty-second year of the reign of the judges, most of the Lamanites had become firm in their faith in God, and *their righteousness did exceed that of the Nephites.*

> *For behold, there were many of the Nephites who had become hardened and impenitent and grossly wicked, insomuch that they did reject the word of God and all the preaching and prophesying which did come among them.* (Helaman 6:2)

The conversion of the Lamanites brought great joy to the members of the Church, allowing them to fellowship one with another. Many of the Lamanites came to the land of Zarahemla and preached to the Nephites with *great power and authority,* sharing their conversion stories and exhorting them to have faith and repent. A significant number of the Nephites were humbled by their teachings and returned to the fold of God.

Nephi and Lehi and many of the Lamanites traveled to the land northward to preach. Then the sixty-third year came to an end.

(Note: Helaman 6:6–10 mentions both the *land northward* and the *land north,* but there is a difference. The *land northward* refers to the far north land where the Jaredites once lived, also called the land Desolation. The *land north* and the *land south* were both south of the land Desolation and refer to the Nephite and Lamanite lands. The Nephites lived in the land north, with Zarahemla as their capital city. The Lamanites lived in the land south, with Nephi as their capital. In Helaman 6:10 we learn that Lehi and his family were led initially to the land south, and Mulek, the son of Zedekiah, and his group were led to the land north. Mulek's people were the original inhabitants of Zarahemla. After the Nephites discovered them, they joined together and the Mulekites were assimilated into the Nephite culture.)

Because of the peace between the Nephites and Lamanites, they were free to travel throughout each other's lands to buy and sell their various goods. Nephites and Lamanites alike became *exceedingly rich,* since both lands had a great abundance of gold and silver and other precious metals. They refined ore, grew great quantities of grain, and raised numerous flocks and herds. The women *did toil and spin* and make cloth of every kind, and the people multiplied on the face of the land.

The sixty-fourth and sixty-fifth years passed away in great joy and peace. In the sixty-sixth year, Cezoram, the chief judge of the Nephites, was murdered *by an unknown hand* as he sat upon his judgment-seat. His son was appointed by the people to replace him and within the same year was also murdered.

The years of peace had allowed the people to set their hearts upon riches. By the sixty-seventh year, they had started to grow wicked again. Living among the people was the secret band formed by Kishkumen and Gadianton that went about engaging in murder, robbery, and plunder. Although members of that band had infiltrated the Nephites, the majority of them were among the *more wicked part of the Lamanites.* It was these Gadianton robbers, as they were called, who had murdered Cezoram and his son.

Upon discovering this band of robbers among them, the Lamanites used *every means in their power to destroy them off the face of the earth.* Most of the Nephites, on the other hand, united with Gadianton's band! They entered into their covenants and oaths and vowed to protect each other with secrecy. They used secret signs and words to distinguish those who had entered into the covenant. This allowed them to murder, steal, plunder, and *commit whoredoms* while under the protection of their band. Any member of the band who revealed their secrets was put to death by the others.

> *Now behold, it is these secret oaths and covenants which Alma commanded his son should not go forth unto the world, lest they should be a means of bringing down the people unto destruction.*
> (Helaman 6:25; refer also to Alma 37:27)

These secret oaths and covenants had not come from the records that were given to Helaman, but were put into the heart of Gadianton by Satan himself.

The Nephites continued to grow in wickedness during the sixty-eighth year, while the Lamanites grew even closer to God, walking *in truth and uprightness before him.* They hunted down the Gadianton robbers until the band was destroyed from among their people. The Nephites did the opposite and allowed them to spread throughout their land until they *had seduced the more part of the righteous.* Now even *they* believed in their works and took part in their *secret murders and combinations* and partook of their *spoils.* By the end of the sixty-eighth year, the Gadianton robbers had taken over *the sole management* of the Nephite government.

·71·

NEPHI PRAYS ON HIS TOWER
HELAMAN 7–10

For six years Nephi had been living in the land northward, preaching and prophesying to the people. He left in the sixty-ninth year to return to Zarahemla because they had rejected all his words. He came home to find his people in an awful state of wickedness and the Gadianton robbers filling the judgment-seats. There was no justice to be found in the courts—they were *condemning the righteous because of their righteousness* and allowing the guilty to go free because of their money. Seeing this great iniquity brought Nephi down into the depths of sorrow, and *he did exclaim in the agony of his soul:*

> *Oh, that I could have had my days in the days when my father Nephi first came out of the land of Jerusalem, that I could have joyed with him in the promised land; then were his people . . . firm to keep the commandments of God. . . .*
>
> *But behold, I am consigned that these are my days, and that my soul shall be filled with sorrow because of this the wickedness of my brethren.* (Helaman 7:7, 9)

Nephi had been praying on a tower in his garden, which overlooked a main highway in the city of Zarahemla. Certain men passing by saw him *pouring out his soul unto God* and ran and told others. Soon there was a whole multitude gathered by the tower, wondering why Nephi was mourning for the wickedness of the people. Nephi noticed the crowd and spared no words in telling them of their evil ways and of the corruption of their government. He pleaded with them to repent. He told them that the Lord had made known to him that their lands would be taken from them and they would *be destroyed from off the face of the earth* unless they repented.

Among the people listening to Nephi's reprimand were judges who belonged to Gadianton's band. They were angry that their secret works of darkness had been exposed. They shouted for the people to seize Nephi so he could be punished for reviling against their law. Even though the judges tried to turn the people against Nephi, some of the people believed in his words and cried out:

> Let this man alone, for he is a good man, and those things which he saith will surely come to pass except we repent.
> . . . If he had not been a prophet he could not have testified concerning those things. (Helaman 8:7, 9)

Seeing that Nephi had supporters in the crowd, the judges dared not haul him away just yet. Nephi was encouraged by this and continued preaching. He mentioned many of the holy prophets who testified of the coming of the Savior. He told those gathered that they had rejected the truth and had rebelled against God and that destruction was *even at [their] doors.* As a testimony that he indeed had the gift of prophecy, he boldly declared that the chief judge Seezoram had been murdered and at that very moment was lying in his own blood! He further stated that the murderer was Seezoram's own brother who wanted the judgment-seat for himself and that both brothers were members of Gadianton's band.

As soon as he said these words, the judges in the crowd sent five men to the judgment-seat to see if their chief judge was dead. Those sent had not believed anything Nephi had said, but on their way they acknowledged that if he were telling the truth about the chief judge, they would have to believe all that he had spoken. They found Seezoram dead, just as Nephi had predicted. Great fear came upon them as they thought about all the other judgments Nephi had pronounced upon their people and *they fell to the earth.*

The slain judge was first discovered by his own servants, who immediately ran and told the people, *raising the cry of murder among them.* A crowd of people arrived back at the judgment-seat just in time to find the five men lying on the floor.

> And now behold, the people knew nothing concerning the multitude who had gathered together at the garden of Nephi; therefore they said among themselves: These men are they who had murdered the judge, and God has smitten them that they could not flee from us. (Helaman 9:8)

The five men were bound and cast into prison. A proclamation was sent abroad proclaiming that the chief judge was slain and his murderers had been apprehended.

The next day the people assembled together to mourn at the burial of their chief judge, Seezoram. Those judges who listened to Nephi preach in his garden were also there and inquired about the five men they had sent to the judgment-seat in response to Nephi's prophecy. The people answered that they knew nothing about those men but that there were five who had been taken into custody. The judges ordered the men brought before them and found them to be the five they had sent. The men explained how they had discovered the chief judge just as Nephi had prophesied and had been so astonished that they had fallen to the earth. Upon recovering, they were charged with the murder. The judges now came to the conclusion that Nephi was the one responsible for the evil deed.

> Behold, we know that this Nephi must have agreed with some one to slay the judge, and then he might declare it unto us, that he might convert us unto his faith, that he might raise himself to be a great man, chosen of God, and a prophet. (Helaman 9:16)

The five (who had been converted through this experience) were liberated, but they rebuked the judges for accusing Nephi. Nevertheless, Nephi was bound and brought before the multitude, and the judges began to question him. They were certain that he had an accomplice and offered him his freedom and money if he would tell them the details of the arrangement. Nephi was filled with anger and lashed out at their wickedness. He told them that they ought to *howl and mourn* because of the great destruction that was awaiting them if they did not repent. He added that because he had testified of the murder as a sign that he knew of their wickedness, they were now seeking his life.

Nephi gave them another sign. The people were told to go to the house of Seantum, who was the brother of the slain judge, and ask him this question:

> Has Nephi, the pretended prophet, who doth prophesy so much evil concerning this people, agreed with thee, in the which ye have murdered Seezoram, who is your brother? (Helaman 9:27)

He would answer no, and then they were to ask him if he had murdered his brother.

And he shall stand with fear, and wist not what to say. And behold, he shall deny unto you; and he shall make as if he were astonished; nevertheless, he shall declare unto you that he is innocent. (Helaman 9:30)

They would then find blood on the *skirts of his cloak* and were to tell him that they knew it was the blood of his brother.

And then shall he tremble, and shall look pale, even as if death had come upon him. (Helaman 9:33)

After witnessing this, they were to say that because of his fear and paleness, they knew he was guilty. At this time he would be even more afraid and he would confess to the murder. He would also tell them that Nephi had nothing to do with the matter *save it were given unto him by the power of God.*

Nephi told the people that when all was said and done just as he prophesied, they would know that he was an honest man sent to them from God.

And it came to pass that they went and did, even according as Nephi had said unto them. And behold, the words which he had said were true; for according to the words he did deny; and also according to the words he did confess. (Helaman 9:37)

Nephi was set free. Some of the people believed he was a prophet; others thought he must be a god, *for except he was a god he could not know of all things.*

And it came to pass that there arose a division among the people, insomuch that they divided hither and thither and went their ways, leaving Nephi alone, as he was standing in the midst of them. (Helaman 10:1)

Nephi headed home, pondering on the things the Lord had shown him.

·72·

NEPHI CALLS DOWN A FAMINE
HELAMAN 10–11

As Nephi walked toward his house, being *cast down* because of the wickedness of the people, the voice of the Lord came to him. He was commended for his tireless preaching and for putting the Lord's will over the safety of his own life. Because of his obedience, a great blessing was about to be pronounced upon him. He was going to be made *mighty in word and in deed*. All things would be done *according to [his] word*, because the Lord knew Nephi would never ask for that which was contrary to the will of God.

> *Behold, thou art Nephi, and I am God. Behold, I declare it unto thee in the presence of mine angels, that ye shall have power over this people, and shall smite the earth with famine, and with pestilence, and destruction, according to the wickedness of this people.*
>
> *And thus, if ye shall say unto this temple it shall be rent in twain, it shall be done.*
>
> *And if ye shall say unto this mountain, Be thou cast down and become smooth, it shall be done.* (Helaman 10:6, 8–9)

Nephi was commanded to go back and tell the people that if they did not repent, they would *be smitten, even unto destruction*. Nephi immediately returned to preach to the people. In spite of the great miracles Nephi had previously performed among them, their hearts remained hardened. They did not believe in Nephi's prophecies and instead tried to put him in prison.

> *But behold, the power of God was with him, and they could not take him to cast him into prison, for he was taken by the Spirit and conveyed away out of the midst of them.* (Helaman 10:16)

Nephi continued to preach to the people, going from multitude to multitude, until they had all been given the message. Still they would not listen, but *were divided against themselves and began to slay one another with the sword.* The seventy-first year ended. The following year saw wars throughout all the Nephite lands, instigated by the Gadianton robbers. In the seventy-third year the warfare continued.

> *And it came to pass that in this year Nephi did cry unto the Lord, saying:*
>
> *O Lord, do not suffer that this people shall be destroyed by the sword; but O Lord, rather let there be a famine in the land, to stir them up in remembrance of the Lord their God, and perhaps they will repent and turn unto thee.* (Helaman 11:3–4)

And so the famine came. As the drought continued into the seventy-fourth year, *the work of destruction* was no longer caused by warfare but by the dry, barren earth. The seventy-fifth year saw no change, and in the more wicked parts of the land the people died by the thousands. Because the people were about to perish, they began to remember the Lord and also Nephi's prophecies. They pleaded with their chief judges to ask Nephi to cry unto the Lord to stop the famine. They were finally humbled and penitent and had even rid themselves of the Gadianton robbers. Nephi prayed mightily to the Lord and asked that the famine now come to an end, since it had turned the people from their wickedness.

In the seventy-sixth year, the Lord caused rain to fall, and fruits and grains were once again harvested in their season. The people throughout the land rejoiced and glorified God, and *did esteem [Nephi] as a great prophet.*

The Nephites began to prosper again and to spread out upon the whole face of the land. The next few years were peaceful, and the church grew. In the seventy-eighth year, contentions arose over a few points of doctrine of the church and grew even worse the following year. Nephi and his brother Lehi and other brethren corrected the falsehoods and the contentions ended.

In the eightieth year, a band of Nephite and Lamanite dissenters began a war with their brethren. They would come out of the hills and murder and plunder, creating great havoc and destruction among the Nephites and the Lamanites, then retreat back into the mountains to their secret hiding places. They had searched out the secret plans of Gadianton, *and thus they became robbers of Gadianton.* Other dissenters added to their numbers daily. An army was sent to find and destroy these robbers but was driven out. When the army went after them again the following year, both sides suffered many casualties, but the army had to retreat because of the great numbers of the Gadianton band that *infested the mountains and the wilderness.* The robbers grew in strength and numbers and defied the armies of the Nephites and Lamanites. They caused great fear to come upon all the land.

> *Yea, for they did visit many parts of the land, and did do great destruction unto them; yea, did kill many, and did carry away others captive into the wilderness, yea, and more especially their women and their children.* (Helaman 11:33)

In the eighty-first year, the great afflictions of the people caused them to turn to God, but only for a short season. By the end of the eighty-fifth year they were *ripening again for destruction.*

·73·

SAMUEL THE LAMANITE
HELAMAN 13–16

I n the eighty-sixth year, the Nephites were still in a state of wickedness, while the Lamanites had remained strict in keeping the commandments of God.

In this same year, a Lamanite named Samuel came to Zarahemla and
began to preach to the people. After many days of calling them to repentance, they cast him out of the city. As he was traveling home, the voice
of the Lord told Samuel to return to the city *and prophesy unto the people
whatsoever things should come into his heart.* Having just been cast out of
the city, he could not enter by way of the city gates, so he climbed upon
the city wall. He *stretched forth his hand* and began to preach in a loud
voice, boldly declaring many things unto the people. He told them that
the *sword of justice* hung over them and that within four hundred years
that sword would fall. Complete annihilation would come by the fourth
generation if they did not repent.

Samuel courageously told the people that their great city of Zarahemla was so wicked that if it were not for the righteous among them,
the Lord *would cause that fire should come down out of heaven and destroy
it.* Not only was Zarahemla wicked, but so were all the cities in the land
round about. Samuel said that like their fathers of old, they mocked and
stoned and cast out the prophets who came to call them to repentance.
But worse than their fathers, they were quick to raise up any man to be a
prophet who spoke flattering words unto them. If a man came along and
told them *do this, and there is no iniquity; . . . walk after the pride of your
own hearts; . . . and do whatsoever your heart desireth,* they would receive
him as a prophet and give him gold and silver and clothe him in costly
apparel!

Because the people set their hearts on their riches instead of on the
word of God, Samuel told them that the day would come when their land

would be cursed. Their treasures would become *slippery,* and the people would not be able to hold on to them. In that day they would say:

> *Behold, we lay a tool here and on the morrow it is gone; and behold, our swords are taken from us in the day we have sought them for battle.* (Helaman 13:34)

Samuel prophesied unto the people that the Savior would be born in five years. As a sign that the time of his birth had come, there would be such *great lights* in the heavens that there would be no darkness the night before he was born.

> *Therefore, there shall be one day and a night and a day, as if it were one day and there were no night; . . . [but] ye shall know of the rising of the sun and also of its setting.* (Helaman 14:4)

A new star would rise, and many other *signs and wonders* would appear in heaven. All these signs were given that they might believe in Jesus Christ and repent *and prepare the way of the Lord.*

Samuel further taught that the Savior must die when his mission on earth was completed so *that salvation may come.* He then gave the signs that would take place when the Savior was crucified.

> *In that day that he shall suffer death the sun shall be darkened and refuse to give his light unto you; and also the moon and the stars; and there shall be no light upon the face of this land, even from the time that he shall suffer death, for the space of three days, to the time that he shall rise again from the dead.* (Helaman 14:20)

During these three days of darkness, there would be *great tempests,* and thunder and lightning would last for many hours. Earthquakes would break up solid rock, causing seams and cracks and *broken fragments* to be found throughout the land. Some mountains would be leveled into valleys and some valleys would become great mountains. Highways would be broken up and many cities would be destroyed. Many graves would be opened, and the resurrected saints would appear unto many. After the people witnessed these signs and wonders, *there should be no cause for unbelief among the children of men.*

In Helaman, chapter 15, Samuel gives a lengthy discourse as to why the Lord would preserve the Lamanites in the land but allow the Nephites to become extinct (see also Alma 9:14–24; Hel. 7:24). He explains that the evil ways of the Lamanites were because of the wicked traditions of their fathers.

> And now, because of [the Lamanites'] steadfastness when they do believe, . . . because of their firmness when they are once enlightened, behold, the Lord shall bless them and prolong their days, notwithstanding their iniquity—
>
> Yea, even if they should dwindle in unbelief the Lord shall prolong their days. (Helaman 15:10–11)

The Nephites, on the other hand, were a chosen people of the Lord and had been shown *mighty works* that had not been shown unto the Lamanites. If they sinned against the light and knowledge given to them and did not repent, the Lord would utterly destroy them.

Samuel prophesied that the Lamanites would again be brought to the knowledge of the truth in the last days, but before that time came *they shall be driven to and fro upon the face of the earth, and be hunted, and shall be smitten and scattered abroad, having no place for refuge* (Helaman 15:12). After these many adversities, the Lamanites would again be *numbered among his sheep.*

Many of those who heard Samuel preach knew he was speaking the truth and went looking for the prophet Nephi so he could baptize them. However, most of the people did not believe Samuel and in their anger sought to kill him. They cast stones and shot arrows at him as he stood upon the wall, but the Lord's Spirit was with him and they could not hit him. Seeing this, more people became converted. Still, the majority of the people did not believe in Samuel's words and attributed his protection to the devil. When they could not hit him with their stones and arrows, they cried for their captains to seize him. As the captains were about to lay their hands on him, he jumped down from the wall and fled, returning to his own country to preach among his own people. Never again was he heard of among the Nephites.

Samuel had come to the Nephites at the end of the eighty-sixth year. During the next few years, the people became *more hardened in iniquity.* In the ninetieth year, the words of the prophets began to be fulfilled as *great signs* and *wonders* were shown to the people. Angels appeared unto many and declared *glad tidings of great joy.*

Except for the more righteous among them, the people continued to harden their hearts. They explained away the manifestations sent from God, saying that the believers simply *guessed right* on some of them and that all the marvelous works prophesied could not come to pass. They also concluded that it was not *reasonable that such a being as a Christ [should] come.* But if so, why would he appear to the people in Jerusalem and not to them?

> But behold, we know that this is a wicked tradition, which has been handed down unto us by our fathers, to cause us that we should believe in some great and marvelous thing which should come to pass . . . in a land which is far distant . . . ; therefore they can keep us in ignorance, for we cannot witness with our own eyes that they are true. (Helaman 16:20)

In spite of the great signs and wonders, Satan had a *great hold upon the hearts of the people upon all the face of the land.*

·74·

THE SAVIOR IS BORN

3 NEPHI 1–2

I t had been six hundred years since Lehi left Jerusalem as the ninety-
second year of the reign of the judges began. Nephi, the great missionary who had called down the famine upon the people, departed
out of the land of Zarahemla and was never heard of again. *Whither he
went, no man knoweth.* Before leaving, he had turned over all the sacred
records to his oldest son, also named Nephi.

In this year the prophecies concerning the coming of the Savior began
to be fulfilled, and the signs and miracles greatly increased. Even so, there
were some who said that the time for the Savior to be born was past and
that the hope and faith of the believers had been in vain. Because of the
uproar that the unbelievers were causing throughout the land, some of the
faithful began to fear that those things that had been prophesied might
not come to pass. Still, they watched *steadfastly* for that night when there
would be no darkness.

> *Now it came to pass that there was a day set apart by the unbe-
> lievers, that all those who believed in those traditions should be put
> to death except the sign should come to pass, which had been given by
> Samuel the prophet.* (3 Nephi 1:9)

When Nephi saw the wickedness of his people, his heart was filled
with sorrow. He bowed down and cried *mightily* to God in behalf of all
those faithful people who were about to lose their lives for trusting in the
prophecies. After he pleaded in prayer all day long, the voice of the Lord
came to him:

> *Lift up your head and be of good cheer; for behold, the time is at
> hand, and on this night shall the sign be given, and on the morrow
> come I into the world, to show unto the world that I will fulfill all*

that which I have caused to be spoken by the mouth of my holy prophets. (3 Nephi 1:13)

As the sun went down that evening there was no darkness. The people in all the land were so astonished that they fell to the earth as if they were dead, just as Samuel had prophesied. Those who had not believed in the words of the prophets were filled with fear because of their wickedness.

All throughout the night there was no darkness; instead *it was as light as though it was mid-day.* When the sun rose in the morning, they knew it was the day the Son of God would be born. Everything foretold by the prophets concerning the birth of the Savior came to pass, including a new star in the heavens.

Satan sent forth *lyings and deceivings* to keep the people from believing in the signs and wonders they had seen. Nevertheless, most of the people were converted and were baptized by Nephi and other leaders of the church, bringing peace throughout the land.

The peace would have continued the following year if it had not been for the Gadianton robbers who created a great deal of havoc among the people. The band of robbers were continually increasing as Nephite dissenters flocked to them. Also, many of the rising generation of the Lamanites were deceived by some of the Zoramites, who persuaded them to join with Gadianton's band.

Within four years of the Savior's birth, the people began to forget the miraculous signs they had witnessed.

> *[They] began to be less and less astonished at a sign or a wonder from heaven, insomuch that they began to be hard in their hearts, and blind in their minds, and began to disbelieve all which they had heard and seen.* (3 Nephi 2:1)

The people attributed the miracles to the power of the devil and grew more and more wicked over the next several years.

(Note: In the Book of Mormon, three different ways to record time were used. For the first 509 years the calendrical system was based on how many years it had been since Lehi left Jerusalem. After the government was changed from kings to judges, the people recorded time according to how many years the judges had reigned. This method lasted 91 years. When Christ was born, the event was so significant that the people began to record their time beginning with the night when there was no darkness. This method for recording time continues throughout the remainder of the book.)

By the thirteenth year, the Gadianton robbers had grown so large in number and *did lay waste so many cities, and did spread so much death and carnage throughout the land,* that the people gathered another army to go against them. They were joined by those Lamanites who had been converted to the Lord. After an unsuccessful start, the Nephites were able to drive the robbers back into the mountains. Gadianton's band came down again the following year, this time getting the upper hand because of wickedness and contentions among the Nephites.

As the fifteenth year ended, the *sword of destruction* hung over the Nephites, who *were about to be smitten down by it.*

·75·

NEPHITES UNDER SIEGE
3 NEPHI 3–5

Lachoneus was the chief judge and governor over the land of the Nephites. In the sixteenth year he received a letter from Giddianhi, who was the leader of the Gadianton robbers.

> *Lachoneus, most noble and chief governor of the land, behold, I write this epistle unto you, and do give unto you exceedingly great praise . . . ; yea, ye do stand well, as if ye were supported by the hand of a god, in the defence of your liberty. . . .*
>
> *And it seemeth a pity unto me, most noble Lachoneus, that ye should be so foolish and vain as to suppose that ye can stand against so many brave men who are at my command.* (3 Nephi 3:2–3)

Giddianhi praised the Nephites for their *noble spirit in the field of battle* but expressed concern for their welfare. He asked that they surrender their people, lands, and possessions rather than be destroyed.

> *Or in other words, yield yourselves up unto us, and unite with us and become acquainted with our secret works, and become our brethren that ye may be like unto us—not our slaves, but our brethren and partners of all our substance.* (3 Nephi 3:7)

Giddianhi swore with an oath that if they surrendered they would be spared, but if they did not they would all be destroyed. He told Lachoneus that the works of his secret society were good and had been handed down to them from ancient times. He also stated that the members of his band had been wronged by the Nephites, who unjustly retained from them their right to govern the people. Unless they surrendered, Giddianhi would *avenge their wrongs.*

After receiving this letter, Lachoneus was very surprised at Giddianhi's boldness in demanding their lands. He was especially incensed at his threats to avenge *the wrongs of those who had received no wrong.* He was not intimidated by the threats of a robber and planned to be prepared for them when they came to war.

Lachoneus sent a proclamation among all his people (which included Lamanites as well), telling them to gather their families, their flocks and herds, and all their provisions into one land for protection. He also admonished them to repent of all their sins and cry unto the Lord for strength. Only then would they be delivered out of the hands of the Gadianton robbers. The people trusted Lachoneus and did as he asked because of his *great and marvelous* words.

It was decided that the people should gather in the combined lands of Zarahemla and Bountiful. (An interesting note: 3 Nephi 3:24 mentions that it was decided against gathering in the land northward where the Jaredites had lived because of the curse that was upon that land.) They marched by the tens of thousands with *their horses, and their chariots, and their cattle, and all their flocks, and their herds, and their grain, and all their substance.* By the end of the seventeenth year, they had all settled into one body in this central area of the Nephite lands.

Lachoneus had strong fortifications built around the land they inhabited and placed armies there to guard against the robbers day and night. He appointed a man named Gidgiddoni to be the chief commander over all the armies. It was the Nephite custom to appoint men who had the spirit of revelation and prophecy to be their chief captains. They considered Gidgiddoni to be a great prophet, and Lachoneus as well.

The people wanted Gidgiddoni to lead them into the mountains where they could attack the Gadianton robbers in their own lands. His answer reflects the Nephite philosophy of war:

> *The Lord forbid; for if we should go up against them the Lord would deliver us into their hands; . . . but we will wait till they shall come against us; . . . if we do this he will deliver them into our hands.* (3 Nephi 3:21)

The people repented of their sins and prayed for deliverance from their enemies—and they prepared for war.

At the latter end of the eighteenth year, the robbers began to *sally forth* from their secret hiding places in the mountains and hills. They took possession of all the cities deserted by the Nephites, but this soon proved to be a hollow victory. The only way the Gadiantons subsisted was to plunder and rob, and the deserted cities had slim offerings. They dared not spread out to raise grain for fear their enemies would come upon them. There was no wild game except in the wilderness. The Nephites, on the other hand, had enough provisions to last seven years, in hopes they could completely destroy the robbers in that time.

In the sixth month of the nineteenth year, Giddianhi found it necessary for his people's survival to go to battle against the Nephites. *Great and terrible* was the appearance of his armies with their heads shorn and their skin dyed in blood.

Upon seeing Giddianhi's army, the Nephites fell to the earth and cried to God for deliverance. The armies of Giddianhi shouted for joy, thinking their enemy had fallen out of fear. They were soon disappointed, as the Nephites met them with strength they had received from the Lord.

> *And great and terrible was the battle thereof . . . insomuch that there never was known so great a slaughter among all the people of Lehi since he left Jerusalem.* (3 Nephi 4:11)

The robbers began to fall before the Nephites and were driven into the wilderness. As the Nephites pursued them, none were spared who fell into their hands. Giddianhi was overtaken and slain, *and thus was the end of Giddianhi the robber.*

The Nephite warriors returned to their fortified lands. For the remainder of the nineteenth year and all of the twentieth, the Gadianton robbers did not come to battle. In the twenty-first year, their new leader, Zemnarihah, ordered his armies to lay siege against the Nephites. He supposed that if they were cut off from their other lands, they would have to surrender. This strategy was unwise, since the Nephites had enough provisions to outlast even a very long siege. The robbers depended upon wild game in the wilderness, which was becoming scarce.

> *And the Nephites were continually marching out by day and by night, and falling upon their armies, and cutting them off by thousands and by tens of thousands.* (3 Nephi 4:21)

When the robbers were about to perish with hunger, their leader, Zemnarihah, gave the command to withdraw. He planned to lead his army far into the land northward and put an end to the great slaughter of his people. Gidgiddoni, the commander of the Nephite armies, found out their plan and positioned an army during the night to block their retreat. The next day when the robbers began their march, they found they were surrounded by Nephites. Many thousands surrendered, and the remainder were slain.

> *And their leader, Zemnarihah, was taken and hanged upon a tree, yea, even upon the top thereof until he was dead. . . . [Then] they did fell the tree to the earth, and did cry with a loud voice, saying:*
>
> *May the Lord preserve his people in righteousness . . . that they may cause to be felled to the earth all who shall seek to slay them because of power and secret combinations.* (3 Nephi 4:28–29)

There was tremendous rejoicing among the people, even *unto the gushing out of many tears.* They praised God for delivering them out of the hands of their enemies. There was not a single person who doubted that Christ had been born because of the many signs given. They forsook all their sins and served God diligently.

The Gadianton robbers had either been taken prisoner or slain—none had escaped. The word of God was preached to them in prison, and those who repented and entered into a covenant to stop murdering were set free. Those who continued to breathe out threats against their brethren were punished according to the law.

> *And thus they did put an end to all those wicked, and secret, and abominable combinations.* (3 Nephi 5:6)

·76·

DIVIDING INTO TRIBES
3 NEPHI 6–7

In the twenty-sixth year, the people returned to their own lands, with their flocks and herds and all their provisions. They even had grain left over. The robbers who had entered into a covenant to keep the peace were given land so they might have the means to support themselves.

Over the next three years the people enjoyed peace and prosperity. New cities were built, existing cities were repaired, and many highways were constructed that led from land to land. Unfortunately, this time of peace would shortly come to an end. The twenty-ninth year marked the beginning of the Nephites' downfall as contentions and persecutions arose because of their *exceedingly great riches*.

> *And the people began to be distinguished by ranks, according to their riches and their chances for learning; yea, some were ignorant because of their poverty, and others did receive great learning because of their riches. . . .*
> *And thus there became a great inequality in all the land.* (3 Nephi 6:12, 14)

By the thirtieth year, the people *were in a state of awful wickedness*. Having been taught the commandments, they did not sin unknowingly but *did wilfully rebel against God*. The organization of the church was destroyed, except among a few of the Lamanites who *were firm, and steadfast* and *would not depart from it*.

Prophets were sent forth to testify of Christ and to warn the people of their wickedness. The chief judges, high priests, and lawyers were angry at this and secretly put them to death. According to the law, no one could be condemned to die without the approval of the governor of the land. These unlawful acts were discovered, and those judges responsible were brought before the governor to be tried for their crimes. The imprisoned judges had many friends and relatives who met with the corrupt lawyers and priests. They entered into a covenant, which *was given and administered by the devil,* to destroy the people of the Lord and prevent the execution of the judges. Included in this covenant were plans to destroy the government and establish a king. They carried out the first part of their plan by killing Lachoneus, the chief judge and governor of the land. (He was the son of that Lachoneus who, as the former governor, had directed all of his people to gather into one land.) Their next move to establish a king did not take place, however, because the people became *divided one against another.*

> And they did separate one from another into tribes, every man according to his family and his kindred and friends; and thus they did destroy the government of the land. (3 Nephi 7:2)

The tribes were very large, and each one appointed a chief, or leader, to make their laws. This great change among the affairs of the people had come about because of the secret combination that had destroyed their government. At this time there were few righteous people to be found.

> And thus six years had not passed away since the more part of the people had turned from their righteousness, like the dog to his vomit, or like the sow to her wallowing in the mire. (3 Nephi 7:8)

The group of people who belonged to the secret combination placed a man named Jacob at their head and called him their king. This wicked band became an enemy to all the other tribes, who were united in their hatred of them. Being greatly outnumbered by their enemies, Jacob commanded his people to flee to the *northernmost part of the land.* His intention was to build his people into a mighty kingdom, being confident they would be joined by dissenters. When they were sufficiently strong, they would come down and wage war with the other tribes. The march of Jacob's people to the land northward was too swift for anyone to stop them.

(Note: We find out what happened to Jacob and his people in 3 Nephi 9:9. They built a great city, but it was one of the many cities destroyed after the crucifixion of the Savior. It was burned with fire because their *secret murders and combinations* were responsible for the collapse of the central government.)

The thirty-first year began with some measure of peace. Even though the tribes had their separate governments, they had very strict laws that prohibited one tribe from trespassing against another. They agreed that there would be no wars between them.

> *Nevertheless, their hearts were turned from the Lord their God, and they did stone the prophets and did cast them out from among them.* (3 Nephi 7:14)

The prophet Nephi was still among the people, (although the last time we heard of him was shortly after the Savior was born. He is the son of that Nephi who called down the famine.) Like his father before him, Nephi was a great spiritual leader who had been visited by angels and had heard the voice of the Lord. He was an *eye-witness* as the people made a swift return from righteousness to wickedness and was filled with sorrow because of it. In this thirty-first year, Nephi went forth among the people. He boldly called them to repentance and ministered unto them *with power and great authority.* The people were angry with Nephi because *he had greater power than they* and they could not *disbelieve his words.*

> *For so great was his faith on the Lord Jesus Christ that angels did minister unto him daily.*
> *And in the name of Jesus did he cast out devils and unclean spirits; and even his brother did he raise from the dead, after he had been stoned and suffered death by the people.* (3 Nephi 7:18–19)

The people saw the miracles that Nephi performed and yet continued to be angry with him. As the thirty-first year ended there were few who had been converted to the Lord, but those who were converted testified that they had been visited by the Spirit of God. Others who had been healed of their sicknesses and infirmities also testified of the power of God.

Nephi continued to preach to the people, and by the end of the thirty-third year, many had been baptized. He also ordained men to help with the ministry.

·77·

TEMPESTS, EARTHQUAKES, FIRES, AND WHIRLWINDS
3 NEPHI 8

As the thirty-third year ended, the people began to *look with great earnestness* for the signs prophesied by Samuel the Lamanite that would accompany the crucifixion of the Savior. Again, just as with the Savior's birth, there *began to be great doubtings and disputations among the people.*

> *And it came to pass in the thirty and fourth year, in the first month, on the fourth day of the month, there arose a great storm, such an one as never had been known in all the land.* (3 Nephi 8:5)

The storm was described as a *great and terrible tempest.* The thunder and lightning were so ferocious that the earth shook *as if it was about to divide asunder.* There were whirlwinds and earthquakes. The storm lasted only three hours, but it caused massive destruction in all the land. The land southward (where the Nephites and Lamanites lived) saw *great and terrible destruction,* but in the land northward (where the Jaredites had once lived), *the whole face of the land was changed.*

> *And the highways were broken up, and the level roads were spoiled, and many smooth places became rough.*
> *And behold, the rocks were rent in twain; they were broken up upon the face of the whole earth, insomuch that they were found in broken fragments, and in seams and in cracks, upon all the face of the land.* (3 Nephi 8:13, 18)

Samuel the Lamanite had prophesied many years before that when the Savior was crucified, if the people had not repented, many of their cities would become *desolate.* By the time the storm was over, sixteen cities were completely destroyed, along with all their inhabitants. Some of these cities had been burned; others were sunk into the depths of the sea. Many cities were swallowed by the earth and covered with valleys or hills and, as in the case of the city of Moronihah, even covered by a *great mountain.*

> *And many [cities] were shaken till the buildings thereof had fallen to the earth, and the inhabitants thereof were slain, and the places were left desolate.* (3 Nephi 8:14)

Not all the cities were destroyed, but those that remained were heavily damaged and many lives were lost. There were people who were carried away in a whirlwind, never to be seen again.

To some, the storm seemed to last a very long time; *nevertheless, all these great and terrible things were done in about the space of three hours.* Then there was darkness upon the face of the land, so thick that the people *could feel the vapor of darkness.* No fires could be kindled; not even a candle could be lit. No light could be seen from the sun, moon, or stars, *for so great were the mists of darkness.*

> *And it came to pass that it did last for the space of three days that there was no light seen; and there was great mourning and howling and weeping among all the people continually; yea, great were the groanings of the people, because of the darkness and the great destruction which had come upon them.* (3 Nephi 8:23)

The people were overcome with guilt and sorrow. If they had just repented *before this great and terrible day,* their friends and loved ones who died during the violent storm might have been spared.

·78·

A VOICE FROM THE DARKNESS
3 NEPHI 9–10

As the people were weeping in the darkness, the voice of the Savior was suddenly heard by every inhabitant of the land—*Wo, wo, wo unto this people . . . except they shall repent.* He told them that the devil was laughing and his angels were rejoicing because his *fair sons and daughters* had been slain; *and it is because of their iniquity and abominations that they are fallen.*

The Lord then named the cities he destroyed, telling how each met its fate: The city of Zarahemla and all of its people were burned with fire. The city of Moroni was sunk in the sea, drowning all who lived there. The city of Moronihah and all of its inhabitants were covered with earth. The city of Gilgal was sunk, burying all of the people in *the depths of the earth.* For the cities of Onihah, Mocum, and Jerusalem, waters came *up in the stead thereof.* The cities of Gadiandi, Gadiomnah, Jacob, and Gimgimno were sunk, and *hills and valleys [were made] in the places thereof,* burying all the inhabitants.

And behold that great city Jacobugath . . . I caused to be burned with fire. This was the city founded by king Jacob, the leader of the secret combination, after he led his people up to the land northward (see 3 Nephi 7:9–13). The Savior explained why he destroyed the city of Jacobugath:

> *Their sins and their wickedness . . . was above all the wickedness of the whole earth, because of their secret murders and combinations; for it was they that did destroy the peace of my people and the government of the land.* (3 Nephi 9:9)

The cities of Laman, Josh, Gad, and Kishkumen and all their inhabitants were burned with fire because they had stoned the prophets sent to tell them of their wickedness, leaving *none righteous among them.*

After naming each city and its fate, the Lord almost always added words similar to these explaining why he destroyed them:

> . . . *that their wickedness and abominations might be hid from before my face, that the blood of the prophets and the saints whom I sent among them might not cry unto me from the ground against them.* (3 Nephi 9:11)

The Lord then told the people that they were spared because they were *more* righteous than those he had slain. He implored them to return unto him and repent of their sins so he could heal them. They were promised eternal life if they would come unto him. Then he identified himself to the people:

> *Behold, I am Jesus Christ the Son of God. I created the heavens and the earth, and all things that in them are . . . and in me hath the Father glorified his name.*
> *I came unto my own, and my own received me not. And the scriptures concerning my coming are fulfilled.* (3 Nephi 9:15–16)

Sacrifices and burnt offerings were now done away, replaced by the covenant to offer to God a sacrifice of *a broken heart and a contrite spirit.*

> *Therefore, whoso repenteth and cometh unto me as a little child, him will I receive, for of such is the kingdom of God.* (3 Nephi 9:22)

The Savior stopped speaking and all was quiet for many hours. People from all across the land had heard his voice *and did witness of it.* They were so astonished *that they did cease lamenting and howling* for their loved ones who had been slain. Then the voice of the Savior broke the silence as he spoke about all the slain people of the cities he destroyed:

> *O ye people of these great cities which have fallen, . . . who are of the house of Israel, how oft* **have** *I gathered you as a hen gathereth her chickens under her wings, and have nourished you.* (3 Nephi 10:4)

The Lord repeated his words a second time, saying instead how often **would** he have gathered them, but they *would not.* Then he repeated his words a third time, directing his words to those who had been spared, saying how often **will** he gather them yet, if they would repent and return unto him *with full purpose of heart.*

When the Savior finished speaking, the people began to weep and howl again for their loved ones who had been slain.

> *And it came to pass that thus did the three days pass away. And it was in the morning, and the darkness dispersed from off the face of the land, and the earth did cease to tremble, and the rocks did cease to rend, and the dreadful groanings did cease, and all the tumultuous noises did pass away.* (3 Nephi 10:9)

The people stopped their weeping and wailing, and *their mourning was turned into joy* as they praised their Redeemer, Jesus Christ.

·79·

THE SAVIOR APPEARS

3 NEPHI 11–12

A few key passages of scripture suggest that many months passed after the people heard the Savior's voice in the darkness before he actually appeared to them. In 3 Nephi 8:5 it says that the great storm came on the fourth day of the **first** month in the thirty-fourth year. In 3 Nephi 10:18 it says that at the **end** of the thirty-fourth year, the Nephites *did have great favors shown unto them, and great blessings poured out upon their heads.* What could have been greater than when Christ came and ministered unto them? There are a few points to consider which make it more likely that Christ came many months later. First of all, after such massive destruction it would take time for the people to take care of their immediate needs, such as attending to the injured, burying their dead, and procuring food and shelter, before they could gather at the temple. It would also take time to recover from their state of shock before they would be in a frame of mind able to comprehend the Savior's teachings. Remember, not only had they lived through catastrophic events and lost loved ones, they had spent three days in complete and total darkness.

During the first day of the Savior's visit, he told them to go back to their homes and ponder upon the things he had said. Would they all have had homes if Christ's appearance immediately followed the devastation?

In 3 Nephi 23:7–13 the Savior asks why it had not been recorded that many saints arose from the dead and appeared unto many at the time of his resurrection. Then he commanded it to be done. How could the Lord have expected this to have been recorded if it had just happened?

A great multitude of people had gathered around the temple in the land of Bountiful. (The group consisted of people from both Nephite and Lamanite descent. It would be another hundred years before a small part of the people would revolt from the church and use the name *Lamanites.* See 4 Nephi 1:17, 20.)

The people were in a state of wonderment as they looked upon the great changes that had taken place in the land. They talked about Jesus Christ and how *the sign had been given concerning his death.*

> *And it came to pass that while they were thus conversing one with another, they heard a voice as if it came out of heaven; and they cast their eyes round about, for they understood not the voice which they heard; and it was not a harsh voice, neither was it a loud voice; nevertheless, . . . it did pierce them to the very soul, and did cause their hearts to burn.* (3 Nephi 11:3)

The voice was heard again, but still they did not understand it. When the voice was heard a third time, the people listened intently and looked toward heaven. This time they understood the marvelous declaration:

> *Behold my Beloved Son, in whom I am well pleased, in whom I have glorified my name—hear ye him.* (3 Nephi 11:7)

As the people gazed upward, they saw a man clothed in a white robe descend out of heaven. Every eye turned to him as he came and stood in the midst of them. He stretched forth his hand and spoke, telling them that he was Jesus Christ, of whom the prophets had testified. He said he was *the light and the life of the world* and that he had glorified the Father by taking upon him the sins of the world. When Jesus had spoken these words, the whole multitude fell to the earth. They remembered that it had been prophesied that the Savior would show himself unto them after his resurrection. Then the Lord spoke to them again, saying:

> *Arise and come forth unto me, that ye may thrust your hands into my side, and also that ye may feel the prints of the nails in my hands and in my feet, that ye may know that I am the God of Israel, and the God of the whole earth, and have been slain for the sins of the world.* (3 Nephi 11:14)

The multitude went forth one by one, thrusting their hands into his side and feeling the prints of the nails in his hands and feet, until every person was able to have a sure witness that he was indeed the Christ. Then the people fell at his feet and worshipped him, crying, *Hosanna! Blessed be the name of the Most High God!*

The prophet Nephi was in the multitude, and Jesus commanded him to come forth. The Lord gave Nephi the authority to baptize. Others were chosen, making twelve disciples in all who were given the authority to baptize. They were told the exact manner in which they were to perform this ordinance so there would be *no disputations* among them. First the person had to repent of his sins and have a desire to be baptized in the name of Christ. Then the one having authority was to stand in the water with the person and, after first calling that person by name, was to say these words:

> *Having authority given me of Jesus Christ, I baptize you in the name of the Father, and of the Son, and of the Holy Ghost. Amen.*
> (3 Nephi 11:25)

The person being baptized was then to be immersed in the water and brought back up. The disciples were admonished that from this point on there were to be no more disputations among the people concerning baptism or any other points of his doctrine, *for he that hath the spirit of contention is not of me, but is of the devil.* Then the Lord explained the essence of his doctrine:

> *Ye must repent, and be baptized in my name, and become as a little child, or ye can in nowise inherit the kingdom of God.* (3 Nephi 11:38)

The twelve disciples were commanded to go among the people, teaching the words of Christ *unto the ends of the earth.* The Lord turned to the multitude and told them to *give heed* unto the words of his chosen disciples. He also told them that after they had been baptized with water by one of the twelve, he would baptize them *with fire and with the Holy Ghost.*

·80·

THE SERMON ON THE MOUNT PART I

3 NEPHI 12

Note: The next two chapters of *And It Came to Pass* cover a discourse given by the Savior to the Nephites. This same discourse is also found in the biblical account of Christ's ministry to the Jews and is commonly referred to as the Sermon on the Mount. Elder Bruce R. McConkie, who was a member of the Twelve Apostles of the current dispensation and one of the foremost scripturians of our time, gives us a clearer understanding of the different recorded accounts of this sermon: "Latter-day Saints have four scripturally recorded versions of this sermon—in Third Nephi, in Luke, in Matthew, and in the Inspired Version of Matthew. . . . All four of these versions follow the same general pattern, present the same general truths, and do it in the same sequence. But in certain particulars, there are radical variations between all versions. Undoubtedly all are accounts of the same sermon, but all are abridgments only, and the same truths were not abridged in every particular into each of the accounts. The most comprehensive and complete report is in the Matthew-Inspired Version record."[1] For purposes of this book, only selective passages of the Savior's discourse are included, with sometimes an added interpretation by one of the General Authorities. All quotations from Elder McConkie are found in volume 1 of his *Doctrinal New Testament Commentary*.

Yea, blessed are the poor in spirit who come unto me, for theirs is the kingdom of heaven. (3 Nephi 12:3)

Elder McConkie defines the *poor in spirit* as "those who are humble and contrite, . . . who are devoid of pride, self-righteousness, and self-conceit."[2]

And again, blessed are all they that mourn, for they shall be comforted.

And blessed are the meek, for they shall inherit the earth. (3 Nephi 12:4–5)

Defining *the meek* as "the godfearing and the righteous," Elder McConkie explains that to *inherit the earth* refers not to our day, "but in that coming day when the earth is sanctified, cleansed from all unrighteousness, and prepared for celestial glory."[3]

And blessed are all they who do hunger and thirst after righteousness, for they shall be filled with the Holy Ghost.

And blessed are the merciful, for they shall obtain mercy.

And blessed are all the pure in heart, for they shall see God. (3 Nephi 12:6–8)

The promise given—the pure in heart shall see God—is clarified by Elder McConkie. It "is to be understood literally. Every living soul who is pure in heart shall see God, literally and personally, in this life, to say nothing of the fact that he shall dwell with and see him frequently in the celestial world hereafter."[4]

And blessed are all the peacemakers, for they shall be called the children of God. (3 Nephi 12:9)

According to Elder McConkie, "In the full sense, only those who believe and spread the fulness of the gospel are peacemakers within the perfect meaning of this Beatitude. The Gospel is the message of peace to all mankind."[5]

Verily, verily, I say unto you, I give unto you to be the salt of the earth. (3 Nephi 12:13)

"Members of the Church have power to become the salt of the earth," teaches Elder McConkie, "that is, to be the seasoning, savoring, preserving influence in the world, the influence which would bring peace and blessings to all others."[6]

Verily, verily, I say unto you, I give unto you to be the light of this people. A city that is set on a hill cannot be hid.

Behold, do men light a candle and put it under a bushel? Nay, but on a candlestick, and it giveth light to all that are in the house;

Therefore let your light so shine before this people, that they may see your good works and glorify your Father who is in heaven. (3 Nephi 12:14–16)

Ye have heard that it hath been said by them of old time . . . that thou shalt not kill. . . .

But I say unto you, that whosoever is angry with his brother shall be in danger of his judgment. (3 Nephi 12:21–22)

"The gospel does more than prohibit and punish," explains Elder McConkie; "it seeks to remove the cause of murder so that men living by the higher standard will not harden themselves to the point of being able to take life."[7]

Behold it is written by them of old time, that thou shalt not commit adultery;

But I say unto you, that whosoever looketh on a woman, to lust after her, hath committed adultery already in his heart. (3 Nephi 12:27–28)

We are reminded by Elder McConkie that "adulterous acts are committed mentally before the physical debauchery ever takes place, and sensual and evil thoughts are in themselves a debasing evil."[8]

And again it is written, thou shalt not forswear thyself, but shalt perform unto the Lord thine oaths;

But verily, verily, I say unto you, swear not at all. . . .

But let your communication be Yea, yea; Nay, nay; for whatsoever cometh of more than these is evil. (3 Nephi 12:33, 34, 37)

This passage of scripture refers to the ancient practice of taking oaths in order to prove your word or verify that you would keep your promise. Elder McConkie explains that "Jesus revealed a higher standard relative to truthfulness in conversation. It was simply that Yea meant Yea, and Nay meant Nay, and that no oath was required to establish the verity of any promise or thing. Every man's every word was to be as true and accurate as if it had been spoken with an oath."[9]

And if any man will sue thee at the law and take away thy coat, let him have thy cloak also;
And whosoever shall compel thee to go a mile, go with him twain.
Give to him that asketh thee, and from him that would borrow of thee turn thou not away. (3 Nephi 12:40–42)

Elder McConkie quotes James E. Talmage here, who said: "These instructions were directed primarily to the apostles. . . . In their ministry it would be better to suffer material loss or personal indignity and imposition at the hands of wicked oppressors, than to bring about an impairment of efficiency and a hindrance in work through resistance and contention."[10]

And behold it is written also, that thou shalt love thy neighbor and hate thine enemy;
But behold I say unto you, love your enemies, bless them that curse you, do good to them that hate you, and pray for them who despitefully use you and persecute you;
Therefore I would that ye should be perfect even as I, or your Father who is in heaven is perfect. (3 Nephi 12:43, 44, 48)

President Joseph Fielding Smith gives us hope concerning the Lord's charge to be perfect: "I believe the Lord meant just what he said: that we should be perfect, as our Father in heaven is perfect. That will not come all at once, but line upon line, and precept upon precept, example upon example, and even then not as long as we live in this mortal life, for we will have to go even beyond the grave before we reach that perfection and shall be like God."[11]

Notes
1. Bruce R. McConkie, *Doctrinal New Testament Commentary* (Salt Lake City, Utah: Bookcraft, 1979), 1:214.
2. Ibid., 215.
3. Ibid., 215.
4. Ibid., 216; see also D&C 93:1; D&C 67:10–14.
5. Ibid., 216.
6. Ibid., 218.
7. Ibid., 222.
8. Ibid., 223–24.
9. Ibid., 226.
10. Ibid., 228.
11. Quoted in Bruce R. McConkie, *Doctrines of Salvation* (Salt Lake City, Utah: Bookcraft, 1982), 2:18.

·81·

THE SERMON ON THE MOUNT
PART II
3 NEPHI 13–14

Verily, verily, I say that I would that ye should do alms unto the poor; but take heed that ye do not your alms before men to be seen of them; otherwise ye have no reward of your Father who is in heaven.

Therefore, when ye shall do your alms do not sound a trumpet before you, as will hypocrites do in the synagogues and in the streets, that they may have glory of men. Verily I say unto you, they have their reward. (3 Nephi 13:1–2)

If ye forgive men their trespasses your heavenly Father will also forgive you;

But if ye forgive not men their trespasses neither will your Father forgive your trespasses. (3 Nephi 13:14–15)

Lay not up for yourselves treasures upon earth, where moth and rust doth corrupt, and thieves break through and steal;

But lay up for yourselves treasures in heaven. . . .

For where your treasure is, there will your heart be also. (3 Nephi 13:19–21)

In Elder McConkie's words, earthly treasures are such things as "money, clothes, jewels, houses, lands, property, business enterprises, honors bestowed by men, social affiliations, and political positions. All these fade away when life ends. . . . Those who gain such attributes of godliness as knowledge, faith, justice, judgment, mercy, and truth will find these same attributes restored to them again in immortality"[1] *No man can serve two masters; for either he will hate the one and love the other, or else he will hold to the one and despise the other. Ye cannot serve God and Mammon. (3 Nephi 13:24)*

"*Mammon* is an Aramaic word for riches," explains Elder McConkie. "Thus Jesus is saying, 'Ye cannot serve God and riches, or worldliness, which always results from the love of money.' "[2]

> *Take no thought for your life, what ye shall eat, or what ye shall drink; nor yet for your body, what ye shall put on. . . .*
> *For your heavenly Father knoweth that ye have need of all these things.*
> *But seek ye first the kingdom of God and his righteousness, and all these things shall be added unto you.* (3 Nephi 13:25, 32–33)

Elder McConkie clarifies that Jesus was giving this counsel to those engaged in missionary work and not to the Church generally. "For the time and season of their missionary service they are to have no concern about business enterprises or temporal pursuits."[3] The last verse of the preceding passage applies to everyone.

> *Verily, verily, I say unto you, Judge not, that ye be not judged.*
> *For with what judgment ye judge, ye shall be judged; and with what measure ye mete, it shall be measured to you again.* (3 Nephi 14:1–2)

We are taught by Elder McConkie that "this is not a prohibition against sitting in judgment either on one's fellowmen or upon principles of right and wrong, for the saints are commanded to do these very things. The sense and meaning of our Lord's utterance is, 'Condemn not, that ye be not condemned.' It is, 'Judge wisely and righteously, so that ye may be judged in like manner.' "[4]

> *Give not that which is holy unto the dogs, neither cast ye your pearls before swine.* (3 Nephi 14:6)

In this scripture, Elder McConkie explains that Jesus is counseling his disciples "to refrain from presenting more of the truths of the gospel than their hearers are prepared to receive." As an example, Elder McConkie uses the sacred teachings revealed in temple ordinances. These are to be "reserved for selected and faithful members of the kingdom who have attained sufficient stability and background to understand them."[5]

Ask, and it shall be given unto you; seek, and ye shall find; knock, and it shall be opened unto you. (3 Nephi 14:7)

Enter ye in at the strait gate; for wide is the gate, and broad is the way, which leadeth to destruction, and many there be who go in thereat;

Because strait is the gate, and narrow is the way, which leadeth unto life, and few there be that find it. (3 Nephi 14:13–14)

The word *strait* in the above scripture means "narrow, strict, or exact." Elder McConkie teaches us that "baptism is the strait gate which puts men on the path leading to the celestial world; [temple marriage] is the strait gate which starts men and women out in the direction of exaltation in the highest heaven of that world."[6]

Beware of false prophets, who come to you in sheep's clothing, but inwardly they are ravening wolves. (3 Nephi 14:15)

Elder McConkie quotes Joseph Smith to illuminate this verse: "False prophets always arise to oppose the true prophets, and they will prophesy so very near the truth that they will deceive almost the very chosen ones."[7]

Not every one that saith unto me, Lord, Lord, shall enter into the kingdom of heaven; but he that doeth the will of my Father who is in heaven. (3 Nephi 14:21)

Elder McConkie quotes the third article of faith to help us understand what the Lord means here: "We believe that through the Atonement of Christ, all mankind may be saved, by obedience to the laws and ordinances of the Gospel."[8] Merely giving lip service is not enough.

Therefore, whoso heareth these sayings of mine and doeth them, I will liken him unto a wise man, who built his house upon a rock—

And the rain descended, and the floods came, and the winds blew, and beat upon that house; and it fell not, for it was founded upon a rock.

And every one that heareth these sayings of mine and doeth them not shall be likened unto a foolish man, who built his house upon the sand.

And the rain descended, and the floods came, and the winds blew, and beat upon that house; and it fell, and great was the fall of it. (3 Nephi 14:24–27)

Elder McConkie teaches us that "those who build their houses of faith on the rock of revelation, rather than on the sands of sectarian delusion, shall have a spiritual structure able to withstand every temptation and turmoil."[9]

Notes

1. Bruce R. McConkie, *Doctrinal New Testament Commentary* (Salt Lake City, Utah: Bookcraft, 1979), 1:239.
2. Ibid., 240.
3. Ibid., 243.
4. Ibid., 245.
5. Ibid., 248–9.
6. Ibid., 250.
7. Ibid., 252.
8. Ibid., 254.
9. Ibid., 255.

·82·

"OTHER SHEEP I HAVE"

3 NEPHI 15–17

After listening to the Savior's teachings, many of the Nephites became confused as to what would now happen to the law of Moses. (This law had been given to Moses to prepare the people for the greater truths that Jesus would bring and did not contain the fulness of the gospel.) Jesus explained to them:

> *Behold, I am he that gave the law, and I am he who covenanted with my people Israel; therefore, the law in me is fulfilled, for I have come to fulfil the law; therefore it hath an end.* (3 Nephi 15:5)

Jesus then spoke about their brethren at Jerusalem and how those people had never been told about the people who had been led to the New World. They had been kept from this knowledge because *of their iniquity.*

> *And verily I say unto you, that **ye** are they of whom I said: Other sheep I have which are not of this fold; them also I must bring, and they shall hear my voice; and there shall be one fold, and one shepherd.* (3 Nephi 15:21; see also John 10:16)

Jesus explained that when the brethren in Jerusalem heard this, they thought the "other sheep" referred to the Gentiles (those not of the house of Israel), not understanding *that the Gentiles should be converted through their preaching.*

Jesus continued his discourse on this subject by revealing that there was yet another group of people who fell under this category of *other sheep.* (The footnotes to the following scripture refer to the ten lost tribes of Israel.)

> *And verily, verily, I say unto you that I have other sheep, which are not of this land, neither of the land of Jerusalem, neither in any parts of that land round about whither I have been to minister.*

> *For they of whom I speak are they who have not as yet heard my voice; neither have I at any time manifested myself unto them.*
>
> *But I have received a commandment of the Father that I shall go unto them, and that they shall hear my voice, and shall be numbered among my sheep, that there may be one fold and one shepherd; therefore I go to show myself unto them.* (3 Nephi 16:1–3)

Jesus taught that in the latter days (referring to the time after the restoration of the gospel) it would be the Gentiles who would receive the fulness of the truth. Through them his teachings would once again be restored to the Jewish people, of whom the Lamanites are a remnant.

Jesus looked around at the multitude and told them it was time for him to return to the Father. He could see that they were too weak to understand all the words he had been commanded to speak unto them. He told them to go back to their homes and *ponder* upon the things he had said and pray unto the Father for understanding. They were to *prepare [their] minds for the morrow* when he would come again.

> *But now I go unto the Father, and also to show myself unto the lost tribes of Israel, for they are not lost unto the Father, for he knoweth whither he hath taken them.*
>
> *And it came to pass that when Jesus had thus spoken, he cast his eyes round about again on the multitude, and beheld they were in tears, and did look steadfastly upon him as if they would ask him to tarry a little longer with them.* (3 Nephi 17:4–5)

Jesus was filled with compassion and asked them to bring their sick to him so he might heal them.

> *Have ye any that are lame, or blind, or halt, or maimed, or leprous, or that are withered, or that are deaf, or that are afflicted in any manner? . . .*
>
> *For I perceive that ye desire that I should show unto you what I have done unto your brethren at Jerusalem, for I see that your faith is sufficient that I should heal you.* (3 Nephi 17:7–8)

With one accord the multitude brought forth all those with afflictions among them, and Jesus healed them. Then everyone bowed down at his feet and worshipped him, and as many as were able *did kiss his feet . . . [and] did bathe his feet with their tears.*

Jesus commanded that their little children be brought to him. *The multitude gave way* until all the children were sitting upon the ground around Jesus. Jesus asked the multitude to kneel, and then he began to pray.

> *And after this manner do they bear record: The eye hath never seen, neither hath the ear heard, before, so great and marvelous things as we saw and heard Jesus speak unto the Father;*
> *And no tongue can speak, neither can there be written by any man, neither can the hearts of men conceive so great and marvelous things as we both saw and heard Jesus speak; and no one can conceive of the joy which filled our souls at the time we heard him pray for us unto the Father.* (3 Nephi 17:16–17)

When Jesus finished praying he arose, and then one by one he blessed each child *and prayed unto the Father for them.* Jesus turned to the multitude and said unto them, *Behold your little ones.* Suddenly, the heavens opened *and they saw angels descending out of heaven as it were in the midst of fire.* The angels gathered around the children and ministered unto them, *and they were encircled about with fire.*

The next day, after more people had gathered at the temple to hear Jesus, the following experience with the children took place:

> *And [the children] did speak unto their fathers great and marvelous things, even greater than he had revealed unto the people; and he loosed their tongues that they could utter.*
> *. . . And they both saw and heard these children; yea, even babes did open their mouths and utter marvelous things; and the things which they did utter were forbidden that there should not any man write them.* (3 Nephi 26:14, 16)

The multitude numbered about twenty-five hundred men, women, and children, and they *did see and hear and bear record* of the glorious events of that day.

·83·

The Sacrament Is Instituted
3 NEPHI 18–24

Jesus sent his disciples for bread and wine. When they returned, he broke the bread and blessed it and passed it to the multitude. Then the wine was passed. (The sacramental prayers are found in Moroni, chapters 4 and 5.)

The following admonition was given by the Savior concerning the ordinance of the sacrament: No one should *knowingly* partake of the sacrament unworthily; otherwise he *eateth and drinketh damnation to his soul.* As to those who are not worthy to partake of the sacrament, Jesus cautioned his twelve disciples not to cast them out but to minister unto them, *for ye know not but what they will return and repent.*

The multitude was counseled by the Savior to *watch and pray always.*

> And whatsoever ye shall ask the Father in my name, which is right, believing that ye shall receive, behold it shall be given unto you. (3 Nephi 18:20)

A great many things had been taught on this first day of the Savior's visit, but it was now time for Jesus to return to the Father. Before he left he gave each disciple the *power to give the Holy Ghost.* Then a cloud came down and *overshadowed the multitude,* and Jesus *departed from them and ascended into heaven.*

The people returned to their homes but immediately began spreading the good news: Jesus had come and ministered unto them and would be returning on the morrow! All that night *it was noised abroad concerning Jesus,* so that by the next day an even greater multitude had gathered to await the arrival of their Savior. There were so many people that they were divided into twelve groups and each group was taught by one of the disciples.

The disciples walked down to the water's edge and the multitude followed them. Nephi went down into the water and was baptized, and then he baptized the other eleven disciples. When they had all come out of the water, *the Holy Ghost did fall upon them.*

> *And behold, they were encircled about as if it were by fire; and it came down from heaven, and the multitude did witness it, and did bear record; and angels did come down out of heaven and did minister unto them.* (3 Nephi 19:14)

Suddenly Jesus was in their midst, and he had all the people kneel. Then he instructed the disciples to pray, and *it was given unto them what they should pray, and they were filled with desire.* Jesus also prayed, and the multitude bore witness that his words were *so great and marvelous . . . that they cannot be written, neither can they be uttered by man.*

Jesus told his disciples that he had not seen such great faith among the Jews. Because of the *unbelief* of the Jews, they had not been shown the great miracles that the Nephites had seen.

Just as had been done the day before, Jesus administered the sacrament to them. This time there was no bread or wine brought by the disciples or the multitude; Jesus miraculously produced it.

The Savior went on to teach many things to the Nephites, such as the great gathering of his covenant people that would take place in the latter days and events that would precede his second coming. He quoted from the prophet Isaiah and commanded the people to search his words (which they had from the brass plates of Laban), *for great are the words of Isaiah.*

Nephi was asked to bring forth the record that had been kept. Jesus reminded them of the prophecy that Samuel the Lamanite made many years earlier—that at the time of his resurrection there would be *many saints who should arise from the dead, and should appear unto many, and should minister unto them.* The disciples confirmed that Samuel's words had all been fulfilled. Then the Savior asked why these things had not been recorded and commanded that it be done.

The Savior quoted many of the words of the prophet Malachi and directed that they be recorded also.

[Daniel H. Ludlow explains: "Malachi, the last writer in our present Old Testament, lived approximately 400 BC. Since his writings were not included on the brass plates of Laban, the Savior gave the words of Malachi to the Nephites."[1]

Included in these writings was this great counsel about tithing:

> *Will a man rob God? Yet ye have robbed me. But ye say: Wherein have we robbed thee? In tithes and offerings.*
>
> *Bring ye all the tithes into the storehouse, that there may be meat in my house; and prove me now herewith, saith the Lord of Hosts, if I will not open you the windows of heaven, and pour you out a blessing that there shall not be room enough to receive it.* (3 Nephi 24:8, 10)

Jesus admonished the people to *give heed* to his words and write them all down. He said that at some future time this record (meaning the Book of Mormon) would *go forth unto the Gentiles.*

Notes

1.   *A Companion to Your Study of the Book of Mormon* (Salt Lake City, Utah: Deseret Book, 1976), 283.

·84·

THE THREE NEPHITES
3 NEPHI 26–29

And now there cannot be written in this book even a hundredth part of the things which Jesus did truly teach unto the people. (3 Nephi 26:6)

The Savior spent three days teaching the multitudes and then returned to his Father in Heaven. He made several appearances to the people after this and *did break bread oft.*

The disciples carried on the work they had been called to, baptizing and teaching *as many as did come unto them.* The people followed all of the commandments Jesus had given them.

And they had all things common among them, every man dealing justly, one with another. (3 Nephi 26:19)

One day when the disciples were gathered together and *united in mighty prayer and fasting,* Jesus appeared unto them and asked what they desired. They asked him by what name the church should be called, because there had been disputations among the people concerning this. In answer to their question, Jesus reminded them of the scriptures that say that we must take upon ourselves the name of Christ. Therefore, whatsoever we do should be in his name, he said, including calling the church after him.

And how be it my church save it be called in my name? For if a church be called in Moses' name then it be Moses' church; or if it be called in the name of a man then it be the church of a man; but if it be called in my name then it is my church, if it so be that they are built upon my gospel. (3 Nephi 27:8)

When it came time for Jesus to leave again, he gave each of his disciples the opportunity to request a specific blessing. One by one, Jesus asked them what it was that they desired of him after he was gone to the Father.

> *And they all spake, save it were three, saying: We desire that after we have lived unto the age of man, that our ministry, wherein thou hast called us, may have an end, that we may speedily come unto thee in thy kingdom.* (3 Nephi 28:2)

Jesus was pleased at their request and told them that when they were each seventy-two years old, he would bring them back into his kingdom where they would find rest. Then he turned to the other three and asked what it was they wanted. *They sorrowed in their hearts* and dared not tell Jesus their request, but he knew their thoughts. They wanted what John the Beloved had been granted. John was one of Christ's apostles in Jerusalem who had asked that he might not die but continue ministering to the people until Christ's return. These three Nephites were granted this same desire.

> *Therefore, more blessed are ye, for ye shall never taste of death; but ye shall live to behold all the doings of the Father unto the children of men, even until all things shall be fulfilled . . . , when I shall come in my glory with the powers of heaven.* (3 Nephi 28:7)

Jesus explained more of this marvelous blessing: They would never endure the pains of death, but when he returned in his glory they would be changed *in the twinkling of an eye* from mortality to immortality. They would not experience pain or sorrow while they sojourned on the earth, except for the sins of the world. They too would inherit the Father's kingdom. Jesus touched each of the disciples with his finger, except for the three *who were to tarry,* and then departed.

> *And behold, the heavens were opened, and [the three Nephites] were caught up into heaven, and saw and heard unspeakable things.*
>
> *And whether they were in the body or out of the body, they could not tell; for it did seem unto them like a transfiguration of them, that they were changed from this body of flesh into an immortal state, that they could behold the things of God.* (3 Nephi 28:13, 15)

Because the prophet Mormon, our narrator, had access to later records, he interjects several interesting facts about the Three Nephites:

- They went forth preaching all across the land, baptizing people into the church.
- They were cast into prison but freed as the prison walls were broken apart.
- They were delivered out of deep pits by the power of God; *therefore [their enemies] could not dig pits sufficient to hold them.*
- Three times they were cast into a fiery furnace, yet received no harm.
- Twice they were cast into a den of wild beasts and *did play with the beasts as a child with a suckling lamb.*
- Mormon saw them, and they ministered unto him.
- *They will be among the Gentiles, and the Gentiles shall know them not. They will also be among the Jews, and the Jews shall know them not.* (3 Nephi 28:27–28)
- Satan could have no power over them.

Mormon gives a stern warning to all who will not hearken to the words of Jesus or to those whom Jesus has sent:

> *It would be better for them if they had not been born. For do ye suppose that ye can get rid of the justice of an offended God, who hath been trampled under the feet of men, that thereby salvation might come?* (3 Nephi 28:35)

> *Yea, wo unto him that shall deny the revelations of the Lord, and that shall say the Lord no longer worketh by revelation, or by prophecy, or by gifts, or by tongues, or by healings, or by the power of the Holy Ghost!* (3 Nephi 29:6)

·85·

A SEASON OF RIGHTEOUSNESS
4 NEPHI

And it came to pass in the thirty and sixth year [from the time of Christ's birth], the people were all converted unto the Lord, upon all the face of the land, both Nephites and Lamanites, and there were no contentions and disputations among them, and every man did deal justly one with another. (4 Nephi 1:2)

The Lord blessed the people and they prospered in the land. They had *all things common among them*, and so there was no distinction between rich and poor. The disciples went about performing great miracles such as healing the sick, raising the dead, causing the lame to walk, and restoring sight to the blind and hearing to the deaf.

The people quickly increased in numbers and became *an exceedingly fair and delightsome people*. They rebuilt many of the cities that had been burned, including *that great city Zarahemla*. They lived righteously, keeping the new commandments the Savior had given them. The disciples continued to perform mighty miracles among the people, and there was peace throughout all the land.

Before one hundred years passed away (the scriptural account is counting time from the birth of Christ), all the disciples Jesus had chosen had returned *to the paradise of God*, except the three who had been allowed to tarry. As each disciple died, another was ordained to replace him. The land was free of contention *because of the love of God which did dwell in the hearts of the people.*

> *Surely there could not be a happier people among all the people who had been created by the hand of God.*
> *There were no robbers, nor murderers, neither were there Lamanites, nor any manner of -ites; but they were in one, the children of Christ, and heirs to the kingdom of God.* (4 Nephi 1:16–17)

In the two hundred and first year, the righteousness of the people began its fateful descent. The people were spread upon all the face of the land and had become *exceedingly rich*. There were those among them who were lifted up in pride, wearing *costly apparel, and all manner of fine pearls*. They separated their possessions, no longer having all things common among them, and were divided into classes. Many denied the true church of Christ and built churches *unto themselves to get gain*.

A few years prior to the two hundredth year, a small part of the people revolted from the church, taking upon themselves the name of Lamanites. *Therefore there began to be Lamanites again in the land.*

By the year 211, many different churches had sprung up. Some claimed to know Christ and yet denied most of his teachings. One church denied the Christ and persecuted the true church, despising the members *because of the many miracles which were wrought among them*. The Three Nephites, who had tarried from the time of Christ, were also subjected to the *power and authority* of the unrighteous. Even after seeing the miracle of the disciples being delivered from harm time and again, the people still hardened their hearts and sought to kill them. *And thus they did dwindle in unbelief and wickedness from year to year.*

> *And now it came to pass . . . in the two hundred and thirty and first year, there was a great division among the people.*
> *. . . In this year there arose a people who were called the Nephites, and they were true believers in Christ. . . .*
> *And it came to pass that they who rejected the gospel were called Lamanites, and Lemuelites, and Ishmaelites; . . . and they did teach their children that they should not believe. . . .*
> *. . . And they were taught to hate the children of God, even as the Lamanites were taught to hate the children of Nephi from the beginning.* (4 Nephi 1:35–36, 38–39)

As time went on, the wicked people became more numerous than the people of God. By the two hundred and sixtieth year, the secret oaths and combinations of Gadianton had again been built up. Among the Nephites, the sin of pride began to show itself because of their great wealth.

> *And from this time the disciples began to sorrow for the sins of the world.* (4 Nephi 1:44)

When three hundred years had passed away, the Nephites and Lamanites were equally wicked. The robbers of Gadianton had spread throughout the land, *and there were none that were righteous save it were the disciples of Jesus.*

In the year AD 321, Ammaron was in charge of all the sacred records that had been handed down from generation to generation. He was *constrained by the Holy Ghost* to hide up the records, where they remained buried for many years until the prophet Mormon took possession of them.

·86·

MORMON COMMANDS THE NEPHITE ARMIES
MORMON 1–2

After hiding the plates, Ammaron came to Mormon, who was just a young boy of about ten. He told Mormon that he perceived him to be *a sober child* and one *quick to observe.* Then he gave him some important instructions: Over the next several years he was to observe the things that happened to the people. When he reached the age of twenty-four, he was to go to the land Antum, to a hill called Shim, and there he would find all the sacred engravings that Ammaron had hidden. He was to remove the plates of Nephi, leaving all the other plates where they were. Upon the plates of Nephi he was to record the previous fourteen years of history.

When Mormon was eleven, his father took him southward to the land of Zarahemla. Buildings covered the land and the people were almost as numerous as *the sand of the sea.*

In the year that Mormon arrived, a war broke out between the Nephites and the Lamanites in the borders of Zarahemla, by the waters of Sidon. The Nephites had gathered an army of more than thirty thousand men and defeated the Lamanites in battle many times during that year. The Lamanites finally withdrew their design, and for the next four years there was peace. Though the people were not at war, *wickedness did prevail upon the face of the whole land.* The Lord took away his beloved disciples, which brought an end to the work of miracles and healing. Even the Holy Ghost did cease to visit the people because of their unbelief.

> *And I [Mormon], being fifteen years of age and being somewhat of a sober mind, therefore I was visited of the Lord, and tasted and knew of the goodness of Jesus.* (Mormon 1:15)

Mormon had a great desire to preach to the people, but he was forbidden by the Lord because *they had wilfully rebelled against their God.*

> *And it came to pass in that same year there began to be a war again between the Nephites and the Lamanites. And notwithstanding I being young, was large in stature; therefore the people of Nephi appointed me that I should be their leader, or the leader of their armies.* (Mormon 2:1)

Mormon was only in his *sixteenth year* when this great responsibility was given to him. It was now the three hundred and twenty-seventh year since the birth of Christ. The Lamanites came upon them with such power that they frightened the Nephite armies, causing them to retreat toward the lands to the far north that were once inhabited by the Jaredites. Under Mormon's command, his men took possession of the city of Angola and fortified the city. The Lamanites still managed to drive them out. The Nephites fled to the land of David but were driven from there also. Then they marched to the land of Joshua, where they attempted to gather the people into one body as fast as possible. This land was filled with Gadianton robbers and Lamanites. *Notwithstanding the great destruction which hung over my people,* they would not repent of their evil ways.

> *Therefore there was blood and carnage spread throughout all the face of the land, both on the part of the Nephites and also on the part of the Lamanites; and it was one complete revolution throughout all the face of the land.* (Mormon 2:8)

The Lamanites, with their army of forty-four thousand, came to battle against Mormon's forty-two thousand. The Lamanites were finally beaten and fled from the Nephite army.

Samuel the Lamanite had prophesied many years before that their treasures would become "slippery," meaning that the people would not be able to keep them from being lost or stolen. That prophecy was now being fulfilled and the people said their land had been cursed. With the Gadianton robbers infesting the land, and also *the magic art and the witchcraft,* it became necessary for everyone to bury their belongings. There was a great *mourning and lamentation* among the people because of these things, and Mormon mistook this for repentance. He rejoiced, thinking that perhaps they would again become a righteous people.

But behold this my joy was vain, for their sorrowing was not unto repentance, because of the goodness of God; but it was rather the sorrowing of the damned, because the Lord would not always suffer them to take happiness in sin. (Mormon 2:13)

Instead of humbling themselves before the Lord, *they did curse God and wish to die.* Mormon lost hope for his people and could see that *the day of grace was passed with them.*

For I saw thousands of them hewn down in open rebellion against their God, and heaped up as dung upon the face of the land. (Mormon 2:15)

In the three hundred and forty-fifth year, the Lamanites again drove the Nephites from their lands and continued to pursue after them. The Nephites were finally stopped in the land of Jashon, which was close to the land where Ammaron had deposited the plates. Mormon was now twenty-four years old, and he retrieved the plates as he had been instructed. He engraved the last fourteen years of history upon the large plates of Nephi. (The Book of Mormon has only Mormon's abridgment of those plates). He sadly comments that *a continual scene of wickedness and abominations has been before mine eyes ever since I have been sufficient to behold the ways of man.*

The Nephites were driven northward again, until they came to the land of Shem. Here they fortified the city and gathered in the people as much as possible to save them from destruction. As the Lamanites came upon them, Mormon inspired the people to stand and fight for their families and their homes instead of fleeing. The Nephites had an army of thirty thousand to contend with the Lamanites' army of fifty thousand, but they stood with such *firmness* that the Lamanites were the ones to flee this time. Mormon's armies pursued after them and beat them again, gaining back some of their land.

In the three hundred and fiftieth year, the Nephites made a treaty with the Lamanites and the Gadianton robbers in which the lands of their inheritance were divided.

And the Lamanites did give unto us the land northward, yea, even to the narrow passage which led into the land southward. And we did give unto the Lamanites all the land southward. (Mormon 2:29)

·87·

A People without Hope
MORMON 3–5

For ten years there were no wars with the Lamanites, although during this time the Nephites were preparing for the next encounter with them. The Lord gave the Nephites one last chance to save their civilization. Mormon was instructed to tell his people that if they would repent and be baptized and build up the church again that the Lord would spare them. Mormon obeyed, but his preaching was in vain because his people had hardened their hearts against God.

In the three hundred and sixtieth year, Mormon received a letter from the king of the Lamanites, warning that they were preparing to come to battle. He had all his people gather in the land of Desolation, to a city that was *by the narrow pass which led into the land southward.* It was Mormon's plan to place his armies in this narrow pass so the Lamanites would be stopped from gaining possession of any Nephite lands to the north. The Lamanites met them in battle, were beaten, and afterward returned to their own lands. The following year they came again to battle, were again beaten, and their dead were thrown into the sea. Because of their great victory, the Nephites *began to boast in their own strength* and to *swear by the heavens* that they would cut their enemies off from the face of the earth.

> *And it came to pass that I, Mormon, did utterly refuse from this time forth to be a commander and a leader of this people, because of their wickedness and abomination.* (Mormon 3:11)

Mormon reflected that in spite of the wickedness of his people, he had loved them and prayed for them *all the day long,* and three times had delivered them from the hands of their enemies. When his people *had sworn by all that had been forbidden them* to avenge the blood of their brethren, the voice of the Lord came to Mormon telling him *vengeance is mine.* Because the people would not repent after having been delivered from their enemies, the Lord was going to destroy them. Mormon did as the Lord commanded and stood by as an *idle witness* that he might testify unto the world of the destruction of the Nephites.

In the three hundred and sixty-third year, the Nephites left the land of Desolation to go to battle against the Lamanites but were driven back to the land of Desolation. While the Nephites were still weary, a fresh army of Lamanites came upon them and a terrible battle ensued. The Lamanites took possession of the city of Desolation, slaying many of the inhabitants and taking others prisoner. The remainder fled to the city of Teancum, which was near the seashore. Mormon tells us that the Lamanites would have had no power over his people if the Nephites had not gone after the Lamanites. (Once again we are reminded of the Nephite philosophy of war—don't attack the enemy in their own territory if you want the Lord's protection.)

In the three hundred and sixty-fourth year, the Lamanites attacked the city of Teancum but were driven back by the Nephites. The Nephites *did again boast of their own strength,* then drove on and took back the city of Desolation. During these battles, thousands of Nephites and Lamanites were slain.

In the three hundred and sixty-sixth year, the Lamanites succeeded in taking possession of the city of Desolation for the second time because they had the larger army. They continued their march, next taking the city of Teancum, where those who had not been able to flee were taken prisoner. The Lamanites took many of the Nephite women and children and offered them up as a sacrifice *to their idol gods.* The following year, angered that their women and children had been sacrificed, the Nephites went against the Lamanites and drove them out of their lands.

> *And it is impossible for the tongue to describe, or for man to write a perfect description of the horrible scene of the blood and carnage which was among the people.* (Mormon 4:11)

It was not just the Lamanites who were committing acts of depravity. Mormon wrote a letter to his son, Moroni, describing the atrocities that were committed on both sides and said that the wickedness of the Nephites did *exceed that of the Lamanites.* This letter is recorded in Moroni, chapter 9, and verses 7–10 describe the tortuous treatment that the Nephites inflicted upon the daughters of the Lamanites.

The Lamanites waited eight years before coming against the Nephites again, but when they did there were so many of them they could not be numbered.

> *And from this time forth did the Nephites gain no power over the Lamanites, but began to be swept off by them even as a dew before the sun.* (Mormon 4:18)

The Lamanites came to the land Desolation to battle, defeating the Nephites and forcing them to flee to the city of Boaz. The Lamanites pursued after them, but the Nephites were able to maintain the city. When the Lamanites came a second time, the Nephites were driven out and there was *an exceedingly great slaughter.* Again, their women and children were sacrificed to idols. All the inhabitants of the towns and villages in that land left with the fleeing Nephites. Mormon went to the hill Shim and gathered up the sacred records because the Lamanites were about to overthrow the land. At this time Mormon *did repent of the oath which [he] had made that [he] would no more assist them* and offered to lead the Nephite armies once again. They looked to him for deliverance, but he was *without hope* because he knew the judgments of God were already upon them. Mormon and his people fled to the city of Jordan. When the Lamanites came upon them, they were able to drive them back. The Lamanites came again, but still the Nephites held the city. Besides the city of Jordan, there were other cities in this area maintained by Nephites. For a time these strongholds prevented the Lamanites from entering the rest of the Nephite territory to destroy their people. All of the Nephite cities and villages south of these strongholds had been burned by the Lamanites, driving the Nephite people north. Those inhabitants who did not join with the fleeing Nephites were killed.

In the three hundred and eightieth year, as the Lamanites came again to battle, the Nephites stood against them boldly. It did little good because of the vast numbers of their enemies who *did tread the people of the Nephites under their feet.*

> *And it came to pass that we did again take to flight, and those whose flight was swifter than the Lamanites' did escape, and those whose flight did not exceed the Lamanites' were swept down and destroyed.* (Mormon 5:7)

Mormon pauses in his narrative to say that he dares not give a full account of the *awful scene of blood and carnage* that he witnessed, but that a knowledge of these things must be recorded. He explains that when the Lord sees fit, this record (the Book of Mormon) will be brought forth in the latter days for the benefit of three groups of people:

(1) The Jews—*that they may be persuaded that Jesus is the Christ.*

(2) The Lamanites—*that they may more fully believe his gospel* after having been driven and scattered by the Gentiles.

(3) The Gentiles, who will receive the gospel first in the latter days. Through them the gospel will be restored to the Jews and the Lamanites. The Gentiles are warned to repent and turn from their evil ways.

·88·

THE FINAL BATTLE AT CUMORAH
MORMON 6–9

ormon wrote a letter to the king of the Lamanites, asking that he be given the time to gather all his people to the land of Cumorah. There they would be ready for battle by the hill that they also called Cumorah. This request was granted. The hill Cumorah *was in a land of many waters, rivers, and fountains,* and here the Nephites thought they would have the advantage. By the end of the three hundred and eighty-fourth year, Mormon had gathered all of his people to this land.

Mormon was an old man and knew that this would be *the last struggle of [his] people.* He hid all the records that had been entrusted to him in the hill Cumorah, except a few plates that he gave to his son, Moroni.

> *And it came to pass that my people, with their wives and their children, did now behold the armies of the Lamanites marching towards them; and with that awful fear of death which fills the breasts of all the wicked, did they await to receive them.* (Mormon 6:7)

The Nephites were filled with terror as the hordes of Lamanites swarmed upon them with their bows and arrows, swords, and axes. Mormon fell wounded in the midst of the dead, but the Lamanites passed him by. The next day, after the Lamanites had returned to their camps, there were only twenty-four Nephites, including Mormon and his son, Moroni, who had survived the battle! (This is not counting a few Nephites who escaped into the south country and those who had deserted over to the Lamanites.)

From the top of the hill Cumorah they surveyed the scene of death and carnage. Mormon had led ten thousand people in the front of the battle and all had been *hewn* down. They could see that the ten thousand men Moroni led were all dead. Mormon goes on to list all of the other captains who died with their ten thousand each: Gidgiddonah, Lamah, Gilgal, Limhah, Jeneum, Cumenihah, Moronihah, Antionum, Shiblom, Shem, Josh, and *ten more . . . with their ten thousand each.*

The dead were left by their enemies to *molder upon the land, and to crumble and to return to their mother earth.* Mormon's *soul was rent with anguish* as he beheld his slain people, and he cried:

> *O ye fair ones, how could ye have departed from the ways of the Lord! O ye fair ones, how could ye have rejected that Jesus, who stood with open arms to receive you!*
> *But behold, ye are gone, and my sorrows cannot bring your return.* (Mormon 6:17, 20)

The last counsel Mormon gives is directed to the Lamanites of the latter days. He reminds them that they are of the house of Israel and urges them to repent and come unto Christ.

Mormon's son, Moroni, then finishes the record of his father. He tells us that after the great battle at Cumorah, those Nephites who escaped into the south country were hunted by the Lamanites *from city to city and place to place* until they were all destroyed. Only Lamanites and robbers were left to exist. Then the Lamanites turned on each other, bringing *one continual round of murder and bloodshed* upon the face of the land. His description of his solitary plight is one of the most heartrending passages to be found in all of scripture:

> *And my father also was killed by them, and I even remain alone to write the sad tale of the destruction of my people. . . . And whether they will slay me, I know not.*
> *. . . My father hath been slain in battle, and all my kinsfolk, and I have not friends nor whither to go; and how long the Lord will suffer that I may live I know not.* (Mormon 8:3, 5)

Moroni tells us that he will continue to write as long as he is able, and then he will hide the plates in the earth. No one will be able to find them and *bring [the record] to light save it be given him of God.* He explains that the plates themselves will be of no monetary worth, because the Lord will not allow anyone to have them *to get gain.* It is the record on the plates that is of *great worth.*

In the remaining passages that he writes in his father's record, Moroni directs his words to those of us who will be living in the last days.

> *Behold, I speak unto you as if ye were present, and yet ye are not. But behold, Jesus Christ hath shown you unto me, and I know your doing. (Mormon 8:35)*

Moroni describes what it will be like in our day when the gospel is restored:

> *It shall be said that miracles are done away. . . .*
> *The power of God shall be denied. . . .*
> *There shall also be heard of wars, rumors of wars, and earth-quakes in divers places.*
> *There shall be . . . all manner of abominations. . . .*
> *There shall be churches built up that shall say: Come unto me, and for your money you shall be forgiven of your sins.*
> *Ye do love money . . . and your fine apparel, and the adorning of your churches, more than ye love the poor and the needy, the sick and the afflicted. (Mormon 8:26, 28, 30–32, 37)*

The last part of Moroni's discourse is directed to the unbelievers—those who do not believe in Christ. Moroni asks if we will continue to deny the Christ on that day when he returns and we are brought to stand before him! He also informs us that it would be more miserable for the wicked to dwell with God *under a consciousness of [their] filthiness* than *to dwell with the damned souls in hell.*

For those who do not believe that revelations and miracles exist today, he reminds us *that God is the same yesterday, today and forever* and is still a God of miracles.

> *And the reason why he ceaseth to do miracles among the children of men is because that they dwindle in unbelief, and depart from the right way, and know not the God in whom they should trust.* (Mormon 9:20)

Moroni asks that we not condemn this work (the Book of Mormon) because of its imperfections. He explains that they have written the record in the characters they called reformed Egyptian. If the plates had been larger, they would have written in Hebrew, and then there would have been no imperfections in the record. He adds that no other people know their language and that God has *prepared means for the interpretation thereof.*

> *And these things are written that we may rid our garments of the blood of our brethren, who have dwindled in unbelief.*
> *. . . And may God the Father remember the covenant which he hath made with the house of Israel; and may he bless them forever, through faith on the name of Jesus Christ. Amen.* (Mormon 9:35, 37)

·89·

ORDINANCE PRAYERS
MORONI 1–6

After adding a few of his own words at the end of his father's record, Moroni abridged the plates of Ether, which is the history of the Jaredites. (This record has been placed at the end of *And It Came to Pass*, instead of between Mormon and Moroni like it is found in the Book of Mormon, so as not to interrupt the storyline.)

Moroni begins his own account by saying, *I had supposed not to have written more, but I have not as yet perished.* It is now months or perhaps years following the last great battle with the Nephites. He describes the present state of the Lamanites:

> *For behold, their wars are exceedingly fierce among themselves; and because of their hatred they put to death every Nephite that will not deny the Christ.* (Moroni 1:2)

Moroni must hide from the Lamanites—*wherefore, I wander whithersoever I can for the safety of mine own life.* He has a few more things he wants to write, *that perhaps they might be of worth unto my brethren, the Lamanites, in some future day.*

In chapter 2 of Moroni's account, he records the words the Savior used when he gave his disciples the power to give the Holy Ghost. In chapter 3, Moroni records a prayer used in ordaining priests and teachers. Chapters 4 and 5 contain the same prayers we use in our sacrament service today to bless the bread and the water:

> *O God, the Eternal Father, we ask thee in the name of thy Son, Jesus Christ, to bless and sanctify this bread to the souls of all those who partake of it; that they may eat in remembrance of the body of thy Son, and witness unto thee, O God, the Eternal Father, that they are willing to take upon them the name of thy Son, and always*

remember him, and keep his commandments which he hath given them, that they may always have his Spirit to be with them. Amen. (Moroni 4:3)

O God, the Eternal Father, we ask thee, in the name of thy Son, Jesus Christ, to bless and sanctify this wine [water] to the souls of all those who drink of it, that they may do it in remembrance of the blood of thy Son, which was shed for them; that they may witness unto thee, O God, the Eternal Father, that they do always remember him, that they may have his Spirit to be with them. Amen. (Moroni 5:2)

(Section 27 of the Doctrine and Covenants explains why we now use water in the sacrament service instead of wine.)

In chapter 6 of Moroni's account, he gives us a discourse on baptism. The people were not baptized until they came forth with *a broken heart and a contrite spirit* and had repented of all their sins. (In *Mormon Doctrine*, page 161, Elder Bruce R. McConkie teaches that "to have a broken heart and a contrite spirit is to be broken down with deep sorrow for sin, to be humbly and thoroughly penitent.") Moroni further states that none were baptized unless *they took upon them the name of Christ, having a determination to serve him to the end.* After being baptized, they were *cleansed by the power of the Holy Ghost.*

Adding more to the subject of repentance, Moroni explained that iniquity could not be tolerated among them. Those who *repented not and confessed not* after being brought before the elders of the church were no longer numbered among their people.

But as oft as they repented and sought forgiveness, with real intent, they were forgiven. (Moroni 6:8)

·90·

FURTHER COUNSEL FROM MORONI
MORONI 7–9

I n chapter 7 of the book of Mormon, Moroni writes *a few of the words of [his] father Mormon,* which were spoken to the people at an earlier time. Mormon begins his counsel by quoting the words of the Savior—*By their works ye shall know them; for if their works be good, then they are good also.* He warns us that even though we may be doing good works, the attitude with which we do them plays an important role. For instance, if we give a gift *begrudgingly,* we may as well have kept the gift. If we do not pray with *real intent,* it will profit us nothing.

We are then taught how to judge whether something comes from God or from Satan.

> *For every thing which inviteth to do good, and to persuade to believe in Christ, is sent forth by the power and gift of Christ; wherefore ye may know with a perfect knowledge it is of God.*
>
> *But whatsoever thing persuadeth men to do evil, and believe not in Christ, and deny him, and serve not God, then ye may know with a perfect knowledge it is of the devil; for after this manner doth the devil work, for he persuadeth no man to do good, no, not one.* (Moroni 7:16–17)

Mormon then explains how *faith, hope, and charity* are tied together.

> *It is by faith that miracles are wrought; and it is by faith that angels appear and minister unto men. . . .*
>
> *. . . How is it that ye can attain unto faith, save ye shall have hope?*
>
> *And what is it that ye shall hope for? . . . Ye shall have hope through the atonement of Christ . . . to be raised unto life eternal. . . .*
>
> *Wherefore, if a man have faith he must needs have hope; for without faith there cannot be any hope.* (Moroni 7:37, 40–42)

As Mormon further explains, we cannot have faith and hope unless we are *meek and lowly of heart.* In order to be *meek and lowly of heart,* we must have charity, which *is the pure love of Christ.*

> *Wherefore . . . if ye have not charity, ye are nothing, for charity never faileth. Wherefore, cleave unto charity, which is the greatest of all.* (Moroni 7:46)

Chapter 8 is a letter that Mormon sent to his son soon after Moroni was called to the ministry. He begins his letter by telling Moroni how he rejoices that he has been called to this holy work and how he prays for him continually. Then Mormon explains the reason he is writing. He has learned that there are *disputations* among the people concerning the baptism of their little children (infants) and tells Moroni that this *gross error* must be corrected. Upon hearing of this practice, Mormon immediately inquired of the Lord about the matter and received this answer:

> *Listen to the words of Christ, your Redeemer, your Lord and your God. Behold, I came into the world not to call the righteous but sinners to repentance; the whole need no physician, but they that are sick; wherefore, little children are whole, for they are not capable of committing sin; wherefore the curse of Adam is taken from them in me.* (Moroni 8:8)

In Mormon's words, baptizing little children is *solemn mockery before God.* The principles of repentance and baptism should be taught to *those who are accountable and capable of committing sin.*

> *For awful is the wickedness to suppose that God saveth one child because of baptism, and the other must perish because he hath no baptism.*
> *Little children cannot repent; wherefore, it is awful wickedness to deny the pure mercies of God unto them.* (Moroni 8:15, 19)

Moroni chapter 9 is a letter that Moroni's father wrote to him at a time when Mormon's army had just been defeated by the Lamanites. He is writing to tell Moroni that he is *yet alive,* but he fears that his people will be destroyed by the Lamanites because they will not repent. When he preaches to them *with sharpness,* they get angry, and when he uses no sharpness, they harden their hearts. Showing his great strength of character, Mormon tells his son that in spite of the hard hearts of the people, they must not *cease to labor for we have a labor to perform whilst in this tabernacle of clay, that we may conquer the enemy of all righteousness. (Moroni 9:6)*

Mormon goes on to describe the depraved conditions of both the Nephites and the Lamanites. In Moroni 9:7–10, we are given chilling details of how the Nephites and Lamanites tortured each other. (These events happened some years before and are also mentioned in chapter 87 herein.) Mormon recalls that not too long ago his people *were a civil and a delightsome people.*

> *And now, my son . . thou knowest the wickedness of this people; thou knowest that they are without principle, and past feeling; and their wickedness doth exceed that of the Lamanites.*
>
> *Behold, my son, I cannot recommend them unto God lest he should smite me.* (Moroni 9:20–21)

Mormon ends his letter by admonishing Moroni not to be weighed down with the wickedness that surrounds him but to be faithful and have the hope of eternal life *rest in [his] mind forever.*

·91·

A TESTIMONY OF THE BOOK OF MORMON

MORONI 10

When Moroni wrote this last chapter of the Book of Mormon, four hundred and twenty years had passed away since the birth of Christ. All of his kinsfolk and friends had been killed, and he had been wandering alone for at least twenty years. During this time he had to hide from the Lamanites to keep from being slain. Still, he managed to accomplish the last of his work on the Book of Mormon— finishing his father's record, abridging the plates of Ether, and then writing his own record, in that order. (This is why the book of Ether is found between the books of Mormon and Moroni.)

Moroni is about to seal up the records for the next fourteen hundred years, until he personally delivers them to Joseph Smith. Before doing this, he has a few last words for us. First, he teaches us how we can gain a testimony of the Book of Mormon.

> *Behold, I would exhort you that when ye shall read these things, if it be wisdom in God that ye should read them, that ye would remember how merciful the Lord hath been unto the children of men, from the creation of Adam even down until the time that ye shall receive these things, and ponder it in your hearts.*
>
> *And when ye shall receive these things, I would exhort you that ye would ask God, the Eternal Father, in the name of Christ, if these things are not true; and if ye shall ask with a sincere heart, with real intent, having faith in Christ, he will manifest the truth of it unto you, by the power of the Holy Ghost.*
>
> *And by the power of the Holy Ghost ye may know the truth of all things.* (Moroni 10:3–5)

Moroni next gives us a discourse on the *gifts of the Spirit*, which are special spiritual blessings given to the faithful by God. He lists many different gifts, such as the gift of *exceeding great faith*, the gift of healing, the gift to work *mighty miracles*, the gift of prophecy, the gift of *beholding of angels and ministering spirits*, the gift to speak with tongues, and the gift to interpret languages. Elder Bruce R. McConkie helps us understand what the gifts of the Spirit are and why we should seek after them:

> By the grace of God—following devotion, faith, and obedience on man's part—certain special spiritual blessings called *gifts of the Spirit* are bestowed upon men. Their receipt is always predicated upon obedience to law, but because they are freely available to all the obedient, they are called gifts. They are signs and miracles reserved for the faithful and for none else. . . . Their purpose is to enlighten, encourage, and edify the faithful so that they will inherit peace in this life and be guided toward eternal life in the world to come. . . . Faithful persons are expected to seek the gifts of the Spirit with all their hearts. They are to "covet earnestly the best gifts" (1 Cor. 12:31; D&C 46:8).[1]

After teaching us about the gifts of the Spirit and other matters, Moroni gives us this admonition:

> *And I exhort you to remember these things; for the time speedily cometh that ye shall know that I lie not, for ye shall see me at the bar of God; and the Lord God will say unto you: Did I not declare my words unto you, which were written by this man, like as one crying from the dead, yea, even as one speaking out of the dust?* (Moroni 10:27)

Moroni urges us to *come unto Christ and lay hold upon every good gift* and to love God with all our *might, mind and strength*. Then he leaves us with these parting words:

> *And now I bid unto all, farewell. I soon go to rest in the paradise of God, until my spirit and body shall again reunite, and I am brought forth triumphant through the air, to meet you before the pleasing bar of the great Jehovah, the Eternal Judge of both quick and dead. Amen.* (Moroni 10:34)

Note
1. Bruce R. McConkie, *Mormon Doctrine*, 2d ed. (Salt Lake City, Utah: Bookcraft, 1966), 314.

·92·

LEAVING THE TOWER OF BABEL
ETHER 1–2

First, a brief explanation of where the book of Ether came from, who the people were, and how this account came to be in the Book of Mormon: In Mosiah chapter 8, we learn that the people of Limhi found a land covered with the bones of men, ruins of buildings, and remnants of war, such as breastplates, swords, and so on. Most important was the discovery of twenty-four gold plates filled with engravings. King Mosiah translated these plates by the use of the Urim and Thummim (the interpreting device, or seer stones, that Joseph Smith would later use to translate the Book of Mormon). Later, the prophet Moroni abridged, or condensed, this record. He wrote that he could not include even a *hundredth part* of what was contained on the plates in his abridgment.

This record is a history of the Jaredite civilization, which lived on this continent from around 2200 BC until 600 BC or later. These people were led to America by the Lord at the time of the Tower of Babel (see Genesis 11:6–9), and because of wars their civilization became extinct. Lehi and his family arrived in America about 589 BC, and the Mulekites arrived a few years later. Coriantumr, the last Jaredite king, lived with the Mulekites for nine months before his death, so the histories of all three groups of people overlapped for a short while.

In just fifteen chapters, the book of Ether covers about fifteen hundred years of Jaredite history, naming a great number of people and events but not providing a lot of detail.

In order to lead into the story of the Jaredites, we must first go to the eleventh chapter of Genesis, where the account of the Tower of Babel is found:

> *And the whole earth was of one language, and of one speech.*

> *And it came to pass, as they journeyed from the east, that they found a plain in the land of Shinar; and they dwelt there. . .*
> *And they said, Go to, let us build us a city and a tower, whose top may reach unto heaven.* (Genesis 11:1–2, 4)

The Lord was angry with the people for building the tower and decided to *confound* their language so they would be unable to understand one another.

> *Therefore is the name of it called Babel; because the Lord did there confound the language of all the earth: and from thence did the Lord scatter them abroad upon the face of all the earth.* (Genesis 11:9)

Living in the city of Babel were the families of a man named Jared and Jared's brother. (The brother's name is never revealed in the scriptural account, but Joseph Smith learned through revelation that his name was Mahonri Moriancumer.) They were forewarned about the judgment the Lord was going to pronounce upon the city.

> *And the brother of Jared being a large and mighty man, and a man highly favored of the Lord, Jared, his brother, said unto him: Cry unto the Lord, that he will not confound us that we may not understand our words.* (Ether 1:34)

The brother of Jared cried unto the Lord concerning their dilemma. The Lord had compassion on the brothers and their families and did not confound their language. Then Jared asked his brother to go again before the Lord and ask that he would *turn away his anger from them who are our friends* and not confound their language either. The brother of Jared prayed to the Lord, and the Lord granted his petition.

> *And it came to pass that Jared spake again unto his brother, saying: Go and inquire of the Lord whether he will drive us out of the land, and if he will drive us out of the land, cry unto him whither we shall go. And who knoweth but the Lord will carry us forth into a land which is choice above all the earth? And if it so be, let us be faithful unto the Lord, that we may receive it for our inheritance.* (Ether 1:38)

In answer to this last prayer, the Lord told the brother of Jared to gather together their flocks, *both male and female of every kind,* and also every kind of seed. The brothers and their families, and also their friends and their families, would then be led by the brother of Jared down into a valley to the north. The Lord promised to meet them in this valley, and from there they would be led *into a land which [was] choice above all the lands of the earth.* In this new land the Lord would bless their people and raise up a great nation, greater than all the other nations of the earth.

This caravan of people and flocks traveled down into a valley called Nimrod, named after *the mighty hunter.*

> And they did also lay snares and catch fowls of the air; and they
> did also prepare a vessel, in which they did carry with them the fish
> of the waters. (Ether 2:2)

Besides hauling live fish and birds with them, they also carried beehives! Moroni gives us the Jaredite word for "honey bee" in his translation, which is *deseret.*

After arriving in the valley of Nimrod, the Lord came down and talked with the brother of Jared, standing in a cloud so as not to be seen. They were told to travel into the wilderness, *into that quarter where there never had man been.* The Lord went before them, giving them directions as he stood in the cloud.

During their journey in the wilderness, they came to *many waters* and were directed to build barges in order to cross them. Finally, Jared and his people arrived at *that great sea which divideth the lands,* and they named the land *Moriancumer.* Here they lived in tents upon the seashore for a period of four years. At the end of the four years, the Lord came to the brother of Jared and talked with him for three hours from the cloud. He chastened him for not calling upon the name of the Lord. The brother of Jared repented and prayed unto the Lord for himself and the others. They were forgiven, but the Lord told them not to sin anymore, for *my Spirit will not always strive with man.* The Lord's intention was to lead these people to the promised land, *a land choice above all other lands*—not to have them dwell in the land of Moriancumer. He then gave them a stern warning concerning the new land: it had been preserved for a righteous people. If the time came that the inhabitants were *ripened in iniquity,* they would be *swept off.* Because Moroni knew the fate of the Jaredites, and also the fate of his own people, the Nephites, he directed this warning to us:

And this cometh unto you, O ye Gentiles, . . . that ye may repent, and not continue in your iniquities until the fulness come, that ye may not bring down the fulness of the wrath of God upon you as the inhabitants of the land have hitherto done.

Behold, this is a choice land, and whatsoever nation shall possess it shall be free from bondage, and from captivity, and from all other nations under heaven, if they will but serve the God of the land, who is Jesus Christ. (Ether 2:11–12)

·93·

THE JAREDITE BARGES
ETHER 2–6

<hr>

After the people had lived in the land of Moriancumer for four years, the Lord gave them instructions to build barges. They were to be patterned after the earlier vessels they built to cross the *many waters* while traveling in the wilderness.

> *And they were small, and they were light upon the water, even like unto the lightness of a fowl upon the water.*
> *And they were built after a manner that they were exceedingly tight, even that they would hold water like unto a dish; and the bottom thereof was tight like unto a dish; and the sides thereof were tight like unto a dish; and the ends thereof were peaked; and the top thereof was tight like unto a dish; and the length thereof was the length of a tree; and the door thereof, when it was shut, was tight like unto a dish.* (Ether 2:16–17)

Eight barges were constructed. Upon their completion, the brother of Jared *cried unto the Lord* concerning two serious problems he perceived with their design. The barges had no light and they had no air! The solution the Lord gave for the lack of air was to *make a hole in the top, and also in the bottom.* When they needed air, they were to unplug one of the holes. If the water came in upon them, they were to plug the hole back up again. (The scriptural account is obviously short on detail here. Just remember that as with Nephi, the Jaredites were using the Lord's blueprints.) The alterations were made that enabled the vessels to have air, but still the second problem remained.

> *Behold, O Lord, wilt thou suffer that we shall cross this great water in darkness?* (Ether 2:22)

The Lord asked the brother of Jared what *he* would suggest be done about the light. The Lord reminded him that they could not have windows, for they would be *dashed in pieces,* nor could they use fire.

> *For behold, ye shall be as a whale in the midst of the sea; for the mountain waves shall dash upon you. Nevertheless, I will bring you up again out of the depths of the sea.* (Ether 2:24)

The brother of Jared went to a very tall mountain they called Shelem. Here he *did molten* sixteen small stones out of the rock, which *were white and clear, even as transparent glass.* He carried these stones to the top of the mountain and called upon the Lord. Showing tremendous faith, he asked the Lord to touch the stones with his finger and make them shine so their vessels might have light.

> *And it came to pass that when the brother of Jared had said these words, behold, the Lord stretched forth his hand and touched the stones one by one with his finger. And the veil was taken from off the eyes of the brother of Jared, and he saw the finger of the Lord; and it was as the finger of a man, like unto flesh and blood; and the brother of Jared fell down before the Lord, for he was struck with fear.* (Ether 3:6)

The Lord asked him why he had fallen. He replied that he had not known that the Lord had a body of flesh and blood, and he was afraid of being smitten. It was explained to him that because of his great faith, he was shown how the Lord would later look with a body of flesh and blood. The brother of Jared was asked if he had seen more than his finger, and he replied, *Nay, Lord, show thyself unto me.* The Lord showed himself to the brother of Jared, introducing himself as Jesus Christ, who had been *prepared from the foundation of the world to redeem [his] people.*

> *Seest thou that ye are created after mine own image? Yea, even all men were created in the beginning after mine own image.*
> *Behold, this body, which ye now behold, is the body of my spirit;*
> *. . . and even as I appear unto thee to be in the spirit will I appear unto my people in the flesh.* (Ether 3:15–16)

(Modern revelation teaches us that our physical bodies are in the likeness of our spirits. See D&C 77:2.)

The brother of Jared was also shown all the people who ever had or ever would live on the earth. The Lord did not want the world to know of the things he had just revealed until a later time, so Jared was commanded to record these things and then *seal them up,* or hide them. Because the brother of Jared would write in a language that others could not understand, the Lord provided *interpreters* (the Urim and Thummim) to be sealed up along with the record.

(In the fifth chapter of Ether, Moroni reveals that the plates containing the writings of the Book of Mormon would be shown to three witnesses, who would assist with the work. The testimony of these three witnesses is found in the introductory pages of the Book of Mormon.)

After beholding his marvelous vision, the brother of Jared came down from the mountain, carrying the sixteen stones that the Lord had illuminated. He placed two stones in each of the eight barges, one in each end, and they provided light for the vessels.

The people prepared food for themselves, for their flocks and herds, *and [for] whatsoever beast or animal or fowl that they should carry with them.* Then they boarded the barges, putting their trust in the Lord. The Lord caused a *furious wind* to blow them towards the promised land, a wind that never stopped until they reached their destination. As they journeyed, the people sang praises to the Lord.

> *And it came to pass that they were many times buried in the depths of the sea, because of the mountain waves which broke upon them, and also the great and terrible tempests which were caused by the fierceness of the wind.*
>
> *And it came to pass that when they were buried in the deep there was no water that could hurt them, their vessels being tight like unto a dish. . . .*
>
> *. . . And no monster of the sea could break them, neither whale that could mar them.* (Ether 6:6–7, 10)

When their vessels were buried deep in the sea, the people would cry unto the Lord and he would bring them to the surface. After being driven upon the sea for 344 days, they landed on the shore of the promised land. They bowed down and shed tears of joy for the *tender mercies* of the Lord.

·94·

SHULE—A RIGHTEOUS KING
ETHER 6–7

The people settled into their new land and began to till the ground. Their leaders taught them *to walk humbly before the Lord*, and they were also guided *from on high*. As their numbers grew, they began to spread upon the face of the land.

When the brother of Jared became old, knowing that his time to die was approaching, he had all the people gather together to be numbered. Jared had twelve sons and daughters, and his brother had twenty-two. The friends of the two brothers, with their families, added to these numbers. Jared and his brother asked the people what they desired of them before they *went down to [their] graves*. The people wanted them to anoint one of their sons to be king.

> *And now behold, this was grievous unto them. And the brother of Jared said unto them: Surely this thing leadeth into captivity.* (Ether 6:23)

Jared persuaded his brother to let them have a king anyway and asked the people to choose one of their sons. Each son refused, except Orihah, who was Jared's son. He was anointed king, and under his reign the people became very rich. Jared and his brother eventually died.

Orihah, a humble ruler who taught his people that the Lord had done great things for their fathers, was a righteous ruler upon the land all his days. Orihah had twenty-three sons and eight daughters; then another son was born to him in his old age. This son was named Kib, and he became the next king.

Kib had a son named Corihor. When Corihor was thirty-two years old, he rebelled against his father and went to live in the land of Nehor. While living there he had sons and daughters, and they were *exceedingly fair.* Corihor drew away a large following and was able to form his own army. He led his army back to the land of Moron, where his father, the king, lived. (Moroni tells us that the land of Moron was near the land that the Nephites called Desolation.) Corihor took his father, Kib, captive and became king over all the people. In his old age, while still living in captivity, Kib had another son and named him Shule.

> *And it came to pass that Shule was angry with his brother; and Shule waxed strong, and became mighty as to the strength of a man; and he was also mighty in judgment.* (Ether 7:8)

Shule went to the hill Ephraim and made swords of steel out of molten rock. He armed his followers with the swords and returned to the city of Nehor, where he engaged in battle with his brother Corihor. Shule was victorious and gave the kingdom back to his father, Kib, who in turn gave the kingdom to Shule. Under Shule's righteous leadership, his kingdom spread throughout the land.

Corihor (the brother of Shule, who had kept their father, Kib, in captivity for many years) repented of his many evils; *wherefore Shule gave him power in his kingdom.* Corihor had a son named Noah, who did not want to live under the rule of his uncle, Shule. Noah rebelled against the king and also against his father, Corihor, and drew away many people. A battle took place that resulted in Noah's gaining possession of the land of Moron. Here Noah became king over his rebel followers. A second battle followed, and this time Noah took Shule captive.

> *And it came to pass as he was about to put him to death, the sons of Shule crept into the house of Noah by night and slew him, and broke down the door of the prison and brought out their father, and placed him upon his throne in his own kingdom.* (Ether 7:18)

Upon the death of Noah, his son, Cohor, became the next ruler. The country was now divided into two kingdoms—Shule's and Cohor's, and the people under the reign of Shule became very prosperous.

Cohor led his people to battle against the kingdom of Shule, but he was slain and his people were defeated. Cohor's son, whose name was Nimrod, then gave his father's kingdom back to Shule! This allowed Nimrod to *gain favor in the eyes of Shule,* and he was permitted to do whatsoever he desired.

During the reign of Shule, the Lord sent prophets among the people to warn them that they would be destroyed if they did not repent. The people only mocked them. Shule was a righteous king and did not tolerate this. He punished those who reviled the prophets and made laws that gave the prophets freedom to preach wherever they pleased. The people finally repented, and so the Lord spared them. They began to prosper again in the land.

And there were no more wars in the days of Shule; and he remembered the great things that the Lord had done for his fathers in bringing them across the great deep into the promised land; wherefore he did execute judgment in righteousness all his days. (Ether 7:27)

·95·

SECRET COMBINATIONS
ETHER 8–9

The next king to reign was Omer, who was the son of Shule. Peace did not continue in the kingdom because of Omer's son Jared. He rebelled against his father and went to live in the land of Heth. *Flattering* the people with his *cunning words,* Jared was able to draw away many followers.

> *And when he had gained the half of the kingdom he gave battle unto his father, and he did carry away his father into captivity, and did make him serve in captivity.* (Ether 8:3)

Throughout the remainder of the book of Ether, there are several more accounts of kings who served in captivity. Dr. Hugh Nibley discusses this strange custom: "Such is the practice, mentioned many times in the book, of keeping a king prisoner throughout his entire lifetime, allowing him to beget and raise a family in captivity, even though the sons thus brought up would be almost sure to seek vengeance for their parent and power for themselves upon coming of age. . . . It seems to us a perfectly ridiculous system, yet it is in accordance with (Asiatic custom). . . . It was the custom of Turkish kings . . . to allow their defeated rivals to sit upon their thrones by day, but lock them up in iron cages for the night!"[1]

Omer spent half his life in captivity, during which time other sons and daughters were born. Two of these sons, Esrom and Coriantumr, later raised an army to fight their brother, Jared, because of his crimes against their father. They came against him in battle, slew his army, and were about to slay their brother. Jared pleaded with them to spare him, and in trade for his life he would give the kingdom back to his father, Omer. Jared was allowed to live, but he became *exceedingly sorrowful* because his heart was set upon the kingdom and *upon the glory of the world.*

Jared had a beautiful yet cunning daughter who approached him with a plan she had devised to get the kingdom back:

> *Whereby hath my father so much sorrow? Hath he not read the record which our fathers brought across the great deep? Behold, is there not an account concerning them of old, that they by their secret plans did obtain kingdoms and great glory?* (Ether 8:9)

She instructed her father to send for Akish, who was a friend of Omer's. She would dance before him, which would please him, and he would ask Jared for permission to marry her. Permission would be granted upon the condition that Akish bring Jared the head of Jared's father, Omer.

Jared's daughter danced before Akish, and he agreed to the conditions stipulated in order to marry her. Akish had all his relatives and friends gather in Jared's house. After *leading them away by [his] fair promises,* he made them all swear to be faithful to him as they carried out his secret plans.

> *And Akish did administer unto them the oaths which were given by them of old who also sought power, which had been handed down even from Cain, who was a murderer from the beginning.*
> *And it came to pass that they formed a secret combination, even as they of old; which combination is most abominable and wicked above all, in the sight of God.* (Ether 8:15, 18)

Following the above scripture, Moroni gives his readers a strong warning about the evils of secret combinations that would exist in our day. Elder Ezra Taft Benson commented on Moroni's words:

"One of the most urgent, heart-stirring appeals made by Moroni as he closed the Book of Mormon was addressed to the gentile nations of the last days. He foresaw the rise of a great world-wide secret combination among the gentiles which '. . . *seeketh to overthrow the freedom of all lands, nations, and countries; . . .*' (Ether 8:25; italics added.) He warned each gentile nation of the last days to purge itself of this gigantic criminal conspiracy which would seek to rule the world. . . .

"The prophet Moroni seemed greatly exercised lest in our day we might not be able to recognize the startling fact that the same secret societies which destroyed the Jaredites and decimated numerous kingdoms of both Nephites and Lamanites would be precisely the same form of criminal conspiracy which would rise up among the gentile nations in this day. . . .

"The Lord has declared that before the second coming of Christ it will be necessary to '. . . *destroy the secret works of darkness,* . . . ' in order to preserve the land of Zion—the Americas. (2 Nephi 10:11–16)."[2] By use of secret combinations, Jared and his friends overthrew the kingdom of Omer.

> *Nevertheless, the Lord was merciful unto Omer, and also to his sons and to his daughters who did not seek his destruction.*
> *And the Lord warned Omer in a dream that he should depart out of the land.* (Ether 9:2–3)

Omer and his family traveled many days and *came over by the place where the Nephites [would later be] destroyed.* Then they turned eastward and came to a place called Ablom, which was by the seashore. Here he and his household pitched their tents.

Notes

1. Hugh Nibley, *Lehi in the Desert and The World of the Jaredites* (Salt Lake City, Utah: Bookcraft, 1952), 201–3.

2. Daniel H. Ludlow, *A Companion to Your Study of the Book of Mormon* (Salt Lake City, Utah: Deseret Book, 1976), 322–23.

·96·

FAMINE AND POISONOUS SERPENTS
ETHER 9

With Omer and his whole household gone, Jared was anointed king. Akish married Jared's daughter, even though he was not able to carry out the plan to behead Omer.

And it came to pass that Akish sought the life of his father-in-law; and he applied unto those whom he had sworn by the oath of the ancients, and they obtained the head of his father-in-law, as he sat upon his throne, giving audience to his people. (Ether 9:5)

This *wicked and secret society* had turned against Jared, and now Akish reigned in his place. Akish became jealous of one of his sons (we are not given the reason why) and shut him up in prison and slowly starved him to death. Another son, named Nimrah, was angry over what his father had done to his brother and fled the land with a small number of men and joined Omer.

Akish had other sons who *won the hearts of the people.* By means of bribery they drew away the majority of their father's followers. A war began between Akish and his sons and lasted so many years that all but thirty people of the kingdom were destroyed! This made it possible for Omer and those who had fled with him to come back to the land, and Omer once more reigned over the kingdom.

Omer had a son in his old age, named Emer, whom he anointed to be the next king. After two peaceful years, Omer died. Over the next sixty-two years they became a strong and prosperous people. They had all kinds of fruits and grains, silks, fine linen, gold, silver, and *precious things.* They had cattle, oxen, sheep, swine, goats, and other kinds of animals that provided them food. There were animals *which were useful unto man,* such as horses and donkeys, but *more especially the elephants and cureloms and cumons.*

Emer served as a righteous king all his days and was even privileged to see *the Son of Righteousness*. He had many sons and daughters, and he anointed one of his sons, Coriantum, to be the next king. Emer lived four more years and then died in peace.

Coriantum was a good king like his father and built many great cities, but he had no children until he was a very old man. After his first wife died, he married a young maid and had sons and daughters. He lived to be 142 years old. His son Com became the next king and reigned for forty-nine years. During Com's reign, the people spread over the face of the land and grew very wicked. Com had a son, named Heth, who turned against him.

> *Heth began to embrace the secret plans again of old, to destroy his father.*
> *And it came to pass that he did dethrone his father, for he slew him with his own sword; and he did reign in his stead.* (Ether 9:26–27)

Prophets came into the land crying repentance and warning the people of a great famine that would destroy them if they did not repent. The wicked king Heth ordered the prophets to be cast out or thrown into pits where they were left to perish.

The famine came, killing the people *exceedingly fast*. (We learn in the following chapter of Ether that Heth and all his household perished in this famine.) Then the Lord sent *poisonous serpents* that killed many people. The serpents also drove their flocks towards the land in the south, *which was called by the Nephites Zarahemla*. Many of the animals perished along the way; others made it to the land southward.

> *And it came to pass that the Lord did cause the serpents that they should pursue [the animals] no more, but that they should hedge up the way that the people could not pass, that whoso should attempt to pass might fall by the poisonous serpents.* (Ether 9:33)

The starving people followed the course of the animals and ate the carcasses that fell by the way *until they had devoured them all*. Once again faced with starvation, the people repented and cried unto the Lord. When the people were sufficiently humbled, the Lord sent rain and there was fruit again in the land.

> *And the Lord did show forth his power unto them in preserving them from famine.* (Ether 9:35)

·97·

A Succession of Kings
ETHER 10–11

I n his book *A Companion to Your Study of the Book Of Mormon*, p. 323, Daniel H. Ludlow suggests that possibly one-third of the Jaredite history is covered in the tenth chapter of Ether.

After the wicked king Heth and all of his household had been killed by the great famine, one of Heth's descendants became the next king. His name was Shez, and he *began to build up again a broken people.*

> And it came to pass that Shez did remember the destruction of
> his fathers, and he did build up a righteous kingdom; for he remem-
> bered what the Lord had done in bringing Jared and his brother
> across the deep; and he did walk in the ways of the Lord; and he
> begat sons and daughters. (Ether 10:2)

Shez built many cities, and the people spread across the face of the land. He lived to a very old age and then died. His son Riplakish was the next to reign.

Riplakish was a wicked king, having many wives and concubines. He laid heavy taxes on the people, which enabled him to build many *spacious buildings* and a beautiful throne. He also built many prisons, where he put those who either refused or were unable to pay their taxes. It was with prison labor that Riplakish obtained *all manner of fine workmanship* and refined all his gold. After he reigned for forty-two years, the people rose up in rebellion against him. In the resulting war, he was killed and his descendants were driven out of the land.

After many years had passed, a descendant of Riplakish, by the name of Morianton, assembled an army of *outcasts* and went to battle against the people. It was a terrible war that lasted many years. Morianton managed to gain many cities, and eventually his power spread over the entire land. He established himself as king. Because he eased the burdens of the people, he gained their favor and they officially anointed him to be their king.

> *And he did do justice unto the people, but not unto himself because of his many whoredoms; wherefore he was cut off from the presence of the Lord.* (Ether 10:11)

Under Morianton's reign, the people became very rich and many cities were built. Morianton lived *to an exceedingly great age,* and during his old age he fathered a son and named him Kim. Kim became the next king and was unrighteous, just as his father had been. Kim's brother rose up in rebellion against him and brought him into captivity, where he remained all the rest of his life. During this time Kim had more sons and daughters, and in his old age a son named Levi was born.

After the death of Kim, Levi served in captivity for forty-two years. Finally, he went to war and won the kingdom back. Levi was a righteous king, and under his reign the people prospered. He lived *to a good old age* and anointed his son Corom to be the next king. Corom was also righteous all his life, *and after he had seen many days he did pass away.* Kish, the son of Corom, reigned next. After Kish died, his son Lib became the next king.

> *And it came to pass that Lib also did that which was good in the sight of the Lord. And in the days of Lib the poisonous serpents were destroyed. Wherefore they did go into the land southward, to hunt food for the people of the land, for the land was covered with animals of the forest. And Lib also himself became a great hunter.* (Ether 10:19)

They built a great city by the narrow neck of land (which is the same narrow neck of land referred to throughout Nephite history). The land northward was covered with inhabitants, and the land southward was preserved *for a wilderness, to get game.*

> *And they were exceedingly industrious, and they did buy and sell and traffic one with another, that they might get gain.* (Ether 10:22)

They dug ore out of the earth, casting *up mighty heaps of earth.* From the ore they made gold, silver, iron, brass, and other kinds of metals, and *they did work all manner of fine work.* They had silks and fine-twined linen. They made all kinds of tools to till the earth, *both to plow and to sow, to reap and to hoe, and also to thrash.* They made all types of weapons and *did work all manner of work of exceedingly curious workmanship.*

During the reign of Lib, the people were blessed by the Lord and they prospered. They knew they were living in a land that was choice above all lands, *for the Lord had spoken it.*

Lib's son Hearthom was the next king. After reigning for twenty-four years, the kingdom was taken from him, and he served all the remainder of his days in captivity.

> *And he begat Heth, and Heth lived in captivity all his days. And Heth begat Aaron, and Aaron dwelt in captivity all his days; and he begat Amnigaddah, and Amnigaddah also dwelt in captivity all his days; and he begat Coriantum, and Coriantum dwelt in captivity all his days; and he begat Com.* (Ether 10:31)

Finally, Com was able to break the cycle of captivity. He managed to draw away half of the kingdom, over which he reigned for forty-two years. Then he went to battle against the king and, after fighting for many years, gained power over the remaining half.

During the reign of Com there again began to be robbers in the land who *adopted the old plans, and administered oaths after the manner of the ancients,* and tried to destroy the kingdom. Com fought against them but never successfully eradicated them. Prophets came, warning the people of their destruction if they did not repent. The people tried to kill them, so the prophets fled to Com for protection.

> *And they prophesied unto Com many things; and he was blessed in all the remainder of his days.* (Ether 11:3)

·98·

PROPHECIES OF DESTRUCTION

ETHER 11–12

Shiblom, who was the son of Com, became the next king. Shiblom's brother rebelled against him, causing a great war in the land. The prophets had testified that a great curse would come upon the people if they did not repent of their wickedness. The resulting destruction would be the worst that had ever come to the land, and their bones would become *as heaps of earth*. Shiblom's brother silenced these prophets by having them all put to death. The warnings of the prophets went unheeded because of the *wicked combinations* embraced by the people, and so the *great calamity* began. There were wars, famines, and pestilences that caused such great destruction *as never had been known upon the face of the earth*. All this came during the reign of Shiblom.

And the people began to repent of their iniquity; and inasmuch as they did the Lord did have mercy on them. (Ether 11:8)

Shiblom was slain, and his son Seth was brought into captivity, remaining there all the rest of his life. Seth had a son named Ahah, who succeeded in obtaining the kingdom. Ahah was a wicked king who caused many lives to be lost, *and few were his days.*

Ethem, a descendant of Ahah, became king and *did execute judgment in wickedness all his days.* During his reign, prophets once again warned the people of coming destruction if they did not repent. No one listened to them, and they *mourned and withdrew from among the people.*

Moron, the son of Ethem, was the next king and was also wicked. During Moron's reign, a rebellion was started by the secret combination. *A mighty man* belonging to this secret society went to battle against Moron and overthrew half the kingdom and ruled over his part for many years. Then Moron overthrew him, and once again his kingdom was intact.

Another powerful man arose who took the kingdom from Moron and forced him to live in captivity for the rest of his life. Moron had a son named Coriantor, who also remained in captivity all his days.

During the days of Coriantor, prophets were again sent to cry repentance. They warned the people that if they did not repent, not only would they be destroyed but the Lord would lead another people to possess the land.

> *And they did reject all the words of the prophets, because of their secret society and wicked abominations.* (Ether 11:22)

Coriantor had a son named Ether, who became a mighty prophet. (Ether lived to see the prophecies fulfilled concerning the destruction of his people, and it was he who recorded the last of their history and hid the plates.)

Ether began to prophesy unto the people during the reign of Coriantumr (not to be confused with Ether's father, who was named Coriantor). Ether felt the Spirit of the Lord so strongly that *he could not be restrained* from preaching to the people. He cried repentance unto them from morning until night, hoping to prevent their destruction. Still, they would not listen.

At this point, Moroni, who is the narrator of this record, interjects his own discourse. (Moroni condensed the lengthy record that Ether left into the thirty-two pages that we now know as the book of Ether.) He first talks about faith.

> *I would show unto the world that faith is things which are hoped for and not seen; wherefore, dispute not because ye see not, for ye receive no witness until after the trial of your faith.* (Ether 12:6)

Moroni gives many examples of others throughout these scriptures who caused miracles to happen because of their great faith, such as Alma, Amulek, and Ammon. Then he speaks of the difficulty of putting their words into writing. He explains that in speaking to the people, the Lord made their words *powerful and great,* but when they attempted to write them, *we behold our weakness, and stumble because of the placing of our words.* Moroni told the Lord, *I fear lest the Gentiles shall mock at our words,* referring to us of the latter days. He received this answer:

Fools mock, but they shall mourn; and my grace is sufficient for the meek, that they shall take no advantage of your weakness;

And if men come unto me I will show unto them their weakness. I give unto men weakness that they may be humble; . . . for if they humble themselves before me, and have faith in me, then will I make weak things become strong unto them. (Ether 12:26–27)

Before summing up the final scenes of Jaredite history, Moroni bids farewell to his readers *until we shall meet before the judgment-seat of Christ.* He tells us that he has seen Jesus, and has talked with him *face to face . . . as a man telleth another in mine own language, concerning these things.*

And now, I would commend you to seek this Jesus of whom the prophets and apostles have written, that the grace of God the Father, and also the Lord Jesus Christ, and the Holy Ghost, which beareth record of them, may be and abide in you forever. Amen. (Ether 12:41)

(At the time of this writing, Moroni thought these would be his final words. However, after he finished abridging the Jaredite record, he found that he had *not as yet perished,* and so he went on to write his own record—the book of Moroni.)

·99·

ETHER'S WARNING

ETHER 13–14

And now I, Moroni, proceed to finish my record concerning the destruction of the people of whom I have been writing. (Ether 13:1)

Great and marvelous were the prophecies of Ether, but still the people rejected his words and cast him out. By day he hid in a cave and finished the remainder of his record; by night he went out and viewed the destruction of his people.

(One of Ether's prophecies concerns the New Jerusalem that will be built upon the American continent. See Ether 13:3–12.)

During Ether's first year of hiding, a great war began. Many mighty men belonging to the secret combinations rose up, hoping to conquer Coriantumr's kingdom. They were instead slain, because Coriantumr had studied *in all the arts of war and all the cunning of the world.*

During Ether's second year of hiding, the Lord commanded him to prophesy unto Coriantumr that if he and his household would repent, the Lord would allow him to retain his kingdom, and the people would be spared.

> *Otherwise they should be destroyed, and all his household save it were himself. And he should only live to see the fulfilling of the prophecies which had been spoken concerning another people receiving the land for their inheritance; and Coriantumr should receive a burial by them;* **and every soul should be destroyed save it were Coriantumr.** (Ether 13:21)

Neither Coriantumr, nor his household, nor the people repented, and the wars continued.

After Coriantumr received the prophecy from Ether, four great contenders rose up against him before the prophecy was fulfilled. The first of these men was Shared. After a three-year battle with Shared, Coriantumr was defeated and brought into captivity. In the fourth year, the sons of Coriantumr overpowered Shared and restored the kingdom to their father.

The war escalated until it spread upon all the face of the land, *every man with his band fighting for that which he desired.* In addition to the warfaring, there were robbers throughout the land, *and all manner of wickedness.*

Three more battles would be fought between Coriantumr and Shared before Shared was finally slain by Coriantumr. Because Coriantumr had been wounded, he did not go to battle again for two years. Nevertheless, during these years of warfare the people were shedding blood everywhere, *and there was none to restrain them.*

> *And now there began to be a great curse upon all the land because of the iniquity of the people, in which, if a man should lay his tool or his sword upon his shelf, or upon the place whither he would keep it, behold, upon the morrow, he could not find it, so great was the curse upon the land.* (Ether14:1; see also Helaman 13:34, which describes a similar Nephite curse)

Consequently, every man held on to his belongings *and would not borrow, neither would he lend.* In order to defend his property and the lives of his family, each man *kept the hilt of his sword in his right hand.*

Two years after Shared was slain, Shared's brother, Gilead, came with his army to battle. Coriantumr drove Gilead's army to the wilderness and thousands were killed in the battle that followed. Then Coriantumr *did lay siege to the wilderness.* One night Gilead and his men came upon part of Coriantumr's army that was drunk and slayed them. Next he marched his army out of the wilderness to the land of Moron, where he placed himself upon Coriantumr's throne.

Coriantumr and his army remained in the wilderness for the next two years, where they grew in number. Gilead's army was also growing in the land of Moron, because of secret combinations. Gilead met his death from an enemy inside his kingdom—his high priest murdered him as he sat upon his throne. Then a man named Lib, who was a member of the secret combination, murdered the high priest while they were in a secret pass. Lib, *a man of great stature, more than any other man among all the people,* now ruled.

During the first year of Lib's reign, Coriantumr brought his army to the land of Moron to battle. In the ensuing conflict, Lib's army was driven to the borders by the seashore, where another terrible battle took place. This time Lib's army gained the advantage and drove Coriantumr's army back to the wilderness of Akish. As Coriantumr fled from Lib, he took all the people with him from that quarter of the land. In the following battle on the plains of Agosh, Coriantumr slew Lib.

Coriantumr now met his final contender, Shiz, the brother of Lib. When the battle became *exceedingly sore,* Coriantumr and his army fled. As Shiz pursued after Coriantumr, he burned the cities in his path.

> *And there went a fear of Shiz throughout all the land; yea, a cry went forth throughout the land—Who can stand before the army of Shiz? Behold, he sweepeth the earth before him!* (Ether 14:18)

All over the land the people divided and flocked to either the army of Coriantumr or the army of Shiz. The war between the two had been going on so long, and had traversed the countryside so swiftly, that no one was left to bury the dead. Bodies covered the face of the land.

> *And the scent thereof went forth upon . . . all the face of the land; wherefore the people became troubled by day and by night, because of the scent thereof.* (Ether 14:23)

Shiz was relentless in his pursuit of Coriantumr for two reasons: first, he had sworn to avenge the blood of his brother, and second, he had heard of Ether's prophecy that Coriantumr could not fall by the sword! Shiz pursued Coriantumr eastward to the borders by the seashore, where they fought for three days. Coriantumr's army caused such terrible destruction that Shiz's army fled in fear to the land of Corihor. In their flight, they *swept off the inhabitants before them* who would not join with them.

Both armies made camp, and then Coriantumr *did sound a trumpet unto the armies of Shiz to invite them forth to battle.* Shiz's army was driven back twice. On their third attempt to defeat Coriantumr's army, *the battle became exceedingly sore.* Shiz attacked Coriantumr and gave him such deep wounds that he fainted from the loss of blood and was carried off as though he were dead.

> *Now the loss of men, women and children on both sides was so great that Shiz commanded his people that they should not pursue*

the armies of Coriantumr; wherefore, they returned to their camp.
(Ether 14:31)

Dr. Hugh Nibley provides us with some important insight concerning Jaredite warfare:

> The insane wars of the Jaredite chiefs ended in the complete annihilation of both sides, with the kings the last to go. . . . This all seems improbable to us, but two circumstances peculiar to Asiatic warfare explain why the phenomenon is by no means without parallel: (1) Since every war is strictly a personal contest between kings, the battle must continue until one of the kings falls or is taken. (2) And yet things are so arranged that the king must be very last to fall, the whole army existing for the sole purpose of defending his person. . . . In the code of medieval chivalry, taken over from central Asia, the person of the king is sacred, and all others must perish in his defense. . . . As long as the war went on, the king could not die, for whenever he did die, the war was over, no matter how strong his surviving forces. . . . Wars of extermination are a standard institution in the history of Asia.[1]

Note
1.   Hugh Nibley, *Lehi in the Desert and The World of the Jaredites*, 235–36.

·100·

CORIANTUMR—THE LAST JAREDITE
ETHER 15

And it came to pass when Coriantumr had recovered of his wounds, he began to remember the words which Ether had spoken unto him.

. . . And he began to sorrow in his heart; yea, there had been slain two millions of mighty men, and also their wives and their children. (Ether 15:1–2)

Coriantumr was finally repentant as he realized that all the words of the prophets had been fulfilled so far, *every whit; and his soul mourned and refused to be comforted.*

Coriantumr wrote a letter to Shiz offering to give up the kingdom if he would spare his people. Shiz replied that he would spare the people only if Coriantumr would surrender himself and allow Shiz to slay him with his own sword. Neither side would compromise, and a battle took place. When Coriantumr's army saw that they were about to fall, they fled to a very large body of water, called the waters of Ripliancum. Here they set up their tents, with the people of Shiz setting up their camp nearby.

The next day, during the *exceedingly sore battle,* Coriantumr was wounded and fainted from the loss of blood. His army was still able to drive their enemy southward to a place called Ogath, where the army of Shiz pitched their tents. Coriantumr's army camped by the hill Ramah, (which is the same hill that the Nephites would later call Cumorah. This is where the Nephites would have their final battle and where Moroni would hide up his sacred records. Centuries later, the prophet Joseph Smith would take the records from this hill and translate them into our present-day Book of Mormon.)

For the next four years the people took a hiatus from their fighting to give the remaining people of the land time to gather to one army or the other. The prophet Ether remained on the sidelines to observe their destruction. Once the people were gathered, the men, women, and children were armed with all manner of weapons and dressed for war with shields, breastplates, and head-plates. Then they marched against each other to battle and fought all that day.

> And it came to pass that when it was night they were weary, and retired to their camps; and after they had retired to their camps they took up a howling and a lamentation for the loss of the slain of their people; and so great were their cries . . . that they did rend the air exceedingly. (Ether 15:16)

They continued the battle the next day, and it was *great and terrible.* When night came they again *did rend the air with their cries, and their howlings, and their mournings* for those slain.

Coriantumr wrote a second letter to Shiz, once again offering him his kingdom if he would spare his people. Because *Satan had full power over the hearts of the people,* no truce was reached and they went to battle instead. After fighting all day, they slept upon their swords, then resumed fighting again on the fourth day.

> And when the night came they were drunken with anger, even as a man who is drunken with wine; and they slept again upon their swords. (Ether 15:22)

They went to battle again on the fifth day, and by that night all had fallen by the sword except fifty-two of the people of Coriantumr and sixty-nine of the people of Shiz. By the end of the sixth day, Coriantumr's people numbered twenty-seven and Shiz's people thirty-two. Those few who had survived *were large and mighty men.* They retired to their camps and *prepared for death on the morrow.*

On the seventh day of the battle, after three hours of fighting, those yet alive had all fainted from the loss of blood. As soon as Coriantumr's men had enough strength to walk, they were about to flee for their lives. Then Shiz and his men arose. Shiz *swore in his wrath that he would slay Coriantumr or he would perish by the sword.* Shiz's small group chased after Coriantumr's few men and finally overtook them the next day. At the end of the final battle, all had been killed except Shiz and Coriantumr, and Shiz had fainted from the loss of blood.

And it came to pass that when Coriantumr had leaned upon his sword, that he rested a little, he smote off the head of Shiz.

And it came to pass that after he had smitten off the head of Shiz, that Shiz raised up on his hands and fell; and after that he had struggled for breath, he died.

And it came to pass that Coriantumr fell to the earth, and became as if he had no life. (Ether 15:30–32)

The Lord commanded Ether to go forth and witness the fulfilling of his prophecy. Then Ether finished his record and hid the plates *in a manner that the people of Limhi did find them.* Ether was now left to wander the earth alone until the Lord saw fit to bring him home.

Upon reaching the end of his abridgment of the record of the Jaredites, Moroni must have felt a strong kinship with the prophet Ether. Both were the lone righteous survivors of their civilizations. Both had been rejected and hunted by their people. Neither knew what would become of him. However, neither seemed to worry too much about his fate because each bore unshakable testimony that at last he would triumph over his current tragic circumstances, as will all who are true and faithful followers of the Lord Jesus Christ.[1]

Note
1.   Joseph Fielding McConkie, Robert L. Millet, and Brent L. Top, *Doctrinal Commentary on the Book of Mormon*, Vol. IV (Salt Lake City, Utah: Bookcraft, 1992), 260.

POSTSCRIPT

The Jaredite history was ending just as the Nephite and Mulekite history was beginning. Ether ends his record with Coriantumr lying unconscious, but we discover through Nephite records what became of him. In Omni 1:20–22 we learn that Coriantumr was found by the Mulekites, the original inhabitants of Zarahemla, and lived with them for nine months, fulfilling the rest of Ether's prophecy. (Ether had prophesied that if Coriantumr did not repent, he would be the last survivor of his people and would receive a burial by another group of people who had been given this land for an inheritance.)

Mosiah 21:25–27 is the account of how the Jaredite land was discovered—a land covered with bones. It was at this time that the plates were found, which contained the history of the Jaredites.

ABOUT THE AUTHOR

Christine Cobb Merrick was born and raised in the Salt Lake Valley. She graduated from Skyline High School and attended the University of Utah and Brigham Young University.

In 1970 she married Randy Guy Merrick and has been a stay-at-home mom ever since. They are the parents of nine children and to date have twenty grandchildren. Over the years they have taken in several teens needing a temporary home. Each was welcomed as part of the Merrick family, whether their stay was a few months or several years.

In 1973 the family moved to Denver, Colorado, and they resided there for seventeen years. They have lived in South Jordan since moving back to Utah in 1990.

Chris is a compulsive journal keeper and in the past twenty-six years has written more than 4400 pages. It is said that nothing helps your writing skills more than just the practice of writing, and this she can attest to.

Her favorite Church callings have always involved teaching. She has always loved to tell a story, and writing this book has allowed her to do both.